## VALUE ADDED TAX IN THE

Adopting distinct and new perspectives to analy book explores the key design challenges and opp tions in the 21st century.

The book shows how the VAT, the world's n tion tax, has failed to live up to the expectation: iterations about a century ago. It identifies anc theory and practice, drawing on lessons from The book begins with an analysis of key desigr ing concessions, registration thresholds and s1 to explore more complex issues, such as the ; supplies, sharing economy transactions, and as well as the treatment of transactions and operate under multiple-tiered systems of go challenges commonly encountered in VAT ju The work outlines innovative and realistic re for a 21st-century economy that are groundec same time, practicable in terms of law, policy particular, the political, technical, and adminis VAT jurisdictions must navigate when develo]

With guidance on VAT design and implei drafters, the book is also a valuable resource tioners interested in VAT policy and practice tax law, policy and economic principles.

# Value Added Tax in the 21st Century

## *Design, Challenges, and Opportunities*

Yige Zu

•HART•

OXFORD • LONDON • NEW YORK • NEW DELHI • SYDNEY

HART PUBLISHING

Bloomsbury Publishing Plc

Kemp House, Chawley Park, Cumnor Hill, Oxford, OX2 9PH, UK

1385 Broadway, New York, NY 10018, USA

Bloomsbury Publishing Ireland Limited, 29 Earlsfort Terrace, Dublin 2, D02 AY28, Ireland



First published in Great Britain 2026



A catalogue record for this book is available from the British Library.

A catalogue record for this book is available from the Library of Congress.

ISBN: HB: 978-1-50996-957-9
ePDF: 978-1-50996-959-3
ePub: 978-1-50996-958-6

Typeset by Compuscript Ltd, Shannon
Printed and bound in Great Britain

*To policymakers, tax administrators, scholars and practitioners dedicated to shaping a better Value Added Tax system for the United Kingdom.*

*To the quiet light that gave this work its colour and warmth – may its hue remain, ever.*

# ACKNOWLEDGEMENTS

This book commemorates ten years of my academic journey in the United Kingdom (UK) – a decade spent learning, teaching and writing about Value Added Tax (VAT). This journey was made immeasurably smoother thanks to the support of my wonderful friends, colleagues and family.

This book builds on my doctoral research, undertaken at Durham University and the University of Leeds between 2015 and 2017, with the thesis completed while I was a lecturer at the University of Exeter in 2018. I must express my sincere thanks to Professor Rita de la Feria, my PhD supervisor, who first sparked my interest in tax and has supported me in many ways since.

The book has developed over many years, and many members of the tax academic community have lent their support at various points along the way. I owe a great debt of gratitude to Professor Rick Krever, whom I regard as the most knowledgeable legal scholar in the field of VAT. There are indeed very few people with whom one can engage in meaningful conversations and debates about VAT, but Rick is one of them. He has provided invaluable feedback and detailed comments on various chapters of this book, for which I am deeply grateful. Professor Joachim Englisch is also owed special thanks for serving as the external examiner of my PhD thesis, for suggesting the possibility of publishing it as a monograph and for his continued support throughout my career. Thanks are also due to Dr Stephen Daly, Professor Dominic de Cogan, Professor Chris Evans, Professor Judith Freedman, Dr Amy Lawton, Dr Leopoldo Parada, Professor Binh Tran-Nam, Professor Edoardo Traversa and Professor John Vella.

I have been extremely fortunate to receive incredible support from colleagues at the universities where I have worked. I am sincerely grateful to my two Heads of Department at the University of Exeter, Richard Edwards and Dr Bill Peng, who made it possible for me to complete the PhD thesis while I was working full time as a lecturer. I am also deeply thankful to Durham University for providing an outstanding academic and cultural environment, along with vital institutional support. I am indebted to Professor Thom Brooks and Professor Ming Du for encouraging me to pursue the publication of this book. Professor Pierre Schammo, who taught me during my LLM at Durham in 2013–14, has since provided unwavering support and has always celebrated my academic milestones. Dr Mike Adcock, a great friend for the past decade, has offered numerous editorial suggestions for the book. Dr Jieying Liang, Professor Federico Lupo Pasini, Professor Bruce Wardhaugh and Professor Olivia Woolley have also offered help in various ways. It has been a privilege to live, work and write in Durham – a charming, historic yet vibrant town in the northeast of England – made all the more special by the generous support of friends and colleagues. Last but not least, I would like to express my heartfelt thanks to the School of Law at City University of Hong Kong for its warm welcome and strong support of my research agenda.

Special thanks are due to policy advisers and professionals at HM Treasury and the Institute of Chartered Accountants in England and Wales (ICAEW) for their interest in and engagement with this book. I am grateful to colleagues at HM Treasury for the invitation to share insights from this book in a policy briefing attended by policy advisers and tax administrators from the Treasury and HM Revenue and Customs. I am particularly thankful to Ed Saltmarsh at ICAEW for involving me in the ICAEW's insightful and impactful 'How to Fix VAT' campaign. These opportunities to engage with policy advisers and professionals have not only offered valuable perspectives, especially on the practical challenges of VAT reform, but perhaps more importantly, provided the final incentive I needed to complete this book – with the hopeful thought that, together, policy advisers, tax administrators, professionals, academics and businesses will shape a VAT system that better serves the UK's future.

Finally, my deepest gratitude goes to my family – my parents and my two four-year-old cats, Kiwi and Coco. Over the years, my parents have made incredible sacrifices for me, my education and my future. My PhD and my achievements in tax would not have been possible without their unconditional love, support, patience, tolerance and understanding. Kiwi and Coco have provided me with invaluable emotional support throughout the writing of this book. Their love and affection have been a constant source of joy in my life. Kiwi, in particular, has helped type a few paragraphs for the book in his cat language, which unfortunately had to be removed from the manuscript. In fact, he might have called for an extension of VAT zero-rating to pet food – a suggestion with which I must respectfully disagree.

Yige Zu
*Durham and Hong Kong*
*January 2026*

# CONTENTS

# TABLE OF ABBREVIATIONS

| | |
|---|---|
| ATO | Australian Taxation Office |
| AUD | Australian Dollar |
| B2B | business-to-business |
| B2C | business-to-consumer |
| CAD | Canadian Dollar |
| CGST | Central GST |
| CJEU | Court of Justice of the European Union |
| CVAT | Compensating VAT |
| DRRs | Digital Reporting Requirements |
| EEC | European Economic Community |
| EU | European Union |
| EUR | Euro |
| FITR | fixed input tax recovery |
| FRS | flat rate scheme |
| GAAR | general anti-avoidance rule |
| GBP | British Pound Sterling |
| GRCM | generalised reverse charge mechanism |
| GST | Goods and Services Tax |
| HFE | horizontal fiscal equalisation |
| HMRC | HM Revenue & Customs |
| HST | Harmonised Sales Tax |
| IOSS | Import One Stop Shop |
| IGST | Integrated GST |
| IMF | International Monetary Fund |

| | |
|---|---|
| LVCR | low value consignment relief |
| LVIG | Low Value Imported Goods |
| MOSS | mini One Stop Shop |
| MTIC | missing trader intra-Community |
| NZD | New Zealand Dollar |
| OECD | Organisation for Economic Co-operation and Development |
| OSS | One Stop Shop |
| PHV | private hire vehicle |
| QRM | Quick Reaction Mechanism |
| QST | Québec Sales Tax |
| RITC | reduced input tax credits |
| RST | retail sales tax |
| SAAR | specific anti-avoidance rule |
| SGD | Singapore Dollar |
| SGST | State GST |
| TOMS | Tour Operators Margin Scheme |
| UKSC | Supreme Court of the United Kingdom |
| US | United States |
| VAT | Value Added Tax |
| ViDA | VAT in the Digital Age |
| VTER | VAT tax expenditures ratio |

# LIST OF FIGURES

# LIST OF TABLES

# TABLE OF CASES

## UK

## EU

**Other jurisdictions**

# TABLE OF LEGISLATION

**UK legislation**

**EU legislation**

**Other legislation**

# 1

# VAT Challenges in the 21st Century

## I. Introduction

Since its introduction in Europe over half a century ago, Value Added Tax (VAT), or Goods and Services Tax (GST) as it is labelled in some Anglo jurisdictions,[1] has become the mainstay of general tax on consumption in more than 170 countries worldwide, including all members of the Organisation for Economic Co-operation and Development (OECD) except for the United States (US) and a large cross-section of developing and transitional nations.[2] VAT has proven to be a key source of revenue for countries around the world and this is particularly true in developing and least developed countries where it commonly accounts for a larger proportion of total tax revenue than elsewhere.[3] Although the adoption of VAT systems was driven by external, internal or hybrid pressures,[4] the remarkable success of the tax in terms of geographical coverage and revenue yields is commonly attributed to the theoretical merits of the tax, notably its complete neutrality in application across all consumption and between domestic sales and imports. The merits derive from three established norms of a model VAT developed mainly on the basis of economic criteria:[5] a single rate and a broad base; self-assessment through an invoice-credit mechanism; and the destination principle in cross-border circumstances.[6]

Ironically, almost all real-world VAT systems fall short of fully incorporating one or more of the design norms underpinning the model that is credited with the stated benefits. Depending on the extent of deviations from the theoretical model,

[1] The term VAT is generally used throughout this book, except where specific reference is made to the taxes that are known as GST in certain jurisdictions, such as Australia, New Zealand, Singapore, Canada and India.

[2] For a list of countries and territories imposing a VAT, see OECD, *Consumption Tax Trends 2024: VAT/GST and Excise, Core Design Features and Trends* (Paris, OECD Publishing, 2024) 271–74.

[3] VAT revenue accounts for over 25% of the total tax revenue in developing and least developed countries, compared to around 21% in OECD countries. See, OECD, 'Global Revenue Statistics Database' (2024), available at www.oecd.org/en/data/datasets/global-revenue-statistics-database.html.

[4] R Krever, 'Designing and Drafting VAT Laws for Africa' in R Krever (ed), *VAT in Africa* (South Africa, Pretoria University Law Press, 2008) 9.

[5] The commonly used criteria include neutrality, equity, simplicity and efficiency (in terms of administrative and compliance costs). This set of criteria is derived from the four canons of taxation established by Adam Smith in A Smith, *The Wealth of Nations* (London, W Strahan and T Cadell, 1776). For modern adaptations of these criteria, see OECD, *Consumption Tax Trends 2024* (n 2) at 18.

[6] OECD, *International VAT/GST Guidelines* (Paris, OECD Publishing, 2017) 14–17; K James, *The Rise of the Value-Added Tax* (New York, Cambridge University Press, 2015) 40–41.

the world's VAT systems can be broadly divided into two camps: the 'traditional VAT' represented by the European Union (EU) VAT system and the 'modern VAT' found in many countries that adopted the tax after New Zealand established the modern VAT model with its introduction of GST in 1986.[7] The division between the two models in practice is mostly centred on the use of concessions in the form of preferential rates and exemptions, with the traditional VAT systems relying more heavily on concessions. Modern VAT systems, seeking to avoid the complexity and economic distortions associated with multiple rates and widespread exemptions in the traditional VAT systems, generally feature a single rate (apart from a zero rate) and fewer and more tightly targeted exemptions.

The gap between VAT in theory and in practice suggests that the model, though grounded in sound economic principles, faces limitations in its practical implementation. In practice, the design of VAT inevitably reflects, to a considerable extent, the political economy reality and technical, administrative and sometimes constitutional constraints that shape tax policy and tax administration in any given country. The theoretical model that disregards these factors arguably does not deal adequately with many complex issues in the real world. In addition, in the modern era, new business models, rapidly evolving market structures, technological advancements and globalisation present new challenges that could not have been foreseen at the time the VAT was first adopted. Therefore, there remains important analytical gaps between the theoretical design norms and real-world policy formulation. The goal of this book is to fill these gaps.

## II. VAT and its Alternatives: A Brief History

The idea of a VAT was first theorised around the 1920s by Wilhelm von Siemens,[8] a German industrialist, and Thomas S Adams,[9] an American economist. The Great Depression and the Second World War distracted governments around the globe from any serious consideration of the theory. At the time, an important source of revenue for almost all Western European countries was a turnover tax, which is administratively simple but widely recognised as the least economically neutral form of sales tax.[10] These turnover taxes applied at low rates to every sale along the

[7] Krever (n 4) at 13–18. Other examples of modern VAT systems include Australia (2000), Canada (1991), South Africa (1991) and Singapore (1994).

[8] W von Siemens, *Veredelte Umsatzsteuer* (translated as 'Refined Sales Tax') (Berlin, Siemensstadt, 1919). The author proposed a refinement to the cascading turnover tax used in Germany at the time, which is considered a precursor to the modern VAT. After the author's death, a second, and expanded, edition of the pamphlet was published by his brother. See CF von Siemens, *Veredelte Umsatzsteuer*, 2nd edn (Berlin, Siemensstadt, 1921).

[9] TS Adams, 'Fundamental Problems of Federal Income Taxation' (1921) 35 *The Quarterly Journal of Economics* 527.

[10] First Council Directive 67/227/EEC of 11 April 1967 on the harmonisation of legislation of Member States concerning turnover tax [1967] OJ 71, Recital.

production and distribution chain, leading to sometimes serious cascading and consequent distortions such as vertical integration of businesses.[11]

The post-war economic rebuilding provided an opportunity for governments to reconsider the merits of VAT. Looking for a means to mitigate the cascading problem of the turnover taxes, in 1948 French authorities experimented with a limited rebate system in one of the turnover taxes to return input tax on purchases to business customers.[12] The idea was later modified and expanded by a French tax administrator, Maurice Lauré, who coined the term 'TVA' (translated as VAT in English) in his book published in 1953.[13] Widely regarded as 'the father of VAT', Lauré played a pivotal role in the introduction of the world's first VAT system in France in 1954.[14] Nevertheless, the cascading turnover taxes continued to prevail elsewhere in Europe.

In cross-border circumstances, the turnover taxes were intended to operate on a destination basis: on the one hand, exports were exempt from the tax, and the tax already charged on exports was rebated in the exporting country; on the other hand, imports were taxed in the same way as domestic products in the importing country. A consequence of the cumulative multi-stage nature of the taxes is that export rebates could not be calculated accurately because it was never possible to know exactly how much tax had been paid on a product. In the earliest stages of the European community, the Member States realised that the distortion of the compounding turnover taxes with respect to cross-border sales was a serious obstacle to the completion of the Common Market, which required that domestic products and goods imported from another Member State be taxed on the same basis.[15]

It was in this environment that the European Economic Community (EEC), the predecessor to the EU, embarked on what proved to be the most successful tax experiment in the modern era, replacing a melange of turnover taxes with an almost uniform VAT across the Member States. Two Directives issued by the EEC Council in 1967 mandated the adoption of VAT systems in all Member States.[16] The EEC followed the path set by France, starting with the turnover taxes with rebates of input taxes to registered businesses. The VAT is imposed on the consideration payable for supplies of goods and services, but registered businesses are allowed to deduct the tax they paid on input purchases from the tax they collected on output sales, leaving the net balance, effectively the tax imposed on their value added, to be remitted to the government. Each supplier is required to issue to the business purchaser an

[11] Krever (n 4) at 10.

[12] CK Sullivan, *Tax on Value Added* (New York, Columbia University Press, 1965) 73.

[13] M Lauré, *La Taxe sur la valeur ajoutée* (translated as 'value-added tax') (Paris, Librairie du Recueil Sirey, 1953).

[14] M Salo, 'The Ideas of Maurice Lauré on VAT in the 1950s' (2014) 3 *World Journal of VAT/GST Law* 130.

[15] 'Tax Harmonization in the European Community' (Community Topics 29, July 1968).

[16] Directive 67/227 (n 10); Second Council Directive 67/228/EEC of 11 April 1967 on the harmonisation of legislation of Member States concerning turnover taxes – Structure and procedures for application of the common system of value added tax [1967] OJ 71.

invoice that specifies the amount of VAT charged, which establishes the purchaser's right to input tax deduction. This operating mechanism is commonly referred to as the invoice-credit method.[17] The tax flows through business transactions and falls on final consumption only, which is exactly proportional to the price of the goods or services, whatever the length of the production or distribution chain. The VAT is therefore designed to achieve neutrality with respect to production and consumption decisions, enabling businesses to make production and investment decisions independent of tax considerations.

In cross-border sales, the neutrality of the VAT is achieved by applying the destination principle: the VAT law zero-rates exports, meaning no tax would be imposed on exported goods or services and exporters would recover all tax on inputs, leaving the exports free of taxation in the country of origin. At the same time, imports are subject to tax in the same manner as locally supplied goods or services. The adoption of VAT was central to the economic integration of the EEC because of the advantage of the tax in achieving equal treatment of domestic and imported supplies with precision through the destination principle.

The EU's experience with the VAT was widely regarded as a significant success by other countries, serving as a powerful catalyst for the global proliferation of VAT during the 1980s and 1990s, a trend that has persisted well into the twenty-first century.[18] The take-up of VAT in developing and transitional countries was also strongly influenced by international organisations, such as the International Monetary Fund (IMF) and the World Bank, which actively promoted the adoption of the tax as part of broader fiscal and tax reform programmes.[19]

In contrast to the EU VAT, which evolved from pre-existing turnover taxes, the US relies on the retail sales tax (RST), an economically equivalent alternative to the VAT for taxing final consumption. The key difference between the two taxes is the collection mechanism through which the goal of taxing final consumption is achieved. The VAT that takes the invoice-credit form is imposed on every sale, whether business-to-business (B2B) or business-to-consumer (B2C), along the supply chain, but intermediary businesses are relieved of tax burden through the invoice-credit mechanism. If a business' credit for input tax exceeds its output tax, it should be entitled to an immediate refund of the excess credit. In contrast, the RST suspends taxation on B2B transactions until the final retail stage by requiring a business customer to provide its supplier with proof of its registration status. As a result, the RST functions as a single-stage tax that is, in theory, imposed only at the point of final sale. With identical rate and coverage, an RST and a VAT would, in principle, impose the same tax burden on taxpayers and yield the same revenue for the government.

[17] L Ebrill and others, *The Modern VAT* (Washington, DC, International Monetary Fund, 2001) 20; OECD, *Consumption Tax Trends 2024* (n 2) at 17. Almost all VAT jurisdictions use the invoice-credit method.

[18] OECD, *Consumption Tax Trends 2024* (n 2) at 271–74.

[19] James (n 6) at 171–73; RM Bird and P-P Gendron, *The VAT in Developing and Transitional Countries* (Cambridge, Cambridge University Press, 2007) 19–20.

The relative merits of a VAT and an RST in their purest forms have long been the subject of debate but neither tax has been implemented in its theoretically optimal form.[20] One of the strongest advantages claimed for the VAT compared to the RST is that the VAT is self-enforcing in that each trader's input tax entitlement is matched by its supplier's output tax liability. As such, the trader has an incentive to ensure that their supplier provides them with an invoice, which entitles them to an input tax credit, and pays the output VAT.[21] Invoices create a paper trail that could serve as a useful tool for tax authorities to detect tax evasion.[22] Moreover, it is often argued that, under an RST, if the final seller evades tax, all revenue due on the supply is lost.[23] By contrast, the fractional nature of VAT means that at any given stage of the supply chain, the revenue at risk due to evasion is limited to the tax on the value added at that stage, assuming that the tax authority would have properly collected the VAT on the value added at earlier stages.[24] For these reasons, the VAT is often regarded as less prone to evasion.[25]

However, the often-cited advantage of VAT in terms of enforcement and integrity stems from the mechanism of first requiring the payment of VAT and then providing an offsetting credit, an approach that significantly increases the complexity of the system. In contrast, the concept of RST is much simpler as it avoids the churning under a VAT. Thus, a great advantage of an RST over a VAT is operational simplicity.[26]

On the whole, turnover taxes are relatively easy to administer, but they are economically distortive. Although the VAT and the RST are conceptually equivalent, the VAT is generally considered to be superior to the RST and has become the most widely adopted form of general consumption tax worldwide.

## III. VAT as a Tax on Final Consumption: Key Challenges

Notwithstanding the intention of taxing final consumption, the real-world VATs often only reach just more than half of the theoretical model VAT base.[27] The

[20] JF Due, 'The Choice Between a Value Added Tax and a Retail Sales Tax' (Faculty Working Paper No 1205, College of Commerce and Business Administration, University of Illinois at Urbana-Campaign, November 1985).

[21] M Keen and S Smith, 'VAT Fraud and Evasion: What Do We Know, and What Can be Done?' (IMF Working Paper WP/07/31, February 2007) 6–7.

[22] H Huizinga, 'A European VAT on Financial Services?' (2022) 17 *Economic Policy* 497, 504.

[23] Keen and Smith (n 21) at 6.

[24] GR Zodrow, 'The Sales Tax, the VAT, and Taxes in Between – or, Is the Only Good NRST a "VAT in Drag"?' (1999) 52 *National Tax Journal* 429, 431.

[25] Criticisms of this view can be found in Due (n 20) at 4–5; and Krever (n 4) at 12–13.

[26] JF Due, 'The Implications for Australia of the Experience in the United States, Canada and Other Countries with Retail Sales Tax' in JG Head (ed), *Changing the Tax Mix* (Sydney, Australian Tax Research Foundation, 1986).

[27] For example, in 2022, the OECD countries, on average, actually collected only 58% of the theoretical potential VAT revenue (the amount that would theoretically be collected if VAT were applied at the standard rate to the potential tax base with perfect compliance). See, OECD, *Consumption Tax Trends 2024* (n 2) at 9.

gap between actual VAT collection and the theoretical potential VAT revenue is mainly a result of poor administration of the tax and deliberately adopted concessions that explicitly reduce or eliminate the VAT payable on designated types of consumption.[28] Real-world experience with VAT has shown that the merits of VAT as a tax on final consumption are not nearly as great as are often claimed. The imperfections of real-world VAT systems compared to the theoretical model can, to some extent, be explained by the failure of the theoretical model to account for factors that are often dominant in tax design in practice.

A prime design norm for an ideal VAT is a single rate that applies to a broad base, with minimal use of exemptions. However, the VAT systems in most countries, and in particular those that have adopted the EU-style VAT, are characterised by more than one rate (apart from the zero rate for exports) and extensive use of exemptions in which no tax is levied on supplies but suppliers are denied credits for input tax included in the price of their acquisitions. In many countries, as is the case with EU Member States, concessions were adopted for historical and political reasons, which aim to replicate the preferential treatment found in former turnover tax systems in order to win the public support necessary for the introduction of VAT. A further important political consideration is associated with the use of concessions to address the perceived regressivity of VAT that falls disproportionately more heavily on the poor. Incomplete taxation of consumption to address equity concerns almost become an inevitable feature of real-world VAT systems, with the only notable exception being New Zealand's GST, which is widely advocated to be the world's 'purest' VAT.[29] Country experience with the use of concessions highlights the political economy realities that cannot be separated from tax policymaking.

Apart from deliberately adopted subsidies in the form of concessions, an important exclusion from the VAT base is created by way of adopting a registration threshold. Most countries apply a registration threshold to relieve small businesses with a turnover below that level from the obligation to register for and remit VAT. This decision is based on a recognition of the uneven distribution of administrative and compliance costs and revenue yields across businesses of different sizes. In other words, the omission of the smallest businesses from the VAT system frees those businesses almost entirely from the costs of complying with VAT obligations, and relieves tax administrations of significant administrative effort, without sacrificing a great deal of revenue. The use of a registration threshold represents a practical departure from the traditional wisdom that VAT should apply to a base that is as broad as possible. Considerations surrounding the use of a threshold illustrate that the effectiveness of tax policy could be considerably constrained by the limitations of administrative and compliance capacities in practice.

[28] M Keen, 'The Anatomy of the VAT' (2013) 66 *National Tax Journal* 424.

[29] R Krever and D White, 'Preface' in R Krever and D White (eds), *GST in Retrospect and Prospect* (Wellington, Brookers Ltd, 2007) viii.

A registration threshold that creates a distinction between businesses above and below it inevitably gives rise to distortions. Some businesses operating below the threshold enjoy a competitive advantage over their competitors above it, as the former group is relieved from both the VAT liability and the associated compliance burden. This competitive distortion was not considered to be significant before the remarkable growth of the sharing economy in recent years. However, the sharing economy allows large groups of small suppliers, most of whom operate below the VAT registration threshold, to access substantial customer base via digital platforms and collectively compete with larger VAT-registered businesses. An increasing number of countries have taken targeted measures to expand the VAT base to capture sharing economy activities carried out by unregistered suppliers in certain sectors, notably ride-sharing and short-term accommodation. These measures typically rely on deeming provisions that treat the digital platform facilitating sharing economy activities as the supplier for VAT purposes. As a result, the platform is required to account for VAT in lieu of the unregistered suppliers. This approach effectively removes any VAT registration requirement for individual sharing economy suppliers and avoids imposing compliance burdens on the small, and often casual, suppliers, while also significantly reducing the number of businesses within the VAT system that the tax authority has to administer directly. In the coming years, the rapid expansion of sharing economy activities across more economic sectors and increasing involvement of platforms in the collection of VAT may prompt governments to re-evaluate the optimal threshold level that is based on the trade-offs between administrative and compliance cost savings, on the one hand, and revenue yields, on the other.

The second design norm of a model VAT requires the tax to operate via an invoice-credit mechanism, which, as noted earlier,[30] is the main difference between a VAT and an RST. While the initial adoption of the invoice-credit mechanism in Europe was driven by the need to transition turnover taxes into a VAT, later justifications were found in favour of the invoice-credit mechanism under a VAT, rather than the suspension system of an RST.[31] The operating mechanism of VAT, however, is relatively complicated, in particular for small businesses. The compliance difficulties are accentuated by the provision of many exemptions and multiple rates in traditional VAT jurisdictions. To reduce the disproportionately high compliance costs faced by small businesses, some countries apply a simplified calculation regime for businesses just above the VAT registration threshold. A notable example is presumptive input tax entitlement regimes, under which a single flat rate applies to business turnover to determine the amount of tax to be remitted to the tax authority. The

[30] See the text following n 19.

[31] See, eg, S Cnossen, 'VAT, RST or a Reverse Charge Mechanism: Which is Best?' (2017) *Tax Notes International* 453; and S Cnossen, 'The Technical Superiority of VAT over RST' (1987) 4 *Australian Tax Forum* 419.

flat rate incorporates a predetermined input tax entitlement, removing the need for small businesses to record input tax on acquisitions.

In addition, the application of the invoice-credit VAT relies on clear identification of explicit prices charged for inputs and outputs, which proved to be practically challenging in the areas of financial supplies and insurance services. Traditional VAT jurisdictions sought to avoid the valuation difficulties by simply applying a wholesale exemption to these supplies, leading to serious economic distortions. A few modern VAT jurisdictions introduced alternative measures to ameliorate the distortions associated with the use of exemptions. Although the new approaches adopted by the modern VAT jurisdictions represent an improvement over the exemption approach used in the traditional VAT jurisdictions, no country has fully resolved the practical difficulties of taxing financial intermediary services.

The third design norm requires the application of the destination principle in cross-border contexts. Under the destination principle, exports are freed from taxation in the exporting country and imports are generally subject to taxation at the customs border in the importing country. The objective of the destination principle is to ensure that the VAT is imposed in the country where consumption takes place. The application of the principle was relatively straightforward at the time the VAT was adopted in the last decades of the twentieth century, when cross-border trade primarily involved B2B sales of goods. However, globalisation and technological advancements in more recent years have led to a surge in the volume of cross-border B2B supplies of services. Unlike goods, intangible services cannot be taxed at the customs border. Furthermore, the rise of e-commerce and the digital economy increasingly enables suppliers to make sales of goods and services remotely to private customers located anywhere in the world. These new developments create significant challenges for the effective implementation of the destination principle. Whilst the invoice-credit mechanism places the liability to pay VAT on business suppliers, it is considerably more difficult to enforce VAT collection on cross-border sales made by foreign suppliers who are out of the reach of national tax administrations.

Countries have responded with bespoke solutions for different types of supplies and suppliers. A common approach to taxing cross-border B2B supplies of services is to apply a reverse charge mechanism, which shifts the liability to pay VAT from the foreign supplier to the domestic importer. In response to the difficulties of taxing cross-border B2C supplies of digital services and low-value goods, many countries have adopted new rules that require foreign suppliers to register and account for VAT in the country in which the private customers are located. These new rules often include deeming provisions, under which online marketplaces that facilitate supplies from large groups of underlying suppliers are deemed to be the suppliers for VAT purposes. As noted above in the context of the sharing economy, the involvement of platforms in the collection of VAT has the potential to deliver significant administrative and compliance cost savings.

As with cross-border supplies of services, similar challenges arise in federal countries, large countries with multiple tiers of government, or economic unions that seek to apply intra-jurisdictional VATs on a destination basis in the absence of physical borders. However, the options available for federations or economic unions may be considerably constrained by the political factors and, in some cases, constitutional limitations specific to each context.

A review of the key challenges in applying the theoretical design norms to policy formulation in the real world suggests that the theoretical norms are often too simplistic in dealing with real-world complexities, particularly those arising from the growth of the digital economy. Meanwhile, opportunities exist in nearly all countries with a VAT system to improve the design of VAT policy to address both longstanding and emerging challenges.

This book examines the extent to which the conventional wisdom about VAT design remains valid in the context of a twenty-first century economy. It also develops a benchmark that sets out the core components of a comprehensive strategy for policymakers to consider in designing and implementing VAT policy. Importantly, although many of the main challenges countries face are broadly similar, there is no single, definitive, one-size-fits-all solution to any of the issues considered in the book. As such, the benchmark inevitably needs to be adapted to reflect the specific circumstances of each jurisdiction. Nonetheless, the benchmark provides a valuable basis for VAT jurisdictions to start the process of evaluating and improving their VAT systems.

## IV. Chapter Outlines

Chapter two engages in a critical analysis of VAT concessions under a conceptual framework. It applies tax expenditure analysis to VAT concessions, recognising that concessions are the equivalent of, and a substitute for, direct spending programmes. The chapter begins by reviewing the key rationales for using concessions and evaluating concessions against three budgetary criteria: fairness, targeting efficiency and budget control. It then examines the negative consequences of concessions in the VAT system in terms of economic distortions, legal difficulties and administrative and compliance costs. The chapter finally outlines a pathway for reform, with particular emphasis on how political economy challenges might be addressed in efforts to remove VAT concessions. Nevertheless, it also considers the second-best option – improving the design of concessions – if their removal proves politically unattainable.

Chapter three discusses the key considerations and challenges involved in setting a VAT registration threshold and the implications of adopting that boundary, as well as the closely related issue of the treatment of small businesses. The chapter starts with a review of the rationale for adopting a registration threshold. It then examines the distortions and inefficiencies caused by a threshold, including the distortion of competition between small businesses above and below the threshold and the behavioural responses of businesses to the threshold. The chapter also discusses three types of commonly used small business regimes: smoothing regimes for small businesses shifting into the full VAT system; simplification regimes for small businesses within the VAT system and an alternative, more rarely used, turnover tax regime for small businesses below the VAT registration threshold.

The central question investigated in chapter four is the appropriate treatment of financial supplies and insurance services under the VAT. The chapter first identifies the theoretically correct outcome in terms of the VAT base concerning these supplies. It continues with an evaluation of the practical challenges of taxing these supplies, and the various approaches adopted by both traditional and modern VAT jurisdictions in response to these challenges. Furthermore, the chapter presents workable options for the effective taxation of financial supplies and insurance services.

Chapter five turns to the cross-border dimensions of VAT, focusing on three key challenges in the international context. The first involves countries' approaches to determining the place of taxation for cross-border sales of goods and services. The second relates to the removal of VAT on business expenses incurred by non-resident businesses. The third concerns the effective collection of VAT on imports. This chapter concludes by exploring the potential for enhanced international cooperation by way of treaties as a solution to some of the cross-border challenges.

Chapter six examines the question of how the VAT functions in the context of federations, economic communities or large countries with multiple levels of government. It evaluates existing models for allocating VAT revenue among sub-central jurisdictions based on the place of consumption, the place of origin, and fiscal equalisation formulas. The chapter then explores possible options for different contexts, depending on factors such as the presence of an overarching fiscal authority and the degree of fiscal autonomy granted to local governments.

Chapter seven addresses a relatively new issue in the VAT – the challenges arising from the growth of the sharing economy. The chapter begins with a discussion of the implications of the expansion of the sharing economy for VAT policy and administration. It then evaluates and compares the existing approaches adopted by several jurisdictions to taxing sharing economy activities. The chapter concludes with an outline of key design criteria that countries should consider if they decide to apply the VAT to sharing economy activities.

Chapter eight summarises the key deviations of real-world VAT systems from the theoretical design norms along with the underlying reasons for these departures, as discussed in the preceding chapters. It also proposes a revised benchmark VAT model, grounded in the traditional design norms and informed by international experience, which can serve as a useful reference for countries seeking to evaluate and reform their VAT systems. The chapter concludes with a consideration of future trends in VAT, drawing insights from past developments and observable patterns.

# 2

# VAT Concessions

## I. Introduction

Two critical issues in Value Added Tax (VAT) design are the level and structure of rates and the appropriate tax base. In principle, a benchmark VAT applies the same tax burden to all types of supplies, so that the tax is neutral in its application to all consumption. Expert advice is almost overwhelmingly in favour of a single rate that applies to a broad base, with minimal use of exemptions. However, the reality is that almost all VAT systems deviate from the theoretical ideal, with deliberately adopted concessions explicitly reducing or eliminating the VAT payable on designated types of consumption.

Most concessions in VAT have been shown to be inefficient subsidy tools, providing misguided benefits, distorting consumption, production and investment decisions, and giving rise to substantial administrative and compliance costs. Experience to date, however, suggests that they are an unavoidable feature of most VAT systems as time and time again politicians opt for VAT concessions as the preferred delivery vehicle to achieve all the rationales for reduced taxation. In this respect, the disconnect between a good VAT in theory and the real VATs in practice can largely be explained in the context of the political economy reality in most countries. This chapter recasts the evaluation of VAT concessions under the conceptual framework of tax expenditure analysis, treating concessions as the equivalent of explicit government outlays. It then develops a realistic pathway for reform in light of the political economy challenges faced by policymakers.

## II. Rationales for VAT Concessions

Concessions in a VAT system can take four forms: (1) taxation at a reduced rate; (2) input taxation only, treating the supply as an exempt supply but denying the supplier any credits for tax included in the price of business purchases; (3) treating the supply as an out-of-scope supply outside the VAT system; or (4) removal of tax completely by zero-rating the supply and allowing full input tax credits. Traditional VAT systems, represented by the European Union (EU), typically uses the first three methods to provide concessions. Some modern VAT systems, such as those in Australia and Canada, use some or all of the second, third and fourth methods. The United Kingdom (UK) employs all four.

Concessions are adopted for a variety of reasons. The most common reason is to address equity concerns. A model VAT that applies the same rate to all types of supplies is often criticised for being a relatively regressive tax, because the same rate applies regardless of the final consumers' circumstances.[1] A prime rationale for concessions is to reduce the regressivity of VAT that is borne disproportionately by lower income persons who apply far greater shares of their income to consumption than their higher income counterparts. Almost all countries, with the notable exception of New Zealand, apply lower rates or exemptions to necessities, in particular food,[2] that are thought to take up a larger share of the budgets of low-income persons. Concessions adopted on equity grounds proved necessary to win the public or political acceptance for VAT adoption in the first place in some countries, such as Australia and Canada.[3] Likewise, in particular in many traditional VAT systems, a key reason for the adoption of concessions was to retain in the VAT system the preferential treatment that existed in the previous turnover taxes replaced by the VAT.[4]

Most countries also use concessions for social or public policy reasons. A second aim of concessions is to subsidise, and hence encourage, the consumption of what the legislature perceives as 'merit supplies' that it believes generate positive externalities, which might not be recognised by consumers faced with a fully taxed supply.[5] The common list of merit supplies include education, cultural activities, health supplies and public transport.[6]

[1] T Clougherty and others, 'A Framework for the Future: Reforming the UK Tax System' (Centre for Policy Studies & Tax Foundation, 2020). It is worth pointing out that the perceived regressivity of VAT is subject to debate. Some commentators argue that the regressivity of VAT depends on the chosen metric – particularly whether it is assessed relative to annual income or lifetime income. While the VAT is generally considered regressive when measured against current income, it tends to appear proportional, or even mildly progressive, when assessed against current consumption, which is used as a proxy for lifetime income. For this view, see E Caspersen and G Metcalf, 'Is a Value Added Tax Regressive? Annual Versus Lifetime Incidence Measures' (1994) 47 *National Tax Journal* 731; and TF Crossley, D Phillips and M Wakefield, 'Value Added Tax' in R Chote and others (eds), *The IFS Green Budget: January 2009* (London, The Institute for Fiscal Studies, 2009).

[2] For example, 31 out of 37 Organisation for Economic Co-operation and Development (OECD) countries provide a reduced or zero rate on food. See, A Thomas, 'VAT Rate Structures in Theory and Practice' (World Bank Policy Research Working Paper 10677, January 2024) 4.

[3] For the Canadian experience, see RM Bird and P-P Gendron, 'Sales Taxes in Canada: The GST-HST-QST-RST "System"' (2010) 63 *Tax Law Review* 517, 529–31; For the Australian experience, see C Alley, D Bentley and S James, 'Politics and Tax Reform: A Comparative Analysis of the Implementation of a Broad-Based Consumption Tax in New Zealand, Australia and the United Kingdom' (2014) 24 *Revenue Law Journal* 14; and M D'Ascenzo, 'Making the Value Added Tax Happen' (2020) 18 *eJournal of Tax Research* 2, 8–10.

[4] An example is the zero-rating of food in the UK, which replicates the preferential treatment available under the UK's former Purchase Tax and was preserved in the UK VAT system through a derogation from the harmonised EU VAT rules. See, G Morse, 'The Origins, Development and Future of Zero-Rating in the UK' in G Loutzenhiser and R de la Feria (eds), *The Dynamics of Taxation: Essays in Honour of Judith Freedman* (Oxford, Hart Publishing, 2020).

[5] Perhaps less commonly, concessions are sometimes used to subsidise particular types of suppliers by reducing the tax burden on their supplies. For example, China treats specified supplies made by disabled persons as exempt supplies. The concession was adopted to provide assistance to disabled persons, which aligns with the country's broader social welfare objectives.

[6] See, the list of exemptions for certain activities in the public interest provided by the EU VAT legislation for example. Council Directive 2006/112/EC of 28 November 2006 on the common system of value added tax [2006] OJ L347/1, Art 132.

A third objective of concessions is to facilitate efficient VAT administration through what might be labelled 'technical concessions' that reduce VAT liabilities associated with abnormally high administrative and compliance costs or where there is uncertainty as to how particular types of transactions can be subject to VAT. Examples include the adoption of a registration threshold to exclude the smallest businesses from the VAT system and the application of exemptions to financial and insurance services. These features are discussed in chapters three and four, respectively.

A fourth objective of concessions is to relieve businesses of the financial burden associated with paying VAT at the time of acquisition but not recovering the tax until input tax credits can be used to offset against the tax payable on sales, or sometimes much later if credits exceed the tax payable and a refund is needed. An example of a tax rule designed to mitigate this burden is the zero-rating or out-of-scope treatment applied to a transfer of a business as a going concern.[7] The acquisition of an entire operating business could normally trigger a substantial VAT liability, and the cost of bridging finance to cover the tax until it is recovered could be significant, potentially derailing many business transfers that would yield benefits for the economy.[8] Removing tax on such supplies would provide a crucial cash flow benefit to the purchaser, who would otherwise need to obtain additional funds to cover the VAT included in the purchase price.

The exclusions from the VAT base aimed at achieving the third and fourth objectives are not explicitly characterised as subsidies. The remainder of this chapter focuses on the concessions adopted to address equity concerns and to advance social or public policy goals.

## III. Concessions as Spending Programmes

Concessions that reduce the VAT payable under a neutral benchmark VAT are treated for national budget purposes as indirect outlays or, as they are labelled in budget documents, 'tax expenditures'.[9] The revenue forgone from incompletely taxed consumption should be treated as revenue that is notionally collected and then immediately remitted as tax expenditures, which are equivalent to direct budget expenditures. As spending measures, concessions in the VAT systems must be evaluated by applying the same (budgetary) criteria that are used in

[7] For example, a transfer of a going concern is treated as an out-of-scope supply under the EU VAT legislation, while the sale of a business as a going concern is GST-free (the equivalent to zero-rated) in Australia. See, Council Directive 2006/112 Arts 19 and 29; and (Australia) A New Tax System (Goods and Services Tax) Act 1999, s 38–325.

[8] J Teoh and R Krever, 'Court Favors Broad Application of Antiavoidance Rule in GST Case' (2013) 70 *Tax Notes International* 737.

[9] Tax expenditures are commonly defined as reductions in tax liabilities relative to a benchmark tax that are implemented by way of tax provisions. See C Heady, 'Tax Expenditures: Definitional and Policy Issues' in L Philipps, N Brooks and J Li (eds), *Tax Expenditures: State of the Art* (Toronto, Canadian Tax Foundation, 2011).

evaluating direct spending programmes, namely, whether the implicit expenditures are distributed in a fair and efficient manner, with minimal collateral distortions.[10] VAT concessions raise serious concerns in terms of fairness, targeting efficiency and budget control.

## A. Fairness

VAT tax expenditures in the form of a reduced rate and zero-rate provide benefits in proportion to the recipient's tax liability. Suppose the standard VAT rate is 20 per cent, a GBP 1 supply of zero-rated food would save 20 pence tax for the rich and 20 pence tax for the poor. This means a concession could potentially provide a larger proportional benefit to the poor if it effectively targeted supplies on which the poor spend a significantly greater share of their incomes (which is unlikely to be the case in practice). However, whatever the type of supply receiving concessional treatment, higher income persons are likely to acquire more in absolute terms than lower income persons.[11] The concession, therefore, provides a larger absolute benefit to the rich.[12] In Australia, for example, the dollar value of Goods and Services Tax (GST) tax expenditures increases as income increases, but GST tax expenditures as a proportion of disposable income decrease as income increases.[13] Table 2.1 presents the distributional incidence of GST tax expenditures on food in Australia for 2015–16.[14] Similar distributional patterns have been observed in other countries.[15] Taken together, this evidence suggests that the zero-rating of basic foods could potentially increase the progressivity of the VAT system.[16] Nevertheless, as spending programmes, the concessions are both unfair in terms of who receives the largest subsidy and illogical from a social welfare perspective.

[10] N Brooks, 'The Under-Appreciated Implications of the Tax Expenditure Concept' in C Evans and R Krever (eds), *Australian Business Tax Reform in Retrospect and Prospect* (Sydney, Thomson Reuters, 2009).

[11] R Krever, 'Designing and Drafting VAT Laws for Africa' in R Krever (ed), *VAT in Africa* (South Africa, Pretoria University Law Press, 2008) 19.

[12] ibid.

[13] 'Tax Benchmarks and Variations Statement 2019' (The Treasury, Australian Government, January 2020), available at treasury.gov.au/publication/p2020-51153.

[14] ibid, 8–9.

[15] For example, a South African report shows that only little more than one-third of the benefits of zero-rating for basic foodstuffs was received by households in the lower five income deciles. See, The Davis Tax Committee, 'Final Report on Value-Added Tax for the Minister of Finance' (March 2018), available at www.taxcom.org.za/docs/20180329%20Final%20DTC%20VAT%20Report%20to%20the%20Minister.pdf; See also OECD, *OECD Economic Survey: Mexico 2007* (Paris, OECD Publishing, 2007) 58.

[16] Earlier studies show that some progressive effects of rate differentiation were found in the UK and other countries. See, S Cnossen, 'The Technical Superiority of VAT over RST' in JG Head (ed), *Australian Tax Reform in Retrospect and Prospect* (Sydney, Australian Tax Research Foundation, 1989) 346–47; and L Ebrill and others, *The Modern VAT* (Washington, DC, International Monetary Fund, 2001) 109.

**Table 2.1** Distributional Incidence of GST Tax Expenditures on Food in Australia, 2015–16

| | **Lowest quintile** | **2nd quintile** | **3rd quintile** | **4th quintile** | **Highest quintile** |
|---|---|---|---|---|---|
| **average weekly value** | $10.26 | $13.54 | $17.46 | $21.04 | $25.54 |
| **as a proportion of disposable income** | 2.76% | 1.24% | 1.03% | 0.86% | 0.63% |

## B. Targeting Efficiency

A prime design objective for any government spending programme is targeting efficiency, which ensures expenditures reach the intended beneficiaries in the least costly manner with minimum spillover to other persons. The targeting efficiency of VAT concessions has two elements. The first, which might be labelled object efficiency, seeks to ensure that subsidies are not wasted where they are not needed and do not distract from desired distributional outcomes. The second, which could be described as class efficiency, involves a two-step process, first determining whether the policy intention is to subsidise suppliers or their customers and then ensuring the benefit reaches the intended class of recipients.

### *i. Object Efficiency*

Different, but parallel, considerations apply to object efficiency where specific types of consumption are targeted to address the regressivity of VAT and where they are targeted to promote the consumption of merit goods or services. Concessions that are used to mitigate the effects of regressivity should not reduce the VAT paid by high-income consumers significantly more than they reduce the VAT paid by low-income persons. Concessions adopted to subsidise merit goods or services should not deliver windfalls to beneficiaries who would have consumed the same amount of these supplies without a subsidy.

To the extent that concessions are intended to address the regressivity of VAT and reduce the proportion of expenditure by lower income persons that is subject to tax, the efficiency goal completely overlaps with the fairness criterion for evaluating tax expenditures. As noted earlier, however, tax expenditures reduce the VAT paid by high-income consumers significantly more than they reduce the VAT paid by low-income persons.

The targeting difficulty results from the inherent inefficiency of addressing regressivity concerns in a general consumption tax. Although it is possible to observe the consumption patterns of different income classes, the policy decisions

In addition, tax expenditures are almost certainly more vulnerable to lobbying and uncontrolled expansion than direct spending programmes that are subject to strict scrutiny.[23] Reduced and zero-rates and exemptions incentivise taxpayers to lobby for further concessions or call for the extension of favourable tax treatment to similar or related supplies to level the playing field. In recent years, following successful campaigns from the publishing industry, the preferential treatment applied to printed books was extended to electronically supplied publications in the UK and the EU.[24] Similarly, lengthy debates over the controversial 'tampon tax', a term used to refer to the application of VAT to women's menstrual hygiene products, led many countries to remove or reduce the VAT on menstrual hygiene products to align the VAT treatment of these products with other goods classified as necessities.[25]

The scope of concessions may also be expanded as a result of court decisions. For example, following litigation, the UK restricted the concession for sports drinks. Under the UK VAT legislation, food of a kind used for human consumption is zero-rated, but beverages are subject to the standard rate as they fall within an exception to the zero-rating rule.[26] The courts had found some sports drinks not to be beverages due to their nutritional content.[27] This created an anomaly in which some sports drinks were subject to the standard rate,[28] whilst others were zero-rated, depending on whether they were consumed for nutritional purposes. The anomaly was addressed in 2012 through a legislative amendment that specifically applies the standard rate to sports nutrition drinks, aligning their VAT treatment with that of other sports drinks.[29] Experiences such as this illustrate how the use of tax expenditures can make government budget control significantly more difficult, if not impossible.

*Shedding Light on Government Spending through the Tax System: Lessons from Developed and Transition Economies* (Washington, The World Bank, 2004).

[23] J Tyson, 'Reforming Tax Expenditures in Italy: What, Why, and How?' (IMF Working Paper WP/14/7, January 2014).

[24] Zero-rating was extended to electronically supplied publications in the UK in 2020. See Value Added Tax Act 1994 c 23, Sch 8, Group 3, Item 7, inserted by 'Value Added Tax (Extension of Zero-Rating to Electronically Supplied Books etc.) (Coronavirus) Order 2020/459', Art 3. The EU introduced legislation to give the Member States the option to apply the same (lower or zero) rates to electronically supplied publications as they apply to printed publications. See, Council Directive (EU) 2018/1713 of 6 November 2018 amending Directive 2006/112/EC as regards rates of value added tax applied to books, newspapers and periodicals [2018] OJ L286/20.

[25] For example, the tax was removed in Canada in 2015, in India in 2018, in Australia in 2019, and in the UK in 2021. Germany reduced the VAT rate that applies to menstrual hygiene products from 17% to 7% in 2020.

[26] Value Added Tax Act 1994 c 23, Sch 8, Group 1, General Item 1, and Excepted Item 4.

[27] See, eg, *SIS (Science in Sport) Ltd v Customs and Excise Commissioners (No.1)* [2000] 3 WLUK 379.

[28] See, eg, *GlaxoDSmithKline Services Unltd v Revenue and Customs Commissioners* [2011] UKUT 432 (TCC).

[29] Value Added Tax Act 1994 c 23, Sch 8, Group 1, Excepted Item 4A, inserted by Finance Act 2012 c 14, Sch 26(1), para 2(2). The policy intention of the legislative amendment is explained in HM Revenue & Customs, 'VFOOD7590 – Expected Items: Beverages: Item 4A: Sports Drinks' (HMRC internal manual: VAT Food, Updated 24 July 2024), available at www.gov.uk/hmrc-internal-manuals/vat-food/vfood7590.

# IV. Distortions in the VAT System

Apart from their troublesome outcomes as spending measures, VAT concessions create significant collateral distortions in terms of their economic, legal and administrative impacts. Each effect presents further compelling rationales for reform.

## A. Economic Distortions

If VAT is imposed on a broad base and at a single rate, all consumption is subject to the same level of tax and other than constraining the total amount of consumption, the tax has no impact on market decisions. The use of VAT concessions undermines neutrality and equality in the VAT system, distorts consumption, production and investment decisions as well as business structure choices. Competitive pressures for innovation and more efficient means of production are removed for suppliers of goods and services enjoying lower VAT rates. Producers, therefore, have incentives to shift production from higher taxed products to lower taxed ones, and to repackage and rebrand in order to shift products from one category of supply to another.

While all types of concessions raise economic efficiency concerns, the distortions caused by exemptions can be particularly pernicious. Since input tax credits are not available for exempt supplies, when exemptions arise at intermediate stages and exempt supplies are used as inputs in making taxable supplies at the subsequent stages of the supply chain, the 'logic of the VAT'[30] is violated as the business-to-business (B2B) chain of tax and offsetting credit is broken. The unrecoverable input tax is likely to be embedded in the cost of subsequent sales and be subject to tax again, leading to tax cascading. The longer the supply chain, the greater the level of cascading there will be. Therefore, the use of exemptions, which results in tax falling on business acquisitions, is a serious violation of the fundamental principle of VAT being a tax on final consumption.

As unrecovered input VAT carried with exempt supplies forms part of the production cost for business purchasers, they are likely to seek fully taxable alternatives that entitle them to input tax credits over acquisitions of exempt supplies. Registered businesses that provide exempt supplies with embedded input tax are therefore at a competitive disadvantage compared with their competitors that provide fully taxable substitutes when selling to business customers.

A further bias created by the use of exemptions is the incentive for self-supply. To avoid input tax on acquisitions, taxable persons making exempt supplies may seek greater vertical integration by bringing services that can be more efficiently outsourced into the business.[31] Exemptions thus potentially encourage in-house

[30] I Crawford, M Keen and S Smith, 'Value Added Tax and Excises' in S Adam and others, *Dimensions of Tax Design: The Mirrlees Review* (New York, Oxford University Press, 2010).

[31] Ebrill and others (n 16) at 86–87.

production, which inhibits specialisation and could lead to the growth of far less efficient businesses.

Exemptions also create a preference for imports by both taxable persons and final consumers.[32] Domestically sourced exempt supplies are input taxed. Imported exempt supplies, in contrast, are completely free of VAT, given that there is no tax in the exporting jurisdiction, where the supplies are treated as zero-rated exports, and no tax on the exempt importation. Firms using exempt supplies as inputs may thus prefer exempt imports to domestically produced supplies.

The magnitude of the efficiency loss associated with all the economic distortions is difficult to gauge, in particular insofar as the exact impact of exemptions on the integrity of the VAT is unclear. Nevertheless, there seems to be little doubt that the inefficiencies are substantial.[33]

## B. Legal Difficulties

The widespread use of concessions is often a prime cause of legislative complexity and a fruitful source of legal disputes. The legal definitions used to identify supplies subject to different tax treatments are not replicated in economic or commercial reality. The flexibility of modern commerce and commercial relations provides almost indefinite opportunities for the repackaging or recharacterisation of supplies. Any rule that carves out particular supplies for concessional treatment, be it exemption, lower rate or zero-rate, creates a legal distinction that raises a host of definitional and interpretative difficulties including boundaries between different treatments and the problem of multi-element supplies, with each element on its own subject to a different tax treatment. In addition, exempt supplies that are accompanied by a denial of input tax credits invite creative business arrangements to bypass the blocked credits.

An initial issue that arises in a system with different VAT treatments is how taxpayers and tax authorities should categorise products that do not clearly fall in one camp or the other. The boundaries between comparable products are often far from intuitive and the indistinct borders both cause confusion and tempt businesses to push the boundaries, sometimes aggressively. Enormous administrative and judicial resources are then needed to draw the lines on a case-by-case basis.

In the UK, for example, where the VAT system is characterised by the extensive use of concessions, deciding which rate should apply to food products is a persistent problem for manufacturers, the revenue authority and courts. Arcane issues arose as to whether, for example, brownies, snowballs and fruit and nut bars

[32] ibid, at 88.

[33] Institute for Fiscal Studies and others, 'A Retrospective Evaluation of Elements of the EU VAT System' (December 2011).

should be characterised as zero-rated cakes or standard-rated confectionary.[34] The definitional problems in the law are exacerbated by the constant development of new and innovative products that do not fit neatly into the pre-existing categories, often leading to curious anomalies with no discernible policy basis.[35] The difficult distinction between flapjacks and cereal bars arose, for example, because flapjacks, the UK term for baked bars prepared with oats, butter and sugar or syrup, were broadly accepted as cakes (zero-rated), whereas cereal bars (currently characterised as standard-rated confectionary)[36] were not widely available at the inception of VAT.[37]

The use of different rates also exacerbates the difficulty of determining the VAT treatment of multi-element supplies. A single notional supply may include components that on their own constitute different categories of supplies in terms of rates or character as fully taxable or exempt supplies. Since a large number of supplies in the contemporary economy are bundled supplies with multiple components, ambiguities exist as to whether a multi-element supply should be treated for VAT purposes as a mixed supply that is separable into differently taxed components or a composite supply that takes on the tax character of the dominant component within the supply. The general approach is that a multi-element supply is considered a composite supply if the elements are integral parts of an overall supply, and a mixed supply if the elements are separately identifiable and each of them serves its own purpose.[38] Ongoing litigation in various jurisdictions, however, shows that the seemingly straightforward distinction between mixed and composite supplies is far from clear-cut in practice.[39] Each case turns on its own facts, making it impos-

[34] See, eg, *Pulsin' Ltd v HMRC* [2018] UKFTT 775 (TC) (chocolate brownies classified as zero-rated cakes); *Lees of Scotland Ltd, Thomas Tunnock Ltd v HMRC* [2014] UKFTT 630 (TC) (snowballs classified as zero-rated cakes); *Swedish Snowball Production Ltd v CC&E* (MAN/86/0305) (snowballs found to be standard-rated confectionery).

[35] In the UK, for example, chocolate milkshake powder is zero-rated but banana and strawberry flavoured milkshake powder is standard-rated (see, *Nestlé UK Ltd v The Commissioners for HM Revenue and Customs* [2018] UKUT 0029 (TCC)); and fruit salad is zero-rated, whilst smoothies made from fruit or frozen fruit desserts are standard-rated (see, eg, *The Frozen Fruit Company Ltd v The Commissioners for Her Majesty's Revenue & Customs* [2016] UKFTT 12 (TC)).

[36] *WM Morrisons Supermarket PLC v The Commissioners for HM Revenue and Customs* [2023] UKUT 00020 (TCC) (fruit and nut bars characterised as standard-rated confectionery).

[37] HM Revenue & Customs, 'VFOOD6200 – Excepted items: Confectionery: The Bounds of Confectionery, Sweets, Chocolates, Chocolate Biscuits, Cakes and Biscuits: The Borderline between Confectionery and Cakes' (HMRC internal manual: VAT Food, Updated 24 July 2024), available at www.gov.uk/hmrc-internal-manuals/vat-food/vfood6200.

[38] For a detailed summary of the UK's judicial approaches to the characterisation of mixed and composite supplies, see M Conlon QC, 'Apportionment of Consideration for Supplies in UK Value Added Tax' (Australian Bar Association Conference Paper, June 2017), available at austbar.asn.au/uploads/pdfs/conference-papers/Conlon%20QC,%20Michael_Apportionment%20of%20GST%20-%20lessons%20from%20the%20UK%20experience%20with%20VAT.pdf.

[39] See, eg, Case C-349/96 *Card Protection Plan Limited v Commissioners of Customs & Excise* ECLI:EU:C:1999:93 [1999] ECR I-00973 (supply consists of standard-rated card handling services and exempt insurance services); *Re Food Supplier and Commissioner of Taxation* [2007] AATA 1550 (Australia) (supply of GST-free food packaged with standard-rated promotional non-food items for a single price).

sible to develop precise boundaries from common law precedents or civil law principles.

Furthermore, the different tax treatments incentivise businesses to push the boundary between mixed and composite supplies, with a view to benefiting from the more favourable treatment. A recent example is *Queenscourt Ltd v Revenue and Customs Commissioners*,[40] in which a dispute arose between the taxpayer and the UK's tax authority, HM Revenue & Customs (HMRC), over the VAT treatment of KFC 'dip pots'. Historically, the taxpayer treated the dip pots as zero-rated supplies of cold takeaway food when sold on their own, but as part of a single standard-rated supply of hot food and dips when sold as part of a meal deal.[41] However, in order to benefit from the zero-rating treatment of cold takeaway food, the taxpayer changed their position and instead argued that the dip pots were separate zero-rated supplies even when sold as part of a meal deal.[42]

Exemptions also invite tax minimisation schemes by suppliers seeking entitlement to input tax credits for acquisitions that ultimately relate to exempt supplies. Additional complexity results from the use of sophisticated intra-group arrangements including internal transfer pricing to maximise input tax entitlements, as the leading Court of Justice of the European Union (CJEU) cases *Halifax*[43] and *BUPA*[44] illustrate. Whilst anti-avoidance rules or judicial doctrines can be relied on by tax authorities to curb the spread of schemes, the long term and more logical solution is to reform the structural features of the law that open the door to avoidance arrangements.

## C. Administrative and Compliance Costs

The use of concessions inevitably leads to an increase in compliance burden for registered businesses and administrative burden for tax administrators, although the exact measurements of the effect of concessions on compliance costs or administrative costs have yet to emerge. The boundaries between different treatments appear to be a main driver of VAT complexity and the resulting administrative and compliance burden.

Registered persons need to divert time and resources to distinguish between fully taxable, reduced rated, zero-rated and exempt versions of often similar supplies. All three types of concession demand further efforts from registered businesses to determine whether multi-element supplies should be characterised as mixed supplies

[40] *Queenscourt Ltd v Revenue and Customs Commissioners* [2024] UKFTT 460 (TC).

[41] See also n 58 below and the accompanying text at n 59.

[42] In this case, the Tribunal dismissed the taxpayer's appeal, holding that the supply of dip pots as part of a meal deal is part of a single standard-rated supply of hot food and dips.

[43] Case C-255/02 *Halifax Plc and others v Commissioners of Customs & Excise* ECLI:EU:C:2006:121, [2006] ECR I-1609.

[44] Case C-419/02 *BUPA Hospitals Ltd, Goldsborough Developments Ltd v Commissioners of Customs & Excise* ECLI:EU:C:2006:122, [2006] ECR I-1685.

or composite supplies. All these issues also increase administrative costs for tax authorities.

In the case of mixed supplies, the price charged for the single transaction has to be apportioned between different component parts to determine the VAT liability. Exemptions may also give rise to an issue of apportionment that arises when businesses make both exempt and taxable supplies. As deductions for input tax are only allowed where an input is used to make a taxable supply, these businesses must track the application of all inputs to apportion the use of inputs between taxable and exempt supplies.

The greatest difficulty, however, arises in relation to the apportionment of residual input tax, that is, tax on acquisitions that are indistinguishably attributable to both taxable and exempt supplies such as overheads.

Many countries allow businesses that make mixed supplies or a combination of exempt and taxable supplies to self-select apportionment methods appropriate to their business models (in some cases subject to the approval of the tax authority).[45] The option to self-select increases compliance costs as taxpayers make calculations based on alternative formulae to achieve an optimal tax result. From an administrative perspective, tax officials must evaluate whether taxpayers' chosen methods produce a fair and reasonable outcome. The legitimacy of businesses' chosen methods is often tested on a case-by-case basis through costly litigation.[46] Apportionment in the case of mixed supplies raised additional concerns over the potential for manipulation by taxpayers of values of components within a single transaction. In the UK, for example, some businesses were found to have exploited the flexibility of non-prescriptive law by apportioning less of the total price to the components that are subject to the standard rate, thereby reducing the amount of VAT payable.[47]

## V. Pathway for Reforms

The tax expenditure analysis of VAT concessions suggests that they are ill-suited tools to achieve social and economic objectives. The negative ramifications of VAT concessions have long been recognised. Tax reform literature almost uniformly advocates their removal as the optimal way to address these problems.[48] Reform-minded policymakers, however, are often faced with two challenges: the

[45] The UK, for example, requires that the apportionment methods for dividing residual input tax between taxable and exempt supplies devised by taxpayers must be approved by HMRC. See, Value Added Tax (Amendment) Regulations 2017, SI 2017/295, reg 102.

[46] See, eg, *Revenue and Customs Commissioners v Lok'nStore Group Plc* [2014] UKUT 288 (TCC) (taxable persons allowed to apportion inputs attributable to taxable sales on the basis of floor space); *Hurlingham Club v Revenue and Customs Commissioners* [2015] UKFTT 76 (TC) (taxable person not allowed to apportion on the basis of floor space).

[47] HMRC, 'VAT and Value Shifting: Consultation' (5 January 2021).

[48] See, eg, AA Tait, *Value Added Tax: International Practice and Problems* (Washington, International Monetary Fund, 1988) 44; S Adam and others, *Tax by Design: The Mirrlees Review* (Oxford, Oxford University Press, 2011) 229.

first is to develop an effective analytical tool for informed policymaking; and the second is to overcome the political barriers to effective base broadening reforms.

## A. Tax Expenditure Reporting and Evaluation

Understanding the revenue impact of VAT concessions is a crucial step in a comprehensive analysis of the effectiveness of using VAT tax expenditures to deliver subsidies. In advanced economies, the revenue cost of VAT concessions is commonly recorded in tax expenditure accounts (as a legal requirement in many countries).[49] The foundation of tax expenditure analysis as a tool to reform tax concessions is full recognition of tax expenditures as government spending programmes. National tax expenditure budgets implicitly recognise total VAT revenue as comprising two components – a portion that is collected and then expended through direct expenditures and a portion that is notionally collected and immediately remitted as tax expenditures. To date, the two components have been analysed in isolation. If they are combined, the actual cost of tax expenditures and direct expenditures can be evaluated in terms of true VAT revenue, comprising both collected tax and tax forgone prior to collection. The proportion of revenue expended by way of tax expenditures can be expressed as a VAT tax expenditures ratio (VTER). In figures, the VTER would be:

$$\text{VTER} = \frac{\text{VAT tax expenditures}}{\text{VAT tax expenditures} + \text{revenue collected}}$$

Tax expenditure reports should also be presented in a way that facilitates comparison of VAT tax expenditures with direct spending programmes. This requires that tax expenditure budgets should not only report the aggregated revenue forgone data, but also detail expenditure breakdown by budget functions applied to direct expenditures.[50] Ideally, the distributional incidence of VAT tax expenditures should be analysed from time to time, as is done in Australia.[51]

In developed countries with good tax expenditure reporting practices, additional efforts are needed to ensure that tax expenditure evaluations are fed back into the policymaking process, potentially offering evidence-based support to future base broadening reforms. Whilst, in recent years, there has been a growing

[49] A Redonda and T Neubig, 'Assessing Tax Expenditure Reporting in G20 and OECD Economies' (CEP Discussion Note 2018/3, November 2018) available at www.cepweb.org/wp-content/uploads/2018/11/Redonda-and-Neubig-2018.-Assessing-Tax-Expenditure-Reporting.pdf.

[50] L Villela, A Lemgruber and M Jorratt, 'Tax Expenditure Budgets: Concepts and Challenges for Implementation' (Inter-American Development Bank Working Paper Series No. IDB-WP-131, April 2010) 42.

[51] See The Treasury, Australian Government (n 13). The US Congressional Budget Office examines the distribution of major tax expenditures in the individual income tax and payroll tax systems. See, 'The Distribution of Major Tax Expenditures in 2019' (The United States Congressional Budget Office, October 2021).

interest in reporting on tax expenditures in the developing world, there is considerable room for improvement in most countries.[52] In developing countries, the priority is to build the practice of reporting tax expenditures as part of the budget process and gradually improve the quality of tax expenditures reports as their political and institutional capacities grow.[53]

## B. Removing VAT Concessions

Once the fiscal cost of concessions is properly evaluated, the challenge is to remove concessions that do not represent value for money and are not appropriate for the original policy purposes.

Although it has long been recognised that VAT concessions are a blunt instrument for addressing distributional concerns, there is a belief that the case for concessions is stronger in developing countries without alternative (spending) instruments to subsidise the poor.[54] This argument, however, has gradually weakened in recent decades in the context of expanding cash transfer schemes in low- and middle-income countries, although the redistributional impact may be limited by the narrow coverage of many schemes.[55] Moreover, employing VAT concessions as a convenient way of pursuing equity objectives does not make problems with the spending programmes disappear. On the contrary, it might reduce the political pressures to fix these problems and hinder the process of developing effective income tax and targeted transfer systems, whilst creating distortions and complicating administration in the VAT system. Low- and middle-income countries should be more cautious when using concessions given that they are more in need of revenue to fund social protection systems, and administration and compliance complexities are often dominant considerations in tax design in these countries. Therefore, developing and least developed countries should be encouraged to continue to invest in targeted welfare programmes, rather than relying on inefficient tax expenditures in lieu of direct spending programmes.

Experience has shown that, once introduced, concessions are difficult to remove and are prone to expansion due to political pressure through business lobbying. The zero-rating of food existed when the VAT was adopted in the UK in 1973 has remained largely unchanged five decades later.[56] The UK's recent experience with

[52] L Kassim and M Mansour, 'Tax Expenditure Reporting in Developing Countries: An Evaluation' (2018) 26 *Revue d'économie du développement* 103.

[53] C Heady and M Mansour, 'Tax Expenditure Reporting and Its Use in Fiscal Management: A Guide for Developing Countries' (IMF How to Notes 19/01, March 2019).

[54] Ebrill and others (n 16) at 75; RM Bird and P-P Gendron, *The VAT in Developing and Transitional Countries* (Cambridge, Cambridge University Press, 2007) 127.

[55] L Abramovsky, D Philips and R Warwick, 'Redistribution, Efficiency and the Design of VAT: A Review of the Theory and Literature' (The Institute for Fiscal Studies, 2017).

[56] HMRC, 'VAT: Addressing Borderline Anomalies' (Consultation document, 21 March 2012), available at webarchive.nationalarchives.gov.uk/ukgwa/20140109143644/http://www.hmrc.gov.uk/budget2012/vat-con-4801.pdf.

attempts to remove VAT concessions further demonstrates the political sensitivity of base broadening reforms.

With an aim to end some borderline anomalies in VAT, the then UK Government announced proposals to remove the zero-rating treatment for certain hot takeaway foods and static holiday caravans in the 2012 Budget.[57] The controversial borderline between 'hot takeaway food' (standard-rated) and 'cold takeaway food' (zero-rated)[58] has been the subject of continual litigation, with the case outcomes often hinging on the temperature at which the food is served.[59] Takeaway food sold to be eaten hot is subject to the standard 20 per cent VAT, whereas baked goods which are put on display warm and subsequently cooled down (rather than being kept hot in a special cabinet) are treated as zero-rated 'cold takeaway food'. The change proposed by the Government, if implemented, would have imposed 20 per cent VAT on food that cools down (including pies, pasties, sausage rolls), which is at a temperature above the ambient air temperature at the time it is provided to the customer. The Budget proposals also included the imposition of VAT at the standard rate on static holiday caravans, which had previously been treated as zero-rated supplies due to a misapplication of the zero-rate that was intended solely for residential caravans.[60] The proposed change aimed to align the VAT treatment of static holiday caravans with that of touring caravans.

The proposals sparked outrage among representatives of the pasty and static caravan industries.[61] The Government, facing significant public opposition, quickly reversed its proposals – the plan to impose VAT on baked goods that cool down naturally was dropped, and the intended 20 per cent VAT charge to static caravans was reduced to five per cent.

The UK's piecemeal and incremental approach to base broadening reforms has almost consistently failed. The UK experience highlights a typical political economy challenge – tax reforms that appear efficient from an economic point of view do not represent a political equilibrium.[62] The unsuccessful attempts can, at least in part, be attributed to the Government's failure to compensate those who were expected to lose out due to the proposed changes.

[57] HM Treasury, 'Budget 2012' (HC 1853, March 2012) 1.202.

[58] Value Added Tax Act 1994 c 23, Sch 8 Group 1, Notes (3)(b).

[59] See, eg, *Pegasus (Manchester) Ltd v Revenue and Customs Commissioners* [2018] UKFTT 126 (TC); *Eat Ltd v Revenue and Customs Commissioners* [2019] UKFTT 67 (TC). See also, HMRC, 'VAT: Addressing Borderline Anomalies' (n 56) at 6.

[60] For the background on this proposed change, see HMRC, 'VAT: Addressing Borderline Anomalies' (n 56) at 20.

[61] See, eg, N Huber, 'Bakers Protest Vote on Pasty Tax' (*AccountingWEB*, April 2012), available at www.accountingweb.co.uk/tax/business-tax/bakers-protest-vote-on-pasty-tax; HC Deb 22 May 2012, vol 545, cols 1098–1104.

[62] E Ilzetzki, 'Tax Reform and the Political Economy of the Tax Base' (2018) 164 *Journal of Public Economics* 197.

The lesson is that a systematic reform of concessions across the VAT legislation, accompanied by a package of measures to compensate the losers, may be necessary to achieve any real success.[63] From a tax policy perspective, a reform programme across an entire area has the advantage of offering greater consistency over isolated piecemeal tinkering with the tax system.[64] As a matter of political economy, it is easier, with a large-scale tax reform combined with compensatory measures, to trade off gains and losses.[65] The recognition of VAT tax expenditures as government spending programmes suggests that the obvious solution is to replace VAT concessions with targeted spending measures. With spending programmes funded by the revenue gains from a broadening of the VAT base, the reform would fully compensate low-income persons for the VAT increase, while still leaving the government with an extra revenue yield.[66]

As the UK experience demonstrates, special interest groups are often very effective in voicing oppositions to base broadening reforms. However, the lobbying incentives of special interest groups may be reduced in a systematic reform, compared to gradual reforms, since no single group is asked to relinquish its preferential tax treatment in isolation.[67] Moreover, effective compensatory measures for low-income persons make it harder for special interest groups to skew the tax system towards their own interests by appealing to redistributive concerns. The opposing opinions could also be weakened substantially due to the greater efficiency gains resulting from a systematic base broadening reform.

The art of successful base broadening reform is, therefore, to construct effective compensation packages for the losers. The most effective way of offsetting the VAT burden for low-income persons is to provide tapered benefits based on income. These can be made directly as welfare payments or indirectly by means of a progressive and refundable tax credit incorporated in the income tax system. The latter may be more cost efficient from an administrative perspective as the same agency measures income and distributes benefits based on that measurement. The Canadian compensatory tapering and refundable tax credit system, known as the GST/Harmonised Sales Tax (HST) credit, provides a working example of this system. The Canadian system provides yearly entitlements paid in four quarterly instalments based on the recipients' marital status, family size and family net income.[68]

[63] R de la Feria and M Walpole, 'The Impact of Public Perceptions on General Consumption Taxes' [2020] *British Tax Review* 637, 666–67.

[64] J Khalizadeh-Shirazi and A Shah, 'Tax Reform in Developing Countries: What Constitutes Successful Tax Reform? A Review of Developing Country Experience' (1991) *Finance & Development* 44.

[65] ibid.

[66] Adam and others (n 48) at 227.

[67] de la Feria and Walpole (n 63) at 664.

[68] See, 'Goods and services tax/harmonised sales tax (GST/HST) credit: payments chart effective July 2025–June 2026 (2024 base year)' (Government of Canada), available at www.canada.ca/en/revenue-agency/services/child-family-benefits/goods-services-tax-harmonized-sales-tax-gst-hst-credit/goods-services-tax-harmonised-sales-tax-credit-payments-chart.html.

Although the Canadian approach has proven to be effective, it has not been widely adopted by other jurisdictions. An alternative option that has gained attention in a few countries in recent years features the introduction of a targeted cashback scheme, through which the VAT is refunded to low-income persons.[69] Advances in digital technology over the past few decades make it possible to refund the VAT in real-time (that is, at the point of purchase) into the (dedicated) bank accounts of those who are in need of financial support.[70] The core attributes of the real-time cashback scheme may not be substantially different from the Canadian GST/HST credit system. What is new is the use of digital technology to alter the frequency and timing of the delivery of subsidies. The method for calculating entitlements used in the Canadian system could serve as a model for determining the refund entitlements in a real-time cashback system. The system would ideally feature a tapered annual refund allowance, which represents the maximum amount of VAT that is refunded to the qualified persons or families. The tapering entitlements would achieve the redistributive objectives, while preventing abuse of the system by higher-income persons. Moreover, the annual refund allowance would eliminate the need for VAT adjustments in cases of cancelled transactions or partial or full refunds of purchase prices.[71]

The proposed real-time cashback scheme appears to be an attractive option for two main reasons. First, it provides an opportunity for encouraging the use of banking or basic payment services by low-income persons, potentially reducing the cash-driven informal economy and tax evasion. Second, compared to the Canadian system that is based on instalment payments, a real-time cashback system makes it easier for beneficiaries to relate the benefits to the VAT, thereby reducing the political resistance to base broadening from the general public.[72] However, it must be pointed out that the initial set-up costs for the tax authorities and financial intermediaries could be very high, not least for a targeted scheme under which the levels of subsidies vary depending on individual circumstances. Furthermore, many countries, in particular developing and least developed countries, may not have the technological infrastructure to enable such a scheme in

[69] For example, a cashback scheme, as part of a significant VAT reform, is being considered in Brazil. See, R Vale and others, 'Distributional Impacts of Brazil's Tax Reform: Scenarios Regarding *Cesta Básica* Exemption' (World Bank Group Poverty and Equity Notes, October 2023).

[70] R de la Feria and A Swistak, 'Designing a Progressive VAT' (IMF Working Paper WP/24/78, April 2024).

[71] The simple method, preferred by de la Feria and Swistak, ibid, under which persons with income falling below a chosen threshold do not pay VAT on their consumption, may give rise to two main difficulties. First, as pointed out by de la Feria and Swistak, the VAT burden suddenly increases for those who have income just above the threshold, which may increase public resistance to the proposal. Second, because persons with income below the threshold do not pay VAT regardless of their consumption, an anti-abuse mechanism would need to be introduced to prevent them from making purchases on behalf of persons who are not qualified for subsidies. In addition, VAT adjustment following a partial or full refund of the purchase price would be needed, which may add a layer of complexity. These issues unavoidably complicate an approach that was meant to be clear-cut and easy to apply.

[72] Bird and Gendron discussed the Canadian experience of failing to establish a clear nexus between the tax credits and the GST concessions which the tax credits were introduced to replace. See, Bird and Gendron (n 3) at 529–31.

the near future. For example, the inadequate digitalisation of payments and banking penetration in Colombia was the key reason behind its preference for a VAT compensation mechanism built into the existing social programmes to deliver cash transfers, rather than a tax refund.[73]

The public, and in particular low-income persons, may be sceptical about the government's claim that the regressive effect of the reform will be fully compensated, or concerned about losing compensations following a change of government. Indeed, previous experiences in New Zealand and Australia, for example, highlight the risk of gradual erosion of compensation.[74] In New Zealand, welfare benefits were sharply cut by a new government four years after the introduction of GST in 1986.[75] Low-income groups may therefore resist base broadening reforms, even if they understand that wealthier individuals benefit more from the VAT concessions. Beneficiaries' concerns about the stability and longevity of direct compensation measures targeted at a minority of voters compared to the perceived stability of universal VAT concessions benefiting a broad political base recognise a simple political equation: removal of VAT concessions is far more difficult than abolition of direct subsidies. Therefore, targeted compensation programmes may need to be more generous than what is strictly necessary to fully compensate the poor, a political price to pay especially if the trust in government is low. Overcompensation would ensure that beneficiaries are better off for some time through higher compensation at the beginning in case of later withdrawal of the compensation policy.[76]

## C. Reforming VAT Concessions

If the complete removal of concessions is politically unattainable,[77] the question then becomes which current concessions can be removed and replaced and which can be retained but improved and, in the case of the latter group, how they can be improved. It may be advisable to use reduced rates in preference to zero-rate and exemptions, especially in developing countries. On the one hand, the use of zero-rate and reduced rates does not break the VAT chain in the way exemptions do, thereby avoiding the cascading problems associated with exemptions. On the other hand, reduced rates and zero-rate increase the likelihood that businesses producing lightly taxed outputs from fully taxed inputs will be entitled to refunds.[78] The refund system is considered 'the most significant

[73] OECD, *Policy Note on the Introduction of VAT Compensation for Vulnerable Households in Colombia* (Paris, OECD Publishing, 2020) 6.

[74] J Daley and D Wood, 'A GST Reform Package' (Grattan Institute, 2015) 19.

[75] P Davidson, 'Tax Reform: A Retrospective' (2000) 23 *UNSW Law Journal* 264.

[76] Daley and Wood (n 74) at 1.

[77] See also M Keen, 'Targeting, Cascading, and Indirect Tax Design' (IMF Working Paper WP/13/57, February 2013) 13, for a discussion of the political difficulty in implementing combined tax-spending reforms as discussed in section V.B.

[78] Crawford, Keen and Smith (n 30) at 291.

vulnerability with the VAT', with fraudulent refund claims being the most obvious way to exploit the invoice-credit mechanism.[79] The control over refunds has proved to be an area of administrative difficulty that is especially pertinent for developing countries with weaker administrative capacity.[80] The problem could be less acute with the use of reduced rates than zero-rate. Where exemptions must be used, they should be restricted to supplies predominantly provided to final consumers so as to more effectively target the intended beneficiaries and minimise the distortionary cascading effects.

While inefficiency and complexity cannot be eliminated entirely so long as concessions remain in the VAT system, a more precisely targeted list of concessionally taxed necessities can help mitigate distortions and reduce the administrative and compliance costs. In many countries, the policy objective is all too often lost in the current approach that relies on broad categories of necessities such as 'food' along with ambiguous or arbitrary distinctions not obviously tied to the objective. The logic between distinguishing chocolate-covered biscuits from chocolate-covered cakes in the UK (as in the well-known 'Jaffa cake' litigation),[81] or treating a supply of six doughnuts as zero-rated food while taxing a supply of five doughnuts at the full rate (as is currently the law in Canada),[82] to target tax relief for lower income persons is at best obscure.

To achieve the intended policy and improve targeting efficiency, broad, vague and often very inconsistent designations that seek to second guess the needs of lower income persons should be replaced with narrowly targeted goods and services that comprise a large percentage of expenditure by lower income persons as identified by objective household expenditure survey data. For example, South Africa (where a relatively narrowly targeted list of food items is used for zero-rating) evaluated whether zero-rating achieves the policy intention by examining the distribution of benefits derived from zero-rating of each food item across low-income households and higher income households, as well as the definitional issues associated with each item.[83] Better targeting in this way avoids excessive leakage of benefits to high-income persons. Efficiency can be enhanced if the targets are reviewed regularly and adjusted as appropriate to changes in the consumption patterns of low-income persons and higher income persons.

Concessions justified on the basis that they apply to merit supplies often extend beyond a rational target for merit goods, which could be a consequence of ambiguous drafting of tax expenditure provisions in VAT laws and

[79] Krever (n 11) at 13.

[80] Bird and Gendron (n 54) at 176.

[81] *United Biscuits (UK) Ltd v CC&E* [1991] LON/91/160.

[82] (Canada) Excise Tax Act (R.S.C., 1985, c. E-15), Sch VI, Part III, para 1(m).

[83] See, eg, Independent Panel of Experts for the Review of Zero Rating in South Africa (n 17) at 40–62.

consequent judicial rulings that misconstrue the intended goals of concessions.[84] As noted earlier,[85] merit supplies that are predominantly consumed by high-income persons may not only have a regressive impact but also be less effective in achieving the intended objective of encouraging the consumption of these supplies. One technique for targeting concessions for merit supplies is to piggy-back the tax expenditure provisions on the relevant direct expenditures laws or laws that tightly regulate a field. Health tax expenditures, for example, could be limited to services that qualify for direct payments under a national health insurance regime.[86] Similarly, education supplies eligible for concessional treatment could be tied directly to well-established and clearly focused education (expenditure) laws, as is done in Australia,[87] rather than relying on ambiguous tests such as the current UK concession for private tuition in 'a subject ordinarily taught in a school or university'.[88] Tightly drafted tax expenditure provisions could improve targeting efficiency and free tax administrators and appeal adjudicators from the almost impossible task of determining the meaning of many vague terms that establish the artificial boundaries in VAT laws.

## VI. Conclusion

Many VAT concessions were adopted to achieve worthy ends, in particular promoting equity or encouraging the consumption of merit supplies. Nevertheless, concessions in the VAT systems more often than not operate as unfair and inefficient subsidy programmes that give rise to significant legal and economic distortions and high administrative and compliance burdens. While often described as sources of revenue loss, concessions should be more appropriately viewed as indirect revenue appropriations that are functionally equivalent to direct budgetary outlays. The ideal reform would see the replacement of VAT

[84] An example is *Harrier LLC v Commissioners for Her Majesty's Revenue and Customs* [2011] UKFTT 725 (TC), in which photography books containing only photographs taken by customers were characterised as zero-rated supplies of books.

[85] See the text at and preceding n 17 (p 17 above).

[86] An example can be found in (Australia) A New Tax System (Goods and Services Tax) Act 1999. Section 38-7 explicitly links tax-free medical services to those that qualify for direct subsidies under the national health insurance scheme.

[87] (Australia) A New Tax System (Goods and Services Tax) Act 1999, s 38–85 and s 195-1 define tax-free secondary and tertiary courses as those qualifying for financial assistance under the Student Assistance Act 1973.

[88] Value Added Tax Act 1994 c 23, Sch 9, Group 6, Item 2. Suppliers of Pilates lessons, belly dancing and Ceroc dancing lessons all have attempted to rely on the provision to characterise their supplies as exempt education supplies. See, eg, *Hocking v Revenue and Customs Commissioners* [2014] UKFTT 1034 (TC); *Cheruvier (t/a Fleur Estelle Belly Dance School) v Revenue and Customs Commissioners* [2014] UKFTT 7 (TC); *The Commissioners for Her Majesty's Revenue & Customs v Anna Cook* [2021] UKUT 0015 (TCC).

concessions with fairer and better targeted direct expenditure programmes. However, the political economy realities in many countries often hinder the implementation of effective base broadening reforms. This chapter suggests that base broadening reforms may be feasible when paired with targeted spending programmes designed to compensate the poor, who are likely to be adversely affected by the removal of VAT concessions. In countries where the complete removal of concessions is unachievable, reform efforts should focus on improving the design of concessions to enhance targeting efficiency and mitigate the adverse effects of these concessions.

# 3

# Thresholds and Small Businesses*

## I. Introduction

In addition to the use of rate differentiation and exemptions discussed in the previous chapter, the treatment of small businesses is a critical aspect of Value Added Tax (VAT) design. Two features common to most VAT systems are the use of a registration threshold based on annual turnover to determine when businesses are subject to the tax and one or more small business regimes that provide specific tax rules for small businesses that have crossed the registration threshold or which sit below the threshold.

The common (but not universal) support for the adoption of a registration threshold does not extend to the level at which it should be set. Registration threshold levels in Organisation for Economic Co-operation and Development (OECD) countries range from zero in Spain, Chile, Turkey, Costa Rica and Mexico to GBP 90,000 in the United Kingdom (UK),[1] with other countries widely scattered between the two extremes. Outside the OECD, Singapore notably applies a significantly higher threshold of SGD 1 million (approximately GBP 575,000), far exceeding the levels adopted in OECD jurisdictions. As is the case with the registration threshold, there is no unanimity on the rules for small businesses. This chapter reviews the key challenges faced by policymakers in setting the registration thresholds. It also examines the potential benefits and costs of using special regimes for small businesses.

## II. Key Considerations for Threshold Setting

The key rationale for a registration threshold is to balance revenue needs against administrative and compliance costs. In principle, a neutral benchmark VAT applies to all types of supplies made by all categories of suppliers. This general principle, however, neglects the uneven distribution of administration and compliance

* This chapter is a revised and updated version of Y Zu, 'VAT/GST Thresholds and Small Businesses: Where to Draw the Line?' (2018) 66 *Canadian Tax Journal* 309.

[1] OECD, *Consumption Tax Trends 2024: VAT/GST and Excise, Core Design Features and Trends* (Paris, OECD Publishing, 2024). In Columbia, there is no registration threshold for incorporated businesses.

costs and tax revenue across businesses of different sizes. A seemingly universal feature in VAT jurisdictions is that small businesses constitute a large proportion of registered persons but contribute only a small proportion of revenue. Put differently, the VAT base is often heavily concentrated among a small number of large businesses. In the UK, for example, about 75 per cent of the total VAT revenue was paid by only two per cent of the registered businesses in 2023–24.[2]

The sheer number of small enterprises in the VAT system requires unnecessarily high administrative resources even as the revenue collected from the group is low. In the UK, more than half of the cost of administering the VAT can be attributed to the administration of the smallest businesses that account for the bulk of taxable persons and a tiny fraction of VAT revenue collected.[3] A United States (US) study considering the implications of adopting a VAT in that country estimated that removal of smaller businesses from the VAT to reduce the number of registrants by more than half could lower administrative costs by one-third while reducing revenue collection by only three per cent.[4]

Compliance costs borne by registered persons should be of an even greater concern than the administrative costs borne by the tax authority, given that compliance costs appear to be much higher.[5] It is well established in empirical studies that VAT compliance costs fall more heavily on small businesses. The disproportionately higher compliance costs for small businesses result to some extent from the fixed component in compliance costs regardless of the size of business.[6] In one study, compliance costs as a percentage of turnover were estimated to be more than 30 times greater for small businesses than for larger firms.[7]

It is clear that small businesses present a special case in the VAT in terms of both administration and compliance costs. From an efficient tax design perspective, even more important than the absolute cost of small business administration and compliance is its magnitude relative to the revenue collected from these enterprises. The total administrative costs incurred by small businesses in respect of calculating and paying the tax and the administrative costs of collecting tax from this sector may well outweigh the VAT revenue generated by this group of enterprises.[8]

[2] HM Revenue & Customs (HMRC), 'Value Added Tax (VAT) annual statistics 2023 to 2024' (6 November 2024), Tables 5a and 5b.

[3] In a study looking at the 1977–78 fiscal year in the UK, Sandford estimated that 55% of administrative resources were allocated to 69% of registered businesses (under GBP 50,000 turnover) from which less than 5% of revenue was collected. See C Sandford, 'The Administrative and Compliance Costs of Taxation: Lessons from the United Kingdom' (1985) 15 *Victoria University of Wellington Law Review* 199.

[4] 'Value-Added Tax: Administrative Costs Vary with Complexity and Number of Businesses' (United States General Accounting Office, May 1993), available at www.gao.gov/products/ggd-93-78.

[5] Sandford (n 3) at 201.

[6] C Evans and R Krever, 'Counting the Costs of VAT Compliance' in RF van Brederode (ed), *Virtues and Fallacies of VAT: An Evaluation after 50 Years* (The Netherlands, Kluwer Law International, 2021) 131.

[7] The study looked at the 1977–78 fiscal year in the UK. See Sandford (n 3) at 201.

[8] L Ebrill and others, *The Modern VAT* (Washington, DC, International Monetary Fund, 2001) 117.

The response in most countries to the high costs and limited revenue associated with the application of VAT to small businesses has been the adoption of a registration threshold to exclude a portion of small businesses from the VAT system. A high threshold allows revenue authorities to concentrate scarce administrative resources on large businesses and relieves small businesses outside the system from VAT compliance burdens. While the outcome seems not to be fully appreciated by countries with relatively low thresholds, the revenue loss from even high thresholds is unlikely to be significant. With no entitlements to credits for the VAT paid on purchased inputs, firms below the threshold are still input-taxed; only the value added by them escapes taxation.

Focusing on the trade-off between revenue, on the one hand, and administrative and compliance costs, on the other, Keen and Mintz developed a simple theoretical rule that the optimal threshold should be set at the level where the marginal revenue gains from bringing more taxpayers into the VAT system equals the additional administrative and compliance costs.[9] The application of the rule has proved more complex in practice, leading to thresholds above, and very often below, the optimal threshold to which the Keen and Mintz approach would point.[10]

A strict balance between revenue and collection costs also provides a case for a lower threshold for sectors with higher value-added-to-sales ratios.[11] Some countries (for example, Ireland and France) apply lower thresholds for goods than for services.[12] This approach, however, should not be advocated as a model for other countries due to the practical difficulties of distinguishing between goods and services, in particular for businesses providing mixed supplies of goods and services.[13] Differentiated thresholds increase administrative and compliance costs, compromising some of the benefits of adopting thresholds in the first place.

An optimal threshold that balances revenue against administrative and compliance costs is inherently transitory. In theory, the threshold should shift downwards if administrative costs fall as capacity grows and compliance costs decrease with advances in technology. This will be increasingly pertinent in the coming years, given the global movement towards digital transformation of tax administration and compliance. A notable development is the growing implementation of real-time reporting and e-invoicing systems, which eliminate the reliance on paper-based invoicing and manual data entry, while progressively

[9] M Keen and J Mintz, 'The Optimal Threshold for a Value-Added Tax' (2004) 88 *Journal of Public Economics* 559.

[10] For example, many EU Member States appear to have a threshold that is lower than the theoretically optimal threshold. See Institute for Fiscal Studies and others, 'A Retrospective Evaluation of Elements of the EU VAT System' (December 2011) 83.

[11] Keen and Mintz (n 9) at 563; Ebrill and others (n 8) at 119.

[12] In Ireland, for example, the registration thresholds are EUR 40,000 for persons supplying services and EUR 80,000 for persons supplying goods.

[13] A Carter (ed), 'International Tax Dialogue: Key Issues and Debates in VAT, SME Taxation and the Tax Treatment of the Financial Sector' (Paris, International Tax Dialogue, 2013).

enabling the automation of pre-filled tax returns.[14] These digital tools have shown positive results in reducing compliance costs and minimising errors across a range of countries, thereby offering significant potential for leveraging digital solutions to enhance the efficiency of tax compliance.[15] Nevertheless, the effective utilisation of digital technology is likely to remain challenging in the near future in some developing and least developed countries due to, inter alia, limited digital infrastructure, low levels of digital literacy and institutional capacity constraints.[16]

At the same time, inflation will cause the nominal turnovers of businesses to rise while their economic size and capacities remain constant, suggesting a rising threshold is appropriate. The UK and Canada represent examples of opposing practices. The VAT threshold in the UK had historically risen annually in line with inflation,[17] leaving the current threshold level in nominal terms 18 times that used when the VAT came into effect in 1973.[18] In contrast, Canada has never changed its threshold since the Goods and Services Tax (GST) was introduced in 1991. In between lie countries with ad hoc threshold lifts.[19]

A system of continual adjustments for inflation appears to disregard the likelihood of reductions in administrative and compliance costs over time. However, the continual reduction of the threshold in real terms in countries that never adjust the threshold brings ever smaller businesses facing relatively higher compliance burdens into the system. The latter approach to some extent explains the unduly low thresholds in some countries. If the goal was to maintain the original choice of balance between revenue and collection costs, a sensible approach would be to periodically review and adjust the threshold, taking into account changes in the real value of money and administrative and compliance costs.

## III. Consequences of a Threshold

A registration threshold can mitigate the relatively high compliance costs that would be faced by small businesses and disproportionate collection costs that would be

[14] For the current state of play on e-invoicing, see OECD, *Tax Administration 3.0 and Electronic Invoicing: Initial Findings* (OECD Forum on Tax Administration, Paris, OECD Publishing, 2022).

[15] See, eg, evidence from the Korean experience in HC Lee, 'Can Electronic Tax Invoicing Improve Tax Compliance? A Case Study of the Republic of Korea's Electronic Tax Invoicing for Value-Added Tax' (World Bank Group Policy Research Working Paper 7592, March 2016) 33–34.

[16] These limitations were identified in O Okunogbe and F Santoro, 'The Promise and Limitations of Information Technology for Tax Mobilization' (2023) 38 *The World Bank Research Observer* 295, 310–17.

[17] It had remained frozen at GBP 85,000 for seven years, before rising to GBP 90,000 in 2024.

[18] The VAT threshold between April 1973 and September 1977 was GBP 5,000.

[19] For example, the registration threshold in New Zealand was increased by 50% in 2009 in response to the global financial crisis.

borne by revenue authorities if all enterprises were subject to VAT. Provided the threshold is set at an appropriate level, these benefits can be achieved with a minimal cost to revenue. There might also be economic costs resulting from the adoption of a threshold, however. The omission of small businesses from the formal VAT system creates a break in the VAT chain if small unregistered businesses buy from or sell to registered businesses. This break may deny revenue authorities a source of information useful for assessment and audit purposes. In addition, the inability of small businesses to issue tax invoices could lead to a cascading problem as unrecovered VAT on their taxable purchases becomes another cost of acquisition for their registered business customers. Most importantly, the differential treatment of firms above and below the threshold in terms of tax liability and compliance burden may give rise to costly distortions to the competitive positions of registered and unregistered businesses making otherwise comparable supplies and induce inefficient changes in business behaviour that cause further economic harm or lead to revenue losses. Policy responses to these problems could in turn yield new problems and distortions.

## A. Distortion of Competition

A registration threshold drives a wedge between businesses in the VAT system and those excluded from the formal VAT system and instead subject to input taxation. It is a given that greatly different tax treatment of two groups of enterprises operating within the same market will result in competitive distortions, but identifying the precise types and levels of distortions has proved difficult. Some firms left outside the VAT by a registration threshold enjoy benefits from exclusion while others are prejudiced by it.

Firms that have lower inputs relative to outputs and sell primarily to final consumers or unregistered businesses are likely to enjoy competitive advantages from being input taxed only with their value-added escaping tax. This competitive advantage will increase as the proportion of final price attributable to a firm's value-added rises. However, the advantage in this respect has generally not been considered a significant concern. This is because although small firms below the threshold may enjoy tax advantages, their prices at the retail stage may still be higher than those of larger firms that are able to reduce costs by exploiting proprietary information and enjoying the economics of scale.

Two types of small firms below the threshold might be disadvantaged relative to firms subject to VAT. The first type is businesses that regularly make supplies to registered businesses. Small firms below the threshold are unable to issue invoices that entitle registered purchasers to input tax credits. Registered businesses will thus be reluctant to purchase from unregistered firms purely for tax reasons.[20] In

[20] Empirical evidence suggests that firms have a stronger incentive to trade with other firms in the same tax regime, meaning that registered businesses would prefer trading with other registered businesses (and unregistered businesses would prefer trading with other unregistered businesses). See,

the absence of a remedy, distortions of business decisions on the choice of suppliers may reduce the overall efficiency in the economy.[21] The second group consists of enterprises with high input costs relative to taxable output sales. Examples include new businesses that incur start-up costs which initially exceed turnover and businesses that make zero-rated export sales. These firms might be entitled to VAT refunds if they were within the VAT system.

To minimise the competitive disadvantage these firms might face, many countries allow voluntary registration by small firms with turnovers below the threshold. The option for voluntary registration, which removes the compliance and administration cost savings that flow from the registration threshold, has markedly different implications for enterprises choosing to enter the tax net and revenue agencies responsible for administering the tax. The former group is voluntarily incurring higher compliance costs and it must be assumed that these firms believe they will enjoy an overall economic benefit from registration after incurring new compliance costs, or they would not have elected to enter the VAT regime.

From a tax collection perspective, in contrast, the result may be reduced revenue and disproportionately high administration costs. Voluntary registrations may constitute a relatively high percentage of total registrations; in several OECD countries, well over one-third of total VAT registrants are voluntary registrants.[22] As a consequence of the self-selection nature of voluntary registration, this group is likely to be disproportionately populated by persons claiming refunds from the revenue authority rather than those paying net tax to the government. For example, in the UK, 41 per cent of the businesses registered for VAT have a turnover lower than the threshold in 2023–24.[23] About 24 per cent of the voluntary registrants reported nil output sales and the VAT receipts from businesses at the bottom of the turnover scale are negative.[24]

Voluntary registration exacerbates considerably the disproportionate cost of administration relative to revenue that is a feature of the imposition of VAT on low turnover enterprises. Disproportionately high administration costs follow two aspects of voluntary registration. The first is the increased risk of refund-related avoidance schemes and outright fraudulent claims for refunds. Refund requests must be vetted carefully, drawing costly additional administrative resources.[25] Secondly, voluntary registration opens the door to whipsaw behaviour by firms that register to claim input tax credits related to start-up costs and then deregister if ongoing business activities

F Gerard and J Naritomi, 'Value Added Tax in Developing Countries: Lessons from Recent Research' (International Growth Centre Growth Brief Series 015, May 2018) 8–9 available at www.theigc.org/sites/default/files/2018/06/IGCJ6046-VAT-Tax-180521_WEB.pdf; See also evidence from India in L Gadenne, TK Nandi and R Rathelot, 'Taxation and Supplier Networks: Evidence from India' (IFS Working Paper W19/21, August 2019).

[21] Gerard and Naritomi, ibid, 8.

[22] Examples include the UK, New Zealand and Australia. See OECD, *Taxation of SMEs: Key Issues and Policy Considerations* (Paris, OECD Publishing, 2009), 122.

[23] HMRC (n 2) Table 5a.

[24] ibid, Tables 5a and 5b.

[25] E Brashares and others, 'Calculating the Optimal Small Business Exemption Threshold for a U.S. VAT' (2014) 67 *National Tax Journal* 283.

yield turnovers below the registration threshold.[26] It is not uncommon for jurisdictions to require voluntary registrants to remain registered for a minimum period of time (commonly between one to five years) to discourage whipsaw behaviour.[27]

As noted,[28] in theory the optimal registration threshold would be set at the level where the marginal revenue gains from bringing more taxpayers into the VAT system equal the increased administrative and compliance costs resulting from the additional registrations. However, the theoretical model disregards the impact on revenue and compliance costs of voluntary registration. These costs must affect the choice of registration threshold. The revenue yield from voluntary registrants below the threshold is likely to be less, and quite probably substantially less, than if the registration threshold were simply lowered to bring the same number of businesses into the VAT system. At the same time, the increased administration costs incurred in respect of voluntary registrants will increase the revenue needs. The task of re-computing the potential impact of voluntary registration becomes a multi-layered undertaking.

There is, however, little evidence of careful consideration of the impact of voluntary registration on the optimal threshold level. While small businesses may seek to register voluntarily for a number of reasons, including trade with registered businesses and market benefits from appearing larger than is actually the case, there are few comprehensive studies of the relative weighing of different factors inducing voluntary registration.[29] It is also unclear how voluntary registration rates would change if registration thresholds were raised or lowered.

These complications may go some way towards explaining why VAT theorists most often ignore the question of voluntary registration when discussing an optimal registration threshold. Policymakers seeking to calibrate the registration threshold in light of the impact of voluntary registration on revenue and administrative and compliance costs therefore face a quandary. However, while exact calculations may not be possible, an effective revenue service should be able to generate sufficient information for authorities to take the probable effects of voluntary registration into account when setting the registration threshold.

## B. Businesses' Behavioural Responses

Not surprisingly, the sharp rise in tax liability and compliance costs for firms that cross the registration threshold prompts behavioural responses by firms enjoying the advantages of sitting outside the formal VAT system. Often co-existing with a VAT registration threshold is the phenomenon of business bunching, with a large number

[26] OECD, *Consumption Tax Trends 2024* (n 1) at 46.

[27] ibid. Fourteen OECD countries, including the UK and New Zealand, do not apply a minimum registration period.

[28] See the text above at n 9.

[29] See, eg, EA Satterthwaite, 'Electing into a Value-Added Tax: Evidence from Ontario Microentrepreneurs' (2018) 66 *Canadian Tax Journal* 761; R Klahr and others, 'Behaviours and Experiences in Relation to VAT Registration: Final Report' (HMRC Research Report Number:446, November 2017).

of businesses reporting turnover just below the threshold level that would require registration. A registration threshold thus creates a 'cliff-edge': a sharp increase in the number of businesses falling into the turnover band just below the threshold compared to the number in the band immediately above the threshold.[30] Figure 3.1 illustrates this pattern based on UK data for 2014–15. Unlike the VAT, the income tax generally has no registration threshold and income tax data in some countries provide unambiguous evidence of small business bunching below the VAT registration threshold.[31] Businesses that are registered for VAT purposes but which qualify for particularly generous small business concessions or beneficial regimes within the VAT system are equally likely to adopt behaviours to ensure their turnover falls below the threshold at which the concessions are withdrawn.[32]

**Figure 3.1** VAT Bunching: Number of Entities by Turnover Band in the UK, 2014–15[33]

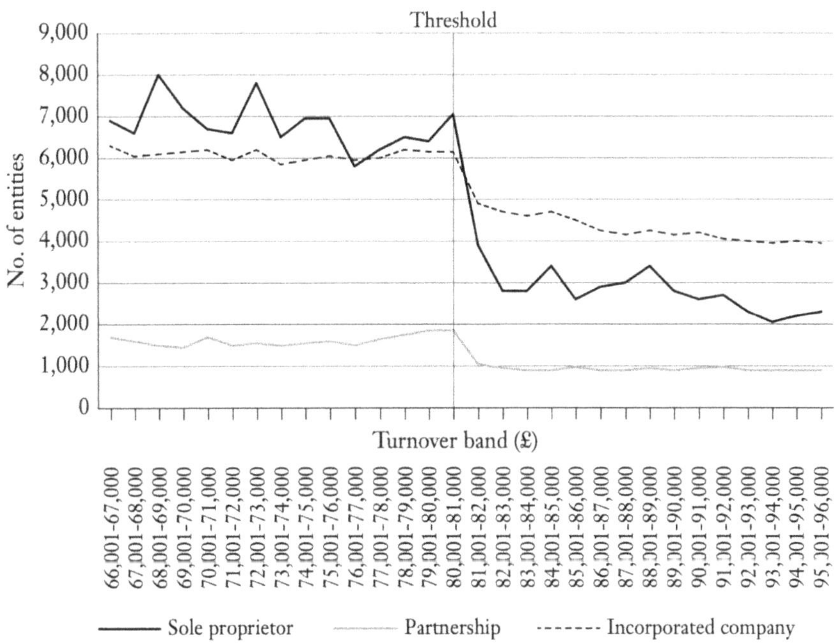


*Source*: United Kingdom, Office of Tax Simplification, *Value Added Tax: Routes to Simplification* (Londan: Office of Tax Simplification, November 2017), at 7.

[30] Office of Tax Simplification, 'Value Added Tax: Routes to Simplification' (2017) 6.

[31] For instance, the evidence was found in the UK, see L Liu and others, 'VAT Notches, Voluntary Registration, and Bunching: Theory and U.K. Evidence' (2021) 103 *The Review of Economics and Statistics* 151; in Finland, see J Harju, T Matikka and T Rauhanen, 'The Effects of Size-Based Regulation on Small Firms: Evidence from VAT Threshold' (CESifo Working Paper No 6115, 2016); and in Brazil, see Gerard and Naritomi (n 20).

[32] For example, evidence of business bunching below the threshold at which concessional treatment was withdrawn under a special regime for small businesses was found in Japan. See, K Onji, 'The Response of Firms to Eligibility Thresholds: Evidence from the Japanese Value-Added Tax' (2009) 93 *Journal of Public Economics* 766.

[33] Office of Tax Simplification (n 30) at 7 (Reproduced under the terms of the Open Government Licence v3).

Businesses seeking to remain below the threshold may adopt one or more of three tactics:

1. deliberately holding back expansion to remain input taxed suppliers;
2. splitting businesses with total turnover above the threshold into smaller separate entities, each of which has a turnover below the threshold; or
3. fraudulently under-reporting sales where actual turnover is above the threshold.

Each of these responses leads to production inefficiency or lost revenue, although their impact varies. While recent empirical studies conducted in the contexts of various jurisdictions successfully document the existence of bunching, their findings differ regarding the extent to which each tactic is used.[34] For most countries, uncertainty as to the prevalence of each tactic compounds the difficulty of devising effective responses.

Much of the emphasis in academic literature and policy discussions is on the first tactic, with concern that restrained production will result in significant efficiency losses from under-utilisation of resources and reductions in potential outputs.[35] The risk of economic harm may be exaggerated, however. Underlying the view that restraint is of prime concern is an assumption that small businesses have unlimited potential and desire for growth. But the reality is that businesses have different initial ambitions towards growth.[36] Those that are capable of ongoing growth will be less tempted to reduce output to stay out of VAT. For these firms, the temporary setback of tax on value added and increase in compliance costs will not outweigh the additional profits from continuing expansion. The threshold will be an inhibition only for small firms with limited prospects for future growth in a no-threshold world. Therefore, the efficiency losses caused by restrained production is unlikely to be as significant as many had anticipated.

An alternative to restraint for an enterprise which is concerned that increased taxation or compliance costs will offset the benefits of higher sales to final consumers is to continue to pursue a total turnover above the registration threshold but artificially split the enterprise into small entities, each of which operates below the registration threshold. Concern over this tactic is not related to economic costs but rather lost revenue from final consumption that should be part of the VAT base.

The most convincing evidence of splitting is found in appeals documenting such behaviour uncovered by revenue authorities. UK cases reveal a number of techniques used by taxable persons who have attempted to split the output of service enterprises to yield multiple turnovers below the registration threshold. One technique is to treat individual service providers within a single operation

[34] A UK study (L Liu, B Lockwood and EHF Tam, 'Small Firm Growth and the VAT Threshold: Evidence for the UK' (IMF Working Paper WP/24/33, February 2024)) and a Finnish study (Harju, Matikka and Rauhanen (n 31)) attribute bunching largely to output restraint, while a Japanese study (Onji (n 32)) suggests splitting is the main cause of bunching in Japan.

[35] See, eg, HM Treasury, 'VAT Registration Threshold: Call for Evidence' (March 2018).

[36] Institute for Fiscal Studies and others (n 10) at 91.

as separate contracted businesses (for example, characterising hairdressers in a hairdressing salon as independent contractors).[37] Another is to attribute different elements of a service to different businesses and business owners (for example, treating a pub meal as separate supplies of food and drink from different related persons).[38] A third technique is to seek to file separate registrations for different businesses operated by the same person (for example, attempting to register a real estate agent business separately from a land developer business).[39]

The concern with the third tactic used to remain below the threshold, under-reporting sales, also involves lost revenue. This behaviour clearly constitutes illegal tax evasion and is most likely to take place in the case of small traders making cash sales to final consumers who do not request invoices.[40]

The implications of each of the three types of behaviour for the setting of the threshold differ.

A change of the threshold level does not remove the temptation to restrain production to stay below the threshold; rather, it simply shifts it to a different group. In theory, the optimal choice of a new threshold will turn on a balance between the potentially increased production by firms with turnovers just below the previous threshold and newly suppressed production by firms with turnovers just below the new higher or lower threshold. If the threshold is raised to a level inhabited by fewer enterprises, there will be a much smaller pool of potential restrainers, prima facie translating to less bunching. Conversely, if the threshold is reduced substantially, the group of businesses that potentially might bunch grows exponentially. On the other hand, if potential restrainers at a lower threshold level and a higher threshold level could grow by the same proportion of their sizes but for the threshold, the absolute value of reduced output caused by a greater number of firms at a lower threshold might be lower. However, restrainers at a higher threshold level might have greater potential for growth, making the overall impact of their restraint more significant. In practice, policymakers are often unable to compare the actual behaviour at both points.

The UK's experience with threshold adjustments provides some insights into how threshold levels might impact on business bunching. Although, as mentioned earlier,[41] the threshold had historically risen in line with inflation, it had been frozen at GBP 85,000 for seven years before it was increased to GBP 90,000 in 2024. Empirical evidence suggests that the number of businesses bunching below the GBP 85,000 threshold had been steadily increasing between 2017 and 2020.[42] While a freeze on the threshold amounts to a reduction in the threshold level in real terms, the UK evidence does suggest that lowering the threshold would increase the scale of bunching below the threshold. However, this does not

[37] See, eg, *Customs and Excise Commissioners v Jane Montgomery (Hair Stylists) Ltd* [1994] STC 256.
[38] See, eg, *Commissioners of Customs and Excise v Marner and Marner* [1977] 1 BVC 1060.
[39] See, eg, *Customs and Excise Commissioners v Glassborow and Another* [1975] QB 465.
[40] D Pomeranz, 'No Taxation without Information: Deterrence and Self-Enforcement in the Value Added Tax' (2015) 105 *American Economic Review* 2539.
[41] See the text above at n 17.
[42] Office for Budget Responsibility, 'Economic and Fiscal Outlook' (March 2023) 67–68.

necessarily point to a higher threshold as a desirable solution to bunching.[43] In countries that do not adjust the threshold in line with inflation, the threshold is decreasing in real terms and the proportion of small businesses with turnovers in the range of the threshold diminish continually to the point at which their numbers become almost insignificant in the larger economy.[44] The difference between raising the threshold and maintaining it at its current level may lie in the timing of the impact: raising the threshold is likely to lead to an immediate reduction in the scale of bunching, whereas maintaining the threshold may yield a similar outcome over time. This suggests that bunching caused by output restraint may be more of a concern in countries in which the threshold is neither too low nor too high.

Finding an optimal threshold level to discourage artificial splitting behaviour is also challenging. One possibility is that a lower threshold would reduce avoidance by artificial splitting.[45] The lower the threshold, the more a growing business would have to split to remain below the threshold. A lower threshold would raise the cost of avoidance by limiting the size of legitimate input taxed businesses. In countries where artificial splitting is not a primary cause of bunching, a more appropriate response may be the use of a dedicated specific anti-avoidance rule (SAAR) to consolidate the output of associated or closely bound enterprises – typically connected through financial, economic and organisational links – as has been done in the UK.[46] Litigation in the UK, however, demonstrates that the tax authority's reliance on the SAAR to challenge artificial splitting schemes has not always been successful.[47]

Wherever the threshold is set, there will be under-reporters with true turnovers above the threshold and consequent administrative costs incurred to protect the integrity of the VAT. The best way to address under-reporting may be to accept this as an inevitable phenomenon whatever the registration threshold, and direct resources to uncover under-reporters and bring those exceeding the threshold into the VAT. Persons under-reporting for VAT purposes are equally likely to under-report for income tax purposes. As thresholds for income tax purposes are uncommon, enhanced enforcement of the income tax for small businesses can be used to reveal under-reporters that should be registered for the VAT. This route is admittedly more difficult in the less common case where the VAT and the income tax are administered by separate agencies.

[43] Kanbur and Keen suggested that to the extent that production restraint is a cause of bunching, a higher threshold would be desirable. See R Kanbur and M Keen, 'Thresholds, Informality and Partitions of Compliance' (2014) 21 *International Tax and Public Finance* 536, 551.

[44] The Office of Tax Simplification in the UK, before its closure in 2022, made a similar point that a significantly reduced threshold would mitigate bunching caused by output restraint. See, Office of Tax Simplification (n 30) at 23.

[45] Ebrill and others (n 8) at 121.

[46] Value Added Tax Act 1994 c 23, Sch 1, para 1A (amended by Finance Act 1997, c 16, s 31(1)).

[47] UK courts have ruled against HMRC in a number of cases concerning business splitting. See, eg, *Charles John Caton v The Commissioners for Her Majesty's Revenue and Customs* [2019] UKFTT 0549 (TC) (a café operated by a husband and a restaurant operated by a wife, located on the same premises, were held to be separate businesses for VAT purposes).

A registration threshold balancing revenue objectives and administrative and compliance costs is a desirable feature of an efficient VAT. There is concern that the bunching problem it creates, and in particular the restraint, splitting and under-reporting tactics adopted by enterprises to fall below the threshold, may yield economic harm for the wider society and revenue losses for the state. Adjustment of the registration threshold has often been suggested or considered as a solution to the problem of business bunching. However, uncertainty remains as to how adjusting the threshold could minimise distortions associated with bunching. The difficulty is enhanced by the absence of reliable empirical evidence on the extent of each type of behaviour that contributes to bunching. A preferable approach is probably to look beyond threshold adjustments when considering responses to bunching.

## IV. Smoothing Regimes for Small Businesses Shifting into the Full VAT

In the absence of any special rules, the consequences of crossing the registration threshold can be significant for small businesses. Compliance costs jump, and the burden of implicit tax built into the price of acquisitions is replaced by liability to remit a higher explicit tax. As noted, the sudden increases in compliance costs and tax burdens were identified as the main causes for the bunching behaviour by small businesses seeking to remain below, or to appear to remain below, the registration threshold. To mitigate this problem, a few countries have adopted, or considered adopting, smoothing mechanisms to cushion the impact of registration on growing businesses by subsidising some of the costs incurred by small businesses shifting into the full VAT. The measures are intended to reduce the barrier to growth caused by VAT registration. The subsidies may, of course, have limited impact on unregistered firms nearing the registration threshold with little prospects for, or interest in, further growth.[48]

The transitional subsidies commonly take the form of a disappearing credit provided to businesses with turnovers that climb over the registration threshold, with the credit phasing out as turnover rises. Japan, for example, had such a regime when its consumption tax, as the Japanese VAT is known, was introduced, but the regime was abolished after eight years. The subsidies provided in the Japanese transitioning regime were particularly generous. At the time of adoption, the consumption tax featured a high registration threshold of JPY 30 million (approximately GBP 150,000) and a vanishing credit for businesses with a turnover between JPY 30 million and JPY 60 million, starting with a full offset for consumption tax otherwise payable by enterprises with turnovers immediately

[48] Institute for Fiscal Studies and others (n 10) at 91.

above the threshold.[49] As a consequence of the high threshold and generous offset, tax savings could be significant and not surprisingly there was a high take-up rate, with 93.3 per cent of eligible registrants signing up for the concessional regime.[50] The concession was found to have an impact on firms otherwise inclined to under-report sales.[51] However, this was achieved at the expense of 88 per cent of the total revenue that would have been raised if all taxpayers within this turnover range had been subject to the normal consumption tax.[52] To limit the windfall gains by businesses with relatively higher turnovers and compliance capacities, Japan lowered the upper limit of the scheme from JPY 60 million to JPY 50 million two years after the introduction of the regime and eventually abolished the regime in 1997.

A less generous regime was adopted in Finland in 2004. Under the Finnish system, the VAT registration threshold was set at EUR 8,500 but a disappearing transition tax relief,[53] in addition to the ordinary input tax credit entitlement, was provided to firms with a turnover between EUR 8,500 and EUR 22,500.[54] The relief was calculated by reference to the net VAT payable. Therefore, the relief was not available to businesses that had a negative VAT liability, which means that, at least some, voluntary registrants could not benefit from the relief.

The Finnish regime had very limited impact on business bunching just below the threshold.[55] It attracted surprisingly little interest from registered firms that were eligible for the relief, with only 31 per cent of the eligible firms applying for the relief when the concessional regime was introduced.[56] The unremarkable impact of the smoothing regime in Finland may be explained by the very limited benefit the concession yields for eligible enterprises.[57] As a result of the low threshold and the relatively low level at which the transitioning relief disappears, the average relief for eligible businesses that did not join the scheme would have been only EUR 617 and 10 per cent of these businesses would have received less than EUR 100 had they joined.[58] The value of incentives compared to the relatively high compliance costs faced by firms entering the VAT system was insufficient to encourage small businesses with limited sales to expand operations and lift turnover above the registration threshold.[59] The regime was abolished at

[49] The transition tax credit was calculated using the following formula: transition tax credit = consumption tax otherwise payable x (JPY 60 million – annual sales)/(JPY 30 million).

[50] H Ishi, *The Japanese Tax System*, 3rd edn (Oxford, Oxford University Press 2001) 292.

[51] WJ Turnier, 'Accommodating to the Small Business Problem under a VAT' (1994) 47 *Tax Lawyer* 963.

[52] Ishi (n 49) at 292.

[53] The tax credit is calculated using the following formula: tax relief = VAT paid – [(turnover – EUR 8,500) x VAT paid]/(EUR 22,500 – EUR 8,500).

[54] The VAT registration threshold and the upper threshold at which level the relief disappears were EUR 15,000 and EUR 30,000 respectively at the end of 2024 when the regime was abolished.

[55] Institute for Fiscal Studies and others (n 10) at 88–89.

[56] ibid at 90.

[57] ibid.

[58] ibid.

[59] ibid at 91.

the end of 2024 as a result of a new EU Directive that mandates the removal of such graduated tax relief across the Member States from January 2025.[60]

The experiences of Finland and Japan illustrate the trade-offs encountered at the margins of smoothing regimes. If the registration threshold is low, a smoothing regime is unlikely to have a significant impact on bunching, as the value of tax relief is low relative to the compliance burden faced by registered businesses. If the registration threshold is high, the corresponding higher value for tax relief may reduce bunching, but the high take-up of the scheme by eligible businesses may lead to substantial revenue cost.

It remains unclear if smoothing regimes designed to reduce bunching incentives could yield better results in VAT systems with thresholds that lie between the two extremes described. However, experience in countries that implemented a smoothing regime suggests that such schemes introduce an additional threshold to monitor and create further complexities for both business taxpayers and revenue authorities.[61] The EU abolished graduated tax relief explicitly on the grounds that it adds complexity and contributes little to reducing the compliance burden for small enterprises.[62] Moreover, it may be possible that bunching will be observed at the new upper threshold, at which level the subsidies are withdrawn. The experience with the application of smoothing regimes to date has been less than encouraging.

## V. Simplification Regimes

Both small businesses facing VAT compliance burden and VAT designers recognise the unfairness of the disproportionate compliance costs faced by the sector compared to that borne by large businesses. The response has been the adoption of a number of 'simplification' systems designed to reduce the cost of compliance for small businesses that have moved into the VAT system. These regimes can operate in conjunction with a VAT threshold, applying to businesses in a defined band above the threshold; or, in the absence of a threshold, they can apply to all businesses with turnovers below the level at which it is agreed the unfairness has largely dissipated.

Simplified regimes may have an impact on the optimal registration level if they operate in conjunction with a registration threshold. The optimal threshold balances revenue against compliance and administrative costs. The reduction in

[60] Council Directive (EU) 2020/285 of 18 February 2020 amending Directive 2006/112/EC on the common system of value added tax as regards the special scheme for small enterprises and Regulation (EU) No 904/2010 as regards the administrative cooperation and exchange of information for the purpose of monitoring the correct application of the special scheme for small enterprises [2020] OJ L62/13, Recital 17.

[61] Deloitte, 'Special Scheme for Small Enterprises under the VAT Directive 2006/112/EC – Options for Review: Final Report Volume I' (European Commission, May 2017) 66–68.

[62] Directive 2020/285 (n 60).

compliance costs for businesses with turnovers at the lower end of the VAT system in theory makes it possible to use a lower threshold while still balancing compliance costs and revenue. Any possible reduction would be limited, however, and possibly negated by the increased administrative costs that would follow if more enterprises entered the VAT system. Even if the goal of reduced costs from simplified rules is not achieved, the professed outcome may provide a rationale for a lower threshold if policymakers seek to tip the balance in favour of increased revenue. Simplified regimes or methods that are commonly used to reduce compliance costs borne by small businesses fall into three groups:

1. less frequent filing and payments;
2. optional cash or payment basis accounting (as opposed to accrual basis accounting);
3. presumptive regimes for small businesses that approximate the VAT that would otherwise be payable under the normal VAT system.

Many countries use more than one of these regimes. The UK, for example, uses all three regimes.

## A. Less Frequent Filing and Payments

Many countries allow small businesses to file and remit less frequently than larger counterparts. The filing and payment periods available vary from jurisdiction to jurisdiction. The UK, Canada and Australia, for example, use monthly, quarterly and annual filing. The assumption is that less frequent filing could significantly reduce compliance costs.[63] However, less frequent, and in particular annual, accounting may even be counterproductive in terms of its simplification goals. In the UK, for example, quarterly filing is the standard option for large and medium-sized businesses,[64] while small businesses with an annual turnover below the current threshold of GBP 1.35 million can elect to file annually under the Annual Accounting Scheme.[65] Anecdotal evidence suggests that in some cases annual return filing increased compliance costs as the single filing prompted poorer record keeping, leaving small businesses struggling to assemble records required to complete one return covering a full year of transactions.[66] As a result, many small businesses that joined the annual accounting scheme later moved back to standard quarterly returns.[67]

For small businesses that file at less frequent intervals, there might be a separate fiscal benefit if tax payments are tied to the filing of returns. Less frequent

[63] OECD, *Taxation of SMEs in OECD and G20 Countries* (Paris, OECD Publishing, 2015) 112.
[64] Value Added Tax Regulations 1995, SI 1995/2518, reg 25.
[65] ibid regs 50(1) and 52(1)(b).
[66] The Office of Tax Simplification, 'Review of Value Added Tax: Progress Report and Call for Evidence' (2017) at 14.
[67] ibid.

tax payments may provide a small cash flow benefit to qualifying taxpayers that could be seen as compensation for the relatively higher compliance costs faced by small businesses.[68] However, there have been concerns over the financial difficulties small businesses tend to have in meeting deferred payment obligations.[69] A compromise solution is to allow optional less frequent filing but require qualifying small businesses to make estimated advance payments at the same frequency as required for other businesses.[70] The Annual Accounting Scheme in the UK, which requires businesses to make advance payments in either nine monthly or three quarterly instalments, provides an example of this approach.[71]

## B. Cash Accounting

VAT systems are generally accrual based, meaning that the VAT is paid (or deducted) when invoices are issued (or received). In many countries, small businesses have the option to use a cash accounting method, accounting for the VAT on the basis of payments received or made.[72] The common practice is to set a threshold based on turnover and allow businesses below that threshold to be eligible to use cash accounting.[73] Businesses with turnovers above that threshold should account for the VAT on an accrual basis. While cash accounting is often advocated as a means of reducing compliance costs,[74] experience in some countries suggests the opposite, that the use of cash accounting actually increases compliance costs.[75] The scheme involves additional accounting obligations as businesses carry out cash-based accounting for VAT calculations in addition to accrual accounting required for general accounting purposes.[76]

The overriding purpose of a cash accounting scheme is more likely to be in providing cash-flow benefits to eligible businesses.[77] Businesses that collect the payments from their customers long after the invoices are issued may benefit greatly as the output tax is not due until the payments are received. Cash accounting may thus avoid bad debt adjustments, as no VAT has been paid on bad debts.[78] However, even from a cash-flow point of view, cash-basis recognition of sales and

[68] OECD, *Taxation of SMEs in OECD and G20 Countries* (n 62) at 112; C Sandford, 'The Administrative and Compliance Costs of the United Kingdom's Value Added Tax' (1990) 38 *Canadian Tax Journal* 1.

[69] AA Tait, *Value Added Tax: International Practice and Problems* (Washington, International Monetary Fund, 1988) 138.

[70] Turnier (n 51) at 984.

[71] Value Added Tax Regulations 1995, SI 1995/2518, reg 50(2).

[72] For a summary of the use of optional cash accounting methods in OECD and non-OECD G20 countries, see OECD, *Taxation of SMEs in OECD and G20 Countries* (n 63) at 111.

[73] For example, in the UK, businesses with a turnover of GBP 1.35 million or less are eligible to use cash accounting. See, Value Added Tax Regulations 1995, SI 1995/2518, regs 57 and 58(1)(a).

[74] OECD, *Taxation of SMEs: Key Issues* (n 22) at 123.

[75] Deloitte (n 61) at 83.

[76] ibid at 91.

[77] ibid at 81.

[78] OECD, *Taxation of SMEs in OECD and G20 Countries* (n 63) at 110.

acquisitions made on a deferred payment basis is a double-edged sword. While one effect is to delay recognition of consideration where a business has sold on a credit basis, it also delays recognition of expenditures yielding input tax credits until payments are made where a business has bought on a credit basis. As such, it is of no benefit to, and may even increase cash flow burden on, small businesses that sell on a cash-on-delivery basis but acquire inputs on credit terms.

Countries that provide a cash accounting option in their VAT systems also need to be wary of the revenue risks the option entails. Concurrent cash and accrual accounting creates a timing mismatch between input tax deduction and output tax liability when a cash-basis supplier makes a supply to an accrual-basis purchaser.[79] The accrual-basis purchaser claims an immediate input tax credit, while the cash-basis seller may defer the payment for a significant period of time or even indefinitely.[80] Evidence was found in the case law in New Zealand and Australia that the accounting basis options were aggressively exploited by related cash- and accrual-basis taxpayers to obtain what were effectively interest-free loans from the government.[81] The schemes were considered avoidance arrangements and were attacked by the tax authorities using the general anti-avoidance rules (GAARs). New Zealand also adopted a SAAR to address the problem.[82] In the UK where the general anti-abuse rule does not apply to the VAT, a SAAR is used to target avoidance schemes associated with the cash accounting option.[83] It is quite possible that the cases uncovered by the Australian and New Zealand authorities represent only the tip of a cash-accrual mismatch abuse iceberg. The problem is avoided in the first place in countries such as Canada where the GST law does not provide the cash accounting option.

## C. Presumptive Input Tax Entitlement Regimes

Presumptive input tax entitlement regimes seek to simplify the calculation of VAT liability by removing the need to record and total input tax on all acquisitions and instead allowing qualifying persons to substitute a predetermined presumptive input tax entitlement. Under presumptive regimes, small businesses charge VAT at regular rates on taxable supplies, but with no right to input tax deduction. A (lower) single flat rate is then applied to the total (VAT-inclusive) turnover to determine

[79] 'Options for Strengthening GST Neutrality in Business-to-Business Transactions' (The New Zealand Inland Revenue and the New Zealand Treasury, June 2008) 29–30.

[80] ibid.

[81] See, eg, *Ch'elle Properties (NZ) Limited v Commissioners of Inland Revenue* [2007] NZSC 73 (New Zealand); *Education Administration Ltd v Commissioner of Inland Revenue* [2010] NZHC 663 (New Zealand); and *VCE and Commissioners of Taxation* [2006] AATA 821 (Australia).

[82] (New Zealand) Goods and Services Tax Act 1985, s 19D.

[83] Value Added Tax Regulations 1995, SI 1995/2518, reg 58 (2)(e) and (f). For a detailed analysis of the anti-avoidance rules in New Zealand, Australia and the UK, see Y Zu and R Krever, 'GST Cash and Accrual Mismatches: Avoiding the Avoidance' (2017) 46 *Australian Tax Review* 271.

the amount of tax to be remitted to the tax authority. This amount is a proxy for the amount of net VAT the eligible business would have remitted after deducting their actual input tax credits from output tax in the ordinary VAT system. The flat rate may vary across industries or sectors, reflecting both the average costs incurred by enterprises in a sector and the extent to which acquisitions within the sector are likely to be exempt, zero-rated or reduced-rated supplies.[84] Importantly, the presumptive regimes do not alter the amount of VAT imposed on supplies and charged to customers. Registered customers of enterprises using the presumptive regime remain entitled to full input tax credits. Consequently, presumptive regimes are fully integrated within invoice-credit VAT systems. Notable examples of such presumptive regimes include the flat rate scheme (FRS) in the UK and the quick method of GST/Harmonised Sales Tax (HST) accounting in Canada. Both regimes are optional for businesses below a specified upper threshold.[85]

An inherent problem in any presumptive regime that determines net VAT payable by the use of a single flat rate applied to turnover is inaccuracy in individual cases. The input tax credits notionally incorporated in the flat rate are based on averages that are by definition not accurate for most individual traders. The finer the group used to determine an average, the more accurate the calculation will be in theory. However, the finer the group, the more boundaries are created. For example, seeking to mitigate the presumed input tax inaccuracy, the UK has calculated different presumptive rates ranging from 4 to 14.5 per cent for 55 categories of industries.[86] The proliferation of rates creates new complexities for businesses that must determine which rate category their business activities fall into and a new set of administrative problems for the tax authority which must police the boundaries between different categories.[87]

Enterprises with higher-than-average inputs that believe they will be unable to recover fully all input taxes under the industry-by-industry flat rate scheme would simply not opt to join the scheme. Deciding whether or not to opt in is not a cost-free exercise. Eligible businesses will regularly incur internal and external costs to estimate and compare VAT liabilities under both the FRS and the normal VAT system before making the decision. These additional costs offset some of the simplification benefits that the FRS was expected to deliver.

The flat rate will provide a tax advantage to businesses of each category with lower-than-average input purchases. The FRS therefore functions in practice as

[84] OECD, *Taxation of SMEs in OECD and G20 Countries* (n 63) at 107.

[85] The upper thresholds are GBP 150,000 in the UK and CAD 400,000 (approximately GBP 223,738) in Canada.

[86] Value Added Tax Regulations 1995, SI 1995/2518, reg 55K (table substituted by Value Added Tax (Amendment) (No 3) Regulations 2010, SI 2010/2940, regs 2, 4).

[87] UK case law provides examples where HMRC or taxpayers incorrectly categorised the taxpayers' businesses for the purposes of the FRS. See, eg, *JJK Engineering Ltd v The Commissioners for Her Majesty's Revenue & Customs* [2016] UKFTT 615 (TC); *IDESS Ltd v The Commissioners for Her Majesty's Revenue & Customs* [2014] UKFTT 511 (TC); *Sll Subsea Engineering Ltd v The Commissioners for Her Majesty's Revenue & Customs* [2015] UKFTT 0043 (TC).

a concessional scheme for some businesses rather than a simplification scheme as intended. In 2016, the UK Government estimated that about 30 per cent of the businesses that used the scheme gained substantial cash benefits relative to the position they would have faced under the ordinary VAT regime.[88] It viewed this business practice as abusive use of the FRS and responded, in 2017, with the introduction of an anti-avoidance measure. A new higher rate of 16.5 per cent (3.5 per cent lower than the standard rate) was introduced for businesses with limited input costs, defined as those whose expenditure on goods is less than two per cent of their turnover.[89] Not surprisingly, the adoption of the new rate, which aims to remove the fiscal benefits enjoyed by service providers with limited input costs, has led to a steady decrease in the take-up rate of the scheme from 25.5 per cent in 2016–17 to 13.5 per cent in 2023–24.[90] The low take-up rate of the scheme shows that the simplification benefits of the FRS might be limited, with the new anti-avoidance rule further increasing the complexity of the scheme that was intended to provide simplification.

The design of the Canadian quick method of accounting may have avoided some of the problems experienced in the UK. Instead of calculating dozens of industry-specific rates, Canada has only two sets of rates, distinguishing between businesses that purchase goods for resale[91] and businesses that provide services, with the former being allowed a higher notional input tax credit by way of a greater retention of output tax. The Canadian system thus avoids much of the complexity found in the UK system as a result of the need to identify each business's specific industry category. However, a sharp distinction between businesses that primarily sell goods and those that primarily sell services may induce inefficient behaviour by enterprises operating near the margin. With its broad sweep approach across all industries, this system has much more scope for inaccuracy in respect of any given enterprise within each rate category.

The Canadian system also illustrates that it is possible to combine a presumptive input tax entitlement scheme with a smoothing regime discussed in section IV above. Under the quick method of accounting scheme, enterprises remit a pre-determined percentage of their taxable sales, with the remainder of the GST collected assumed to equal the input tax related to the supply. Additionally, as a phasing in concession, enterprises are entitled to a one per cent credit on the first CAD 30,000 of eligible sales each fiscal year, resulting in a maximum reduction of CAD 300 in the GST/HST payable.[92] Presumably, the concession represents a recognition of the sudden increase in the tax liability and compliance burden for

[88] (UK) Explanatory Memorandum to the Value Added Tax (Amendment) Regulations 2017.

[89] Value Added Tax Regulations 1995, SI 1995/2518, reg 55KA (inserted by Value Added Tax (Amendment) Regulations 2017, SI 2017/295, regs 2, 7).

[90] The take-up rate measures the total number of businesses within the FRS as a percentage of the total number of eligible businesses. For the original statistics, see HMRC (n 2) Table 7.

[91] The costs of goods purchased must be at least 40% of the businesses' annual turnovers from taxable supplies (including the GST/HST).

[92] (Canada) Streamlined Accounting GST/HST Regulations (SOR 91-51), s 17(1).

those above the threshold compared to small businesses who are excluded from the GST/HST system by the threshold.

The number of rates used in a presumptive regime, to a degree, reflects a government's perception on the balance between neutrality and simplicity. The quest for greater accuracy, and fewer tax savings opportunities, in the presumptive regime in the UK, for example, has had an impact on its effectiveness as a simplification scheme. Cost savings from the UK FRS were initially estimated to average GBP 750 per business,[93] but a later evaluation estimated average compliance cost savings to be only GBP 45.[94] Potential savings are likely to diminish even further with the increased computerisation of cash registers and accounting systems, which, as noted earlier,[95] has been shown to reduce compliance costs in many countries.[96] These technological changes cannot obviate the need for simplification schemes entirely, however. Technology helps to reduce compliance burden where systems can automatically record tax attributes of sales or acquisitions – for example, whether supplies are taxable or exempt and, in the former case, whether they are subject to standard, reduced or zero-rates. They offer no savings where judgments are required such as the apportionment of input tax credits by businesses that make both taxable and exempt supplies. Simplification regimes will continue to play a cost reduction role in these cases.[97] From a tax policy perspective, the reliance on simplification regimes in these circumstances underscores the need to address the underlying complexity of a VAT system burdened with concessions.

## VI. Alternative Regimes for Small Businesses

Commonly, jurisdictions adopt simplified rules for small businesses above the threshold. However, in some countries, in particular developing countries and least developed countries, a different approach to simplification for small businesses is used, with the registration threshold replaced by a turnover border that distinguishes larger businesses subject to full VAT and smaller businesses subject to an alternative turnover tax system.[98] Under the turnover tax, a lower rate is

[93] HM Customs and Excise, 'Easing the Impact of VAT: Consultation on a Flat Rate Scheme for Small Firms: HM Customs and Excise Summary of the Responses to the Consultation Document Issued in June 2001' (Parliament Deposited Paper Dep 02/956, 2002).

[94] HMRC, 'VAT Flat Rate Scheme (FRS): Impact Assessment of Changes to the Flat Rate Percentages in January 2010' (7 December 2009) available at www.legislation.gov.uk/ukia/2009/327/pdfs/ukia_20090327_en.pdf.

[95] See text at nn 14–15 above.

[96] This point was made in the UK context in The Office of Tax Simplification, 'Review of Value Added Tax' (n 66) at 11.

[97] ibid at 11.

[98] The turnover tax may be used to substitute strictly for the VAT, as is done in China, or may be used as a surrogate tax for both income tax and VAT liabilities, as is done in South Africa. See also, L Abramovsky, D Philips and R Warwick, 'Redistribution, Efficiency and the Design of VAT: A Review of the Theory and Literature' (The Institute for Fiscal Studies, 2017) 9.

applied to gross receipts, with no recognition of input tax credits. The turnover tax is sometimes mistakenly labelled a 'simplified VAT' system.[99]

There is no doubt that, compared to a full VAT, a turnover tax imposed solely on sales without regard to input purchases is easier to administer and comply with. It is equally clear, however, that subjecting small businesses to a turnover tax is not as simple as the alternative of removing the businesses from the VAT system entirely and leaving them subject to input taxation. From a revenue raising perspective, a lower rate turnover tax on small businesses allows a government to raise the threshold at which a higher rate VAT applies. This explains the attractiveness of the turnover tax to developing countries – the tax is revenue neutral and politically feasible; it frees small businesses from VAT obligations without losing revenue.

In addition to revenue and simplification considerations, other possible rationales are offered for the application of so-called simplified regimes to small firms. A common explanation for the alternative turnover tax is to bring informal businesses into the 'formal' economy, but advocates of this view often offer no example of formality apart from formally paying taxes.[100] In theory, tax authorities could pass details of known enterprises on to other authorities responsible for business licences or other attributes of the formal economy; in practice, however, particularly in developing economies, channels for the automatic exchange of data between ministries are limited. It is possible that if appropriate information channels were established, incorporation of small businesses into the formal taxpaying economy could provide the government with a better understanding of the overall economy, allowing it to make more informed macro-economic decisions.

A second explanation for simplified turnover tax regimes for small businesses is to provide these businesses with basic fiscal skills as preparation for compliance should they grow sufficiently to cross the full VAT border.[101] The expectation is that an introduction to simple turnover accounts could mature into more sophisticated record keeping at a later stage.

A turnover tax regime is known as 'the economically most distorting form of sales tax'.[102] It applies to all sales, leading to serious tax-on-tax cascading along the supply chain. As noted in chapter one,[103] concerns over the economic distortions resulting from the use of turnover taxes were one of the key drivers for members of the European Economic Community to replace their turnover taxes with a common VAT system in the 1960s. In countries where a small business turnover tax is used as a supplement to the formal VAT system, registered businesses in the VAT system that purchase from suppliers in the turnover tax system are

[99] China provides an example of this practice, as explained in N Li, J Teoh and R Krever, 'VAT Reform in China Reaches a Critical Turning Point' (2016) 82 *Tax Notes International* 387, 397.

[100] Kanbur and Keen (n 43) at 539.

[101] RM Bird and P-P Gendron, *The VAT in Developing and Transitional Countries* (Cambridge, Cambridge University Press, 2007) 187.

[102] ibid at 30.

[103] See the text at nn 15–16 in chapter one.

unable to claim input tax credits. The turnover tax, therefore, becomes a cascading non-recognisable cost of acquisition for enterprises in the formal VAT system. The cascading effect is noticeably higher than that encountered when small businesses are simply left outside the VAT system but incur input taxation on acquisitions.

## VII. Conclusion

VAT thresholds and small business regimes remain as two of the most difficult areas of VAT design, presumably because the evidence on the extent of the problems associated with them and business responses to attempted solutions are so ambiguous. Subject to this caveat, however, a number of tentative conclusions can be reached. First, the adoption of a registration threshold is the most efficient measure to balance the need to protect revenue with the need to safeguard the efficiency of tax administration and avoid undue compliance burden for businesses. A relatively high threshold with the option of voluntary registration is generally preferable to a lower threshold with concessional or simplified regimes for small businesses just above the registration threshold. Input taxation for enterprises with turnovers below the registration threshold rather than alternative turnover taxation is more desirable. Second, the costs of simplification schemes often outweigh their benefits. In countries where simplified rules for small businesses with turnovers above the registration threshold are considered necessary (for political reasons, for example), less frequent filing tends to be the least problematic option among simplification measures that are commonly used. Third, experience with the use of smoothing schemes to transition small enterprises into the formal VAT system has generally been unsuccessful. The distortions and inefficiencies caused by a threshold may need to be accepted as a necessary trade-off for securing administrative and compliance cost savings, at least until more conclusive evidence emerges regarding the negative consequences of a threshold and the associated policy implications.

# 4

# Financial Supplies and Insurance Services

## I. Introduction

The application of Value Added Tax (VAT) to financial supplies and insurance services in the context of an invoice-credit system was considered 'the last unconquered frontier' in the design of VAT.[1] Whilst legislated definitions of financial supplies differ across jurisdictions, the two core types, in broad conceptual terms, common to all are intermediary loan services and the issuance and transfer of financial instruments. Insurance services typically include general insurance services and life insurance services.

The theoretical benchmark as applied to financial and insurance supplies is simple – services related to loans, insurance and the transfer of financial securities should be fully taxed as are all other services to the extent that they represent final consumption, while there should be full recovery of any tax in the case of business-to-business (B2B) supplies and the acquisition of savings. Translating this theory into practice has confounded tax designers for almost 60 years since the adoption of VAT in Europe in the mid to late 1960s. Officials in traditional VAT jurisdictions were uncertain about how to apply the VAT to a wide range of services and intangible supplies and adopted a stop-gap solution that saw all financial supplies treated as exempt supplies to keep them out of VAT calculations. The most challenging practical issue is to identify the value added in the case of intermediary services that are normally charged in the form of interest spreads. The problem is further complicated by the conceptual difficulty as to what constitutes consumption in financial and insurance supplies, as well as by the varying nature of different types of supplies.

The rationale for continuing incomplete taxation of financial supplies has weakened as policymakers increasingly recognised the distortions and inefficiencies of the exemption approach. Consequently, a variety of alternative approaches that depart from the exemption approach have been adopted for selected financial supplies and insurance services in a few modern VAT systems.

This chapter discusses the theoretically optimal tax base for intermediary loan services, financial assets, general insurance and life insurance. It also suggests workable options for the VAT treatment of each type of supply, drawing on an evaluation of the existing models and proposals.

[1] P-P Gendron, 'Policy Forum: Canada's GST and Financial Services – Where Are We Now and Where Could We Be?' (2016) 64 *Canadian Tax Journal* 401.

# II. Financial Supplies

## A. Intermediary Loan Services

Intermediary loan services, which channel funds from lenders to borrowers to accommodate different timing preferences for consumption by both parties, represent the most common form of financial intermediation. The appropriate tax base of intermediary loan services is one of the main conceptual issues that have yet to be resolved satisfactorily. This section takes traditional banking services of deposit-taking and loan-making as an example to illustrate the conceptual and practical challenges.

### *i. Conceptual Difficulty*

One distinct feature of intermediary loan services is that they are not charged explicitly. Rather, the value of intermediary services is reflected in the spread between the higher interest rate charged to borrowers and the lower interest rate paid to depositors. As is shown in Figure 4.1, loan payments comprise three main components: repayment of the loan principal, pure interest and the interest spread. The interest spread, in turn, consists of an intermediary service charge and a risk premium. The conceptual question is which of these four elements constitutes consumption and should therefore be included in the VAT base.

**Figure 4.1** Composition of Loan Payments

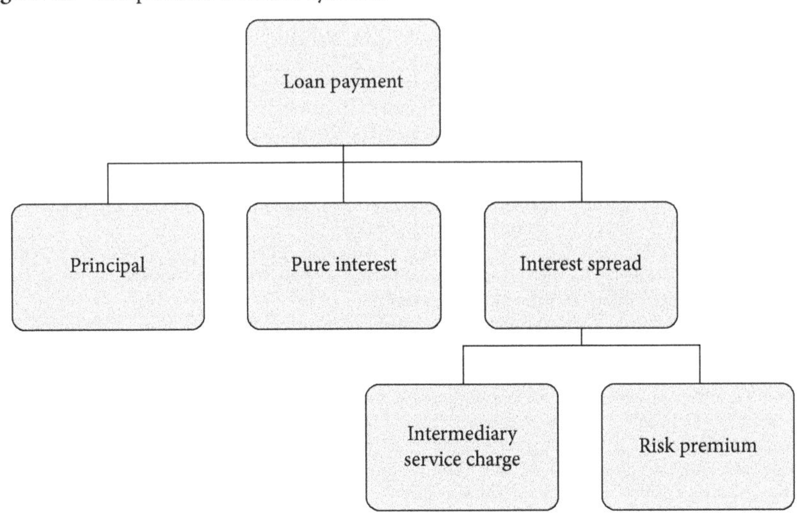

It is universally accepted that the loan principal and the pure interest components should not be taxed under a VAT.[2] The loan principal only represents the transfer of funds via the bank from the depositor to the borrower, which involves no consumption and should not incur VAT.[3] The pure interest rate is the rate that would be imposed on a loan if there were no intermediary services. The pure interest payments are compensation for deferring consumption for savers and the cost of moving forward consumption for borrowers.[4] This component is merely a reflection of the time value of money and should not form part of the VAT base.

The inconsistencies in the conceptual literature stem from issues concerning the two components of the interest spread: the intermediary service charge and, to a lesser extent, the risk premium. The key conceptual debate has focused on whether financial intermediary services should be subject to VAT like all other services and goods. One view is that financial intermediary services function in a similar way as pure interest rates – they only act to smooth the time preferences of consumption between borrowers and lenders, while yielding no consumer utility.[5] Under this view, financial intermediary services are not consumption goods and should be excluded from the VAT base.[6] This view was challenged by Auerbach and Gordon on the grounds that the production of financial services uses real resources, and 'all primary factors that enter into the production of a good' should be taxed under the VAT.[7] From the perspective of alternative consumption choices of individuals and revenue implications for the government, Grubert and Krever[8] reached the conclusion that financial intermediary services provided to borrowers should be subject to VAT.[9] If the borrowers were not acquiring the financial services, they would have used the funds to acquire other goods or services that were subject to tax, and the capital and labour inputs used in the acquisition of financial services would have been used to provide

[2] H Grubert and R Krever, 'VAT and Financial Services: Competing Perspectives on What Should be Taxed' (2012) 65 *Tax Law Review* 199.

[3] ibid, 319–20.

[4] S Poddar and M English, 'Taxation of Financial Services Under a Value-Added Tax: Applying the Cash-Flow Approach' (1997) 50 *National Tax Journal* 89, 91.

[5] NC Chia and J Whalley, 'The Tax Treatment of Financial Intermediation' (1999) 31 *Journal of Money, Credit and Banking* 704; and H Grubert and J Machie, 'Must Financial Services be Taxed Under a Consumption Tax?' (2000) 53 *National Tax Journal* 23.

[6] Through a different line of reasoning, Jack reached a similar conclusion that financial intermediary services charged by means of margin should not be taxed under the VAT. The underlying assumption is that the prices of all consumption goods should be increased by the same percentage in response to the VAT. However, since the (net of tax) price of margin-based financial services are increased in proportion to the nominal value of the underlying transaction, imposing a tax on these services would mean that their prices increase proportionately in response to the tax. This would distort the relative prices of consumption goods. See, W Jack, 'The Treatment of Financial Services Under a Broad-Based Consumption Tax' (2000) 53 *National Tax Journal* 841.

[7] A Auerbach and R Gordon, 'Taxation of Financial Services Under a VAT' (2002) 92 *The American Economic Review* 411.

[8] Grubert initially argued that financial intermediary services should not be taxed under the VAT. See, Grubert and Machie (n 5). He later recanted his view in Grubert and Krever (n 2).

[9] Grubert and Krever, ibid at 217–18.

taxable non-financial goods or services.[10] Therefore, only if financial intermediary services acquired by the person who accelerates consumption are taxed can the government obtain the same amount of tax revenue from accelerated or deferred consumption.[11]

Over time, the extreme challenge to the taxation of financial intermediary services under the VAT has not gained further support. The conceptual literature, however, diverges as to whether the entire value of intermediary services should be subject to VAT. Although Auerbach and Gordon, and Grubert and Krever, both opposed the view that financial intermediary services should be completely excluded from the VAT base, their positions yield different results with respect to lenders. It is widely accepted that the costs of intermediary loan services are borne by both depositors and borrowers. Nevertheless, the literature has been largely silent as to whether the two components of intermediary services, namely, those provided to savers and borrowers, should be taxed alike. If the view of Auerbach and Gordon were accepted, it would be equally logical to subject intermediary services provided to both savers and borrowers to VAT. Proposals for taxing financial intermediary services under the VAT explicitly take the view that the VAT should be applied to intermediary services provided to both savers and borrowers.[12]

The approach adopted by Grubert and Krever, however, requires careful consideration to be given to the distinct nature of financial intermediary services provided to each side of a loan transaction. While intermediary services provided to both savers and borrowers use real resources, savers are not acquiring the inputs as an alternative to the consumption of other goods or services as is the case with borrowers.[13] Rather, the expenses incurred by savers in applying the resources are part of the costs of generating further savings for future consumption.[14]

In addition to the charge for intermediary services, the interest margin includes an element of risk premium to cover the risk of default by borrowers.[15] The risk premium is functionally equivalent to insurance for lenders, covering the unpaid principal and interest in the event of borrower default. If characterised as principal repayments and interest payments by other borrowers on behalf of defaulters, the amounts should be excluded from the VAT base, just as direct repayments and interest are.[16] While this view gained substantial support in

[10] ibid.

[11] ibid at 218.

[12] See, eg, Poddar and English (n 4); and HH Zee, 'A New Approach to Taxing Financial Intermediation Services Under a Value-Added Tax' (2005) 58 *National Tax Journal* 77, 88–89.

[13] Grubert and Krever (n 2) at 218.

[14] ibid.

[15] ibid.

[16] Poddar and English (n 4); LA Hoffman, SN Poddar and J Whalley, 'Taxation of Banking Services Under a Consumption Type, Destination Basis VAT' (1987) 40 *National Tax Journal* 547; A Schenk, 'Taxation of Financial Services Under a Value Added Tax: A Critique of the Treatment Abroad and

the literature, a subsequent contribution offered a different perspective, suggesting that risk assessment requires the use of real resources and should therefore be regarded as an element of financial intermediary services.[17] However, this conclusion may reflect a confused commingling of the risk premium, which functions as an element of insurance in intermediation between borrowers and lenders, on the one hand, and the intermediary's activities of assessing default risk that is an integral part of intermediary services, on the other hand.

In sum, there is a broad consensus that repayment principal, pure interest and risk premium should remain out of the VAT base, while intermediary services provided to borrowers should be subject to VAT. However, there are differing views on whether intermediary services provided to savers should be taxed under a VAT.

### *ii. Practical Difficulties*

The conceptual debates have no doubt provided the important theoretical basis for the design of VAT rules for financial services. Nevertheless, the differing views on the correct treatment of intermediary services provided to savers may not have significant practical implications, given that the practical challenges arising from accurately identifying the value of intermediary loan services appear too difficult to overcome.

Under an invoice-credit VAT, tax is imposed on the value of a supply. The invoice-credit mechanism is used to remove the burden of the tax from intermediate acquisitions along the supply chain. The proper functioning of VAT relies on the identification of explicit prices charged for taxable sales and business acquisitions so that the VAT liability can be determined.[18] The charges for intermediary loan services, however, are hidden in interest spreads and cannot be identified on a transaction-by-transaction basis. The margin could be measured on an aggregate basis at the institution level by taking the sum of wages and profit, as illustrated by the 'addition' method used in Israel. However, there is no readily achievable measure to allocate the value of intermediary services to any particular transaction, leaving business borrowers unable to claim input tax credits for the intermediary services they receive.[19] These peculiar problems presented by the financial sector led to the assertion by some, in the early days of VAT adoption, that a VAT is ill-suited for taxing financial services.[20]

the Proposals in the United States' (1994) 9 *Tax Notes International* 823; R Carroll and A Viard, 'Value Added Tax: Basic Concepts and Unresolved Issues' (2000) 126 *Tax Notes* 1117, 1125.

[17] HH Zee, 'VAT Treatment of Financial Services: A Primer on Conceptual Issues and Country Practices' (2006) 34 *Intertax* 458, 462.

[18] ibid, 461.

[19] L Ebrill and others, *The Modern VAT* (Washington, D.C., International Monetary Fund, 2001) 95.

[20] See AA Tait, *Value Added Tax* (McGraw-Hill Book Company, 1972) 20; *Report of the Committee on Turnover Taxation* (Cmnd 2300) para 185.

## *iii. Country Practices*[21]

The fallback approach adopted in the traditional European VAT system about six decades ago, a broad exemption for most financial supplies and insurance services to avoid valuation difficulties,[22] was the starting point for almost all subsequent VAT systems. But while exemption remains a central design feature of most VAT systems, modifications and variations have appeared in some modern VAT systems. Moreover, exemption is not universal. China, for example, started with a comprehensive taxation approach and applies VAT to financial services broadly, making limited use of exemptions.

### a. Full Exemption: European Union (EU)

The technical difficulties of applying VAT to financial services are a key rationale for the exemption approach adopted in the EU,[23] although the initial choice of exempting these supplies was more likely driven by the need to retain the preferential treatment afforded under the pre-existing turnover taxes in the founding Member States.[24] The EU exemption approach was subsequently followed widely by other countries adopting VAT in later years.

As discussed in chapter two, the use of exemptions gives rise to economic distortions, and administrative and legal difficulties.[25] Although these problems are associated with exempt supplies across any economic sector, it is believed that the problems are particularly acute in the financial sector.[26] The spillover effects of the economic distortions in the financial sector may be strong, given the significant role the sector plays in supporting the real economy.[27]

[21] The proposals that remain untested in practice are not discussed in this chapter. These include the cash-flow method developed by Hoffman, Poddar and Whalley (above n 16) and modified reverse-charging method developed by Zee (n 12).

[22] Council Directive 2006/112/EC of 28 November 2006 on the common system of value added tax [2006] OJ L347/1, Art 135, 1. An exception to this general rule is that the Member States may grant taxable persons an option to tax otherwise exempt financial supplies under Art 137, 1(a). However, not many Member States have implemented such an option.

[23] R de la Feria and M Walpole, 'Options for Taxing Financial Supplies in Value Added Tax: EU VAT and Australian GST Models Compared' (2009) 58 *International & Comparative Law Quarterly* 897.

[24] It was explained in the European Commission's proposal for a sixth VAT Directive that 'The other exemptions, …, relate to specific fields, such as insurance, provision of credit and dealings in currency and on the stock exchange, where they are justified for reasons of general policy common to all the Member States.' See European Commission, 'Proposal for a Sixth Council Directive on the harmonization of Member States concerning turnover taxes – Common system of value added tax: uniform basis of assessment' COM (73) 950.

[25] The economic distortions and legal difficulties arising from the application of exemptions to financial supplies have been discussed in the EU context in de la Feria and Walpole (n 23).

[26] See S Poddar, 'Consumption Taxes: The Role of the Value-Added Tax' in P Honohan (ed), *Taxation of Financial Intermediation* (Washington and New York, The World Bank and Oxford University Press, 2003) 352; Zee (n 17) at 463.

[27] Poddar, ibid, at 352.

Exemptions have mixed impacts on financial service providers and their business and private customers. Although exempt supplies do not attract a tax liability, no credit is provided for the VAT paid on inputs related to these supplies. The irrecoverable input tax will thus become an element of the business costs. The tax component will be passed on to customers through higher service charges, unless it is absorbed by a reduction in the profit margin of financial suppliers.

Private customers (or borrowers, if Grubert and Krever's view discussed earlier is adopted)[28] are undertaxed, as they bear the tax burden only on the inputs acquired by their suppliers,[29] while being relieved of tax on the value added by the suppliers. The undertaxation of final consumers may exacerbate the regressivity of the VAT, given that the use of financial services tends to increase with income.[30] In contrast, registered businesses that acquire exempt financial supplies to make taxable supplies are overtaxed and the inclusion of irrecoverable tax in their cost base leads to cascading in the VAT system. Financial institutions thus have an incentive to avoid paying the irrecoverable input tax by vertically integrating businesses or self-supplying inputs that could have been more efficiently purchased from outside suppliers. Exemptions therefore discourage specialisation and reduce economic efficiency in the financial sector.

As noted, the primary justification for treating intermediary loan services as exempt supplies lies in administrative convenience. Under the exemption approach, financial intermediaries are relieved of the burden of calculating the value of intermediary services and allocating it between depositors and borrowers. However, these compliance cost savings are partly offset by the significant complexity involved in defining the scope of exemptions and apportioning input tax between taxable and exempt supplies. Once those additional costs are taken into account, the administrative benefits of the exemption approach appear to be outweighed by its shortcomings.

#### b. Exemption with Partial Input Tax Credits: Australia and Singapore

One way to ameliorate the problem of cascading or self-supply bias in countries that adopt an exemption approach is to allow financial institutions to claim credits for a proportion of the input tax they paid on acquisitions used to make exempt supplies. Australia and Singapore provide examples of two different partial recovery systems operating alongside the general exemption approach.

[28] See the text above at n 9.

[29] Contrary to the prevailing view that private customers are undertaxed under the exemption approach, Grubert and Krever's analysis suggests that private savers, to whom exempt intermediary services are supplied, are overtaxed. For the mainstream position, see S Cnossen, *Modernizing VATs in Africa* (Oxford, Oxford University Press, 2019) 199.

[30] H Huizinga, 'A European VAT on Financial Services?' (2022) 17 *Economic Policy* 497, 501 and 520–21.

The Australian regime, known as the reduced input tax credits (RITC) system, was adopted with the primary aim to remove the self-supply bias created by the full exemption rule.[31] Under the RITC regime, financial service providers are entitled to a reduced credit for their input tax paid on certain specified acquisitions relating to exempt financial supplies. The reduced input tax credit is generally equal to 75 per cent of the Goods and Services Tax (GST) payable on a qualifying acquisition,[32] providing a partial relief of the full input tax burden. The RITC regime may be effective in neutralising the bias against outsourcing and reducing tax cascades. Nevertheless, it does not eliminate cascading.

Concerns over the cascading effects of exemptions prompted Singapore to adopt a different partial input tax recovery regime.[33] This system, known as the fixed input tax recovery (FITR) method, allows financial institutions to claim a credit for a fixed percentage of their total input tax. The fixed input tax recovery rate varies for banks holding different types of banking licences. The fixed recovery rates are broadly determined on the basis of the estimates of the shares of inputs used by each type of bank to make supplies to registered businesses and non-resident customers, which are calculated using proxy industry statistics and are reviewed annually.[34]

The fixed recovery rates seem to have been set with an intention to approximate the effect of zero-rating B2B supplies made by financial institutions.[35] However, the benefits of the FITR may be spread amongst registered and private customers if financial institutions do not charge separate prices for services rendered to business and private customers, leaving business customers still carrying some irrecoverable input taxes. The FITR method could thus reduce the degree of over-taxation for business customers, rather than achieving an equivalent of zero-rating B2B supplies that completely eliminates cascading.

### c. Exemption with Zero-Rating of B2B Financial Services: New Zealand

An alternative approach to addressing the cascading problem that results from exemptions is found in New Zealand. Financial service providers are given the option to zero-rate the financial services (including but not limited to intermediary loan

[31] For a detailed description of the RITC regime, see R Krever and J Teoh, 'Financial Loan Intermediary Services: Australia' in RF van Brederode and R Krever (eds), *VAT and Financial Services: Comparative Law and Economic Perspectives* (Singapore, Springer, 2017).

[32] A 55% recovery rate is provided for certain trustee services. See, A New Tax System (Goods and Services Tax) Regulations 1999, reg 70-5.03.

[33] 'Report of the Select Committee on the Goods and Services Tax Bill' [Bill No 14/93] (Eighth Parliament of Singapore).

[34] 'GST: Guide for The Banking Industry', 6th edn (Inland Revenue Authority of Singapore, 7 March 2024) note 1. The current rates are 74% for a Full Bank and 94% for a Wholesale and Merchant Bank.

[35] S Poddar, 'VAT on Financial Services – Searching for a Workable Compromise' in R Krever and D White (eds), *GST in Retrospect and Prospect* (Wellington, Brookers Ltd, 2007).

services)[36] made to registered businesses whose taxable supplies account for at least 75 per cent of their total supplies in a given period.[37] The burden of ascertaining whether business customers are entitled to the zero-rating treatment falls on the financial institutions. As B2B zero-rating is only allowed where supplies made by the recipient of financial supplies are predominantly taxable, the treatment is generally not available for supplies made between financial service providers. To overcome this limitation, New Zealand's GST Act provides a special rule that allows financial service providers a pro-rated deduction of input tax for exempt financial supplies rendered to other financial service providers, to the extent that the recipient financial institution uses these supplies to make taxable supplies to registered business customers.[38]

Compared with the Australian and Singaporean regimes, New Zealand's rules that provide full input tax recovery for B2B supplies made by eligible financial institutions are more effective at reducing cascading. However, New Zealand's zero-rating rules for B2B financial services replicate the operating mechanism of a retail sales tax (RST).[39] One of the main advantages of a VAT over an RST is that under a VAT, suppliers are not required to distinguish between business and private customers for tax purposes. New Zealand's approach thus leads to increased compliance costs, as financial institutions are burdened with identifying the registration status of customers and ascertaining whether their registered customers meet the 75 per cent threshold, which are complexities that Singapore intended to avoid by adopting an implicit zero-rating approach.[40] The different approaches used by Singapore and New Zealand reflect the inherent trade-offs in tax design, in particular between the objectives of neutrality (or economic efficiency) and simplicity, with New Zealand's system placing greater emphasis on neutrality.

### d. Exemption with VAT on Financial Supplies Charged by Explicit Fees: South Africa

While the conceptual and practical difficulties are associated with margin-based activities, the value of financial services for which explicit fees and commissions are charged can be readily identified and subject to tax. South Africa exempts only financial services charged by way of margin, whilst imposing full taxation on fee- or commission-based services. This approach intends to limit the scope and distortionary effects of exemptions. The effectiveness of the measure, however,

[36] For the meaning of the term 'financial services', see (New Zealand) Goods and Services Tax Act 1985, s 3(1).

[37] ibid, s 11A(1)(q) and (r).

[38] ibid, s 20C.

[39] RF van Brederode and R Krever, 'Taxing Loan Intermediary Services: Theory and Design Considerations' in van Brederode and Krever (n 31) 25.

[40] G Jenkins and R Khadka, 'Value Added Tax Policy and Implementation in Singapore' (1998) 9 *VAT Monitor* 35, 40–41.

may depend on the mix of margin and fee-based services in the financial sector[41] and the ability of financial suppliers to substitute exempt margin-based services for taxable fee-based services for private customers. Nevertheless, the risk may not raise a serious concern in practice because business customers would prefer fee-based services to maximise their input tax deduction, and it may be impractical for financial institutions to differentiate arrangements for business and private customers.[42]

#### e. Reduced Rate: China

While traditional VAT jurisdictions broadly exempt financial supplies and a few modern VAT jurisdictions devised methods to address some of the shortcomings of the exemption approach, China is one of the first countries to apply VAT broadly to financial services.

China applies a reduced rate at six per cent (seven per cent lower than the standard rate) to gross loan interest and explicit fees and commissions charged for financial services. Business borrowers, however, are not entitled to input tax deduction for loan interest or fees and charges paid to lenders for services directly related to loans. These rules raised two main concerns. First, it has been rightly noted that tax on gross interest leads to overtaxation of loan services as only intermediary services should be subject to tax.[43] Second, the denial of input tax credits for business borrowers increases the cost of business financing and brings tax cascading into the real economy.

The Chinese approach must be understood within its particular political economy context. The VAT on financial supplies was introduced in 2016 as part of a comprehensive VAT reform implemented between 2012 and 2016, which replaced China's predecessor turnover tax with a VAT on services. However, rather than drawing on the experience of modern VAT jurisdictions, the Chinese Government adopted a politically and technically simpler path by essentially replicating the previous turnover tax rules in the VAT treatment of financial supplies. This approach is arguably no better than the EU's exemption approach. The two systems share a common weakness – the cascading problem that some modern VAT systems attempted to fix.

### *iv. Possible Options*

The regimes in New Zealand, Singapore and Australia have improved upon the EU exemption approach by introducing measures to mitigate the cascading effects of

[41] Poddar (n 35) at 188.

[42] P Jenkins, 'VAT Treatment of Financial Services' (2006) 866 *Tax Journal* 15. However, Poddar noted that attempts to tax fees and commissions on foreign exchange transactions in Russia prompted a shift from explicit fees to margins or a move of these supplies into the untaxed, informal economy. See, Poddar (n 26) 377.

[43] Y Xu and R Krever, 'Applying VAT to Financial Services in China: Opportunities for China and Lessons for the World?' (2016) 45 *Australian Tax Review* 38.

exemptions. The policy decision regarding the optimal regime would broadly come down to a government's perception on the appropriate balance between simplicity and economic efficiency. The Australian model, which applies an arbitrary pre-determined input tax recovery rate unrelated to the actual proportion of acquisitions used to make exempt supplies, is arguably the simplest but also the least effective in mitigating cascading effects. By contrast, New Zealand's zero-rating approach most effectively addresses the cascading problem but, at the same time, imposes a higher compliance burden on financial institutions. Overall, while the approaches adopted in the three countries alleviate certain negative consequences of the exemptions, they do so at the cost of increased complexity in rules and revenue loss from providing input tax credits.

Although the recent Chinese reform appears to have been a missed opportunity, the Chinese rules can be readily amended to establish a model for other countries, in particular developing economies. The Chinese approach coincidentally resembles 'the separate rate' approach proposed by Bakker and Chronican in 1985, which involves applying a reduced VAT rate to the gross interest on loans in order to approximate the tax consequence of applying the standard rate to the proportion of interest that constitutes the intermediary service charge.[44] Under the separate rate approach, registered businesses would be entitled to input tax credits as normal. This method requires an estimate of the industry-average proportion of interest that reflects the value of intermediary services, which is then used to determine the applicable reduced rate.

The separate rate approach has some advantages over the existing approaches. First, a reduced rate would completely remove the cascading resulting from exemptions. Second, the separate rate approach could provide greater simplicity than the existing approaches in terms of administration and compliance. The main technical challenge with respect to the separate rate approach would be the initial determination of the applicable reduced rate. However, the accuracy of the rate would not have significant practical impact. Business customers of financial institutions would be indifferent to the applicable VAT rate so long as they are entitled to full input tax deduction. How accurately the rate is set would only matter for private customers. Therefore, greater accuracy is likely to be achieved in countries where intermediary services are primarily provided to business rather than private customers. On balance, this approach may be a particularly attractive option for developing countries with limited administrative capacities.

In countries that have a long history of exempting financial supplies, the main impediment to reform may be concerns over the revenue consequences. Empirical estimates of the revenue impact of abolishing VAT exemptions yield mixed outcomes. Some studies find that moving from exemptions to full taxation for financial supplies would result in revenue gains.[45] In contrast, one

[44] C Bakker and P Chronican, *Financial Services and the GST – A Discussion Paper* (Wellington, Victoria University Press for the Institute of Policy Studies, 1985).

[45] See, eg, Institute for Fiscal Studies and others, 'A Retrospective Evaluation of Elements of the EU VAT System' (December 2011) 73. A study focused on Germany estimates that replacing the

study suggests that replacing VAT exemptions with full taxation for the core financial intermediation services of banks in the EU may result in little change in revenue or even lead to revenue loss.[46] The potential revenue loss can be explained by the irrecoverable input tax and cascading effect associated with exempt financial supplies. The revenue impact in a given country, therefore, may be negative if the proportion of business borrowings is significantly higher than that of private borrowings, given the outsized role business borrowings play in the economy.[47] In countries where revenue loss is a significant concern, exemptions, however flawed they are, may be seen as a way of ensuring that at least some revenue is collected from financial services.[48]

## B. Financial Securities

The trading and issuance of financial securities raise a distinct conceptual issue that is seldom addressed in the academic literature. Three types of supply may be acquired in the process of trading financial instruments: the direct acquisition of investments, intermediary services (provided by brokers), and ancillary services such as investment advice and financial analysis.

The direct acquisition of investments is simply an investment activity with no personal consumption element and should, therefore, be kept outside the VAT base. In the case of financial instruments traded through a broker, the investor acquires intermediary services from the broker, with the commission fee for brokerage service payable as a fixed amount or a percentage of the transaction amount. In theory, intermediary services in securities trading and supplies ancillary to the acquisition of investments should be treated in the same way as intermediary services provided to savers in loan services. Therefore, these supplies should either be subject to full taxation or no taxation, depending on whether the acquisition of intermediary services related to savings is recognised as consumption.

In practice, however, most countries broadly exempt the issuance and transfer of financial instruments and related services from the VAT. Moving to either zero-rating or full taxation for these services would remove cascading for downstream B2B taxable supplies. The choice between the two options only affects business investors acquiring the services to make exempt supplies and private investors. Countries facing revenue constraints would prefer the full taxation approach over zero-rating. In addition, the zero-rating approach that removes the VAT

exemptions of financial supplies in Germany would increase revenue yields by EUR 1.7 billion or 1.3%. See, T Buettner and K Erbe, 'Revenue and Welfare Effects of Financial Sector VAT Exemption' (2014) 21 *International Tax and Public Finance* 1028.

[46] PwC, 'How the EU Exemptions Impact the Banking Sector: Study to Assess Whether Banks Enjoy a Tax Advantage as a Result of EU VAT Exemption System' (18 October 2011), available at www.pwc.com/gx/en/financial-services/pdf/2011-10-18_vat_study_final_report.pdf.

[47] L Abramovsky, D Philips and R Warwick, 'Redistribution, Efficiency and the Design of VAT: A Review of the Theory and Literature' (The Institute for Fiscal Studies, 2017) 10.

[48] Gendron (n 1) at 409.

entirely from investments may intensify the existing public perception that the VAT is regressive, given that private investors are more likely to be higher income persons.[49] This, however, may not be an important consideration in VAT design because the role of VAT is to raise revenue in a neutral manner without explicit consideration for vertical equity.[50]

# III. Insurance Services

Insurance services are pooling services offered by insurers that collect premiums from a group of policyholders and use the funds to satisfy indemnity claims by insured persons who suffer property or profit losses (in the case of general insurance, or casualty insurance as it is sometimes called), or by the beneficiaries upon the death of the insured persons (in the case of life insurance). In the cases of both general and ordinary term life insurance, premiums pay for coverage over a fixed period and the policy has no cash value at the end of that period. By contrast, whole life insurance, also known as whole-of-life insurance, includes a savings component in addition to the regular premium during the initial years of the policy. The savings element enables the insurer to maintain level premiums even as the actual cost of insurance increases over time, while also building a cash value that the insured person can access if they choose to cash out the policy prior to death. Different types of insurance carry distinct VAT implications.

## A. General Insurance

The premiums paid to the insurer for general insurance include two components: the proportion that will be transferred to a pooled fund to cover the insured risks and the charge for the pooling services offered by the insurer. As is the case with intermediary loan services, the pooling services utilise real resources and should form part of the VAT base. Registered policyholders should be entitled to input tax credits for the pooling services they acquired. Where claims are satisfied in cash, the indemnity payments made by the insurer to the claimants include the VAT that will be later paid by the claimants on the repair or replacement of assets. This VAT component should be collected from all the policyholders. If the insured person is a final consumer or registered business making exempt supplies (with no right to input tax deduction), the VAT will be remitted to the tax authority when the replacement goods or services are purchased. If the insured person is a registered business making taxable supplies, the VAT should be remitted to the tax authority

[49] R Krever, 'VAT and Financial Investments' in RF van Brederode and R Krever (n 31) 193.
[50] A similar point was made in Gendron (n 1) at 408.

at the time the indemnity is paid, as the subsequent repair or replacement will be acquired for business use and thus effectively VAT-free.

Insurance services are broadly exempt under the EU VAT on the grounds of the technical difficulty of separating the charge for pooling services from the proportion of the premium transferred to the common pool at the level of individual policies.[51] However, experience of a few modern VAT jurisdictions, such as New Zealand and Australia, has shown that the correct outcomes in terms of service charge and indemnity payments can be achieved under an invoice-credit VAT.

New Zealand applies its GST to general insurance on a net cash flow basis at the level of insurers, treating general insurance as comprising two distinct transactions for VAT purposes: a taxable supply upon receipts of premiums and a deemed acquisition when an indemnity payment is made. The GST is imposed on the insurance premiums paid by both registered businesses and unregistered individuals. The insurer remits the GST to the tax office in respect of the premiums received, while issuing invoices to registered business policyholders. The GST on premiums paid by registered businesses is recovered by them through the ordinary input tax credit system and the GST paid by unregistered policyholders is effectively used to gross up benefits to cover the GST-inclusive cost of repairs and replacements.[52] The indemnity payments received by both registered and unregistered claimants are deemed to be creditable acquisitions by the insurer, giving rise to input tax credits for the insurer and a GST liability for the registered insured.[53] The net tax remitted by the insurer is the GST on the pooling services. Where the insured person is an unregistered individual, the tax authority collects the tax on repair or replacement when the insured person uses the proceeds of the indemnity payment to purchase goods or services. New Zealand's approach, therefore, achieves the correct outcome by taxing the margin between the premiums and the settlements on a pooled basis. This method is fully integrated into an invoice-credit VAT system, while avoiding the valuation difficulties associated with determining the value of pooling services on an individual policy basis.

Figure 4.2 illustrates this process in respect of registered business policyholders.[54] Suppose the premium is 120, and the GST-inclusive indemnity payment is 1200. The GST rate is 20 per cent. When the policy is issued, the insurer remits 20 GST and the insured business claims an input tax credit of 20. At the settlement stage, the insured business is deemed to have made a taxable supply and

[51] As an alternative, most EU Member States adopted an Insurance Premium Tax to compensate for the lost revenue (if any) resulting from the perceived undertaxation of these supplies under the VAT.

[52] T Edgar, 'The Search for Alternatives to the Exempt Treatment of Financial Services under a Value Added Tax' in R Krever and D White (eds), *GST in Retrospect and Prospect* (Wellington, Brookers Ltd, 2007) 157.

[53] See (New Zealand) Goods and Services Tax Act 1985, s 5(13).

[54] For an illustration of how the GST applies to general insurance in the case where the insured person is an unregistered individual, see 'GST and general insurance' (The Treasury, Australian Government) 53–54, available at treasury.gov.au/sites/default/files/2019-03/4gst.pdf.

charged a GST-inclusive price of 1200. The settlement amount paid to the insured business includes a GST element of 200. The insured business remits 200 GST and the insurer claims an input tax credit of 200.

**Figure 4.2** Insurance Claim by a Registered Business

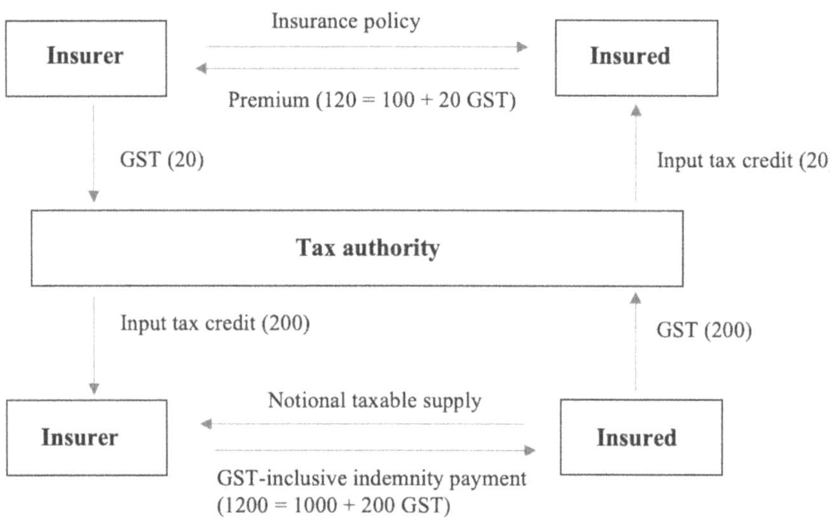


An alternative approach, used in Australia, was modelled on New Zealand's approach but intends to simplify the process in terms of settlements made to the registered insured person by requiring the insurer to pay the registered claimant the GST-exclusive value of repairs or replacements (1000 in the example given above) as the settlement payment.[55] This system therefore removes the deemed supply and avoids the circular flow of GST among the tax authority, the insurer and the registered insured person at the settlement stage required under New Zealand's model. However, the purported simplicity of the Australian approach is questionable, as the system requires insurers to distinguish between registered and unregistered claimants in order to determine the correct value of the settlement payment.[56]

## B. Life Insurance

In one sense, taxing the intermediary pooling services of a life insurer should be simpler than taxing similar services rendered by a casualty insurer as almost all holders of life insurance policies are final consumers, although in some cases

[55] ibid, 55–57, available at treasury.gov.au/sites/default/files/2019-03/4gst.pdf.
[56] R Krever and J Teoh, 'GST and Insurance: Australia' in RF van Brederode and R Krever (n 31).

registered businesses could also be the policyholders. This conclusion holds true for pure term life insurance where annual premiums provide coverage for only a year. The picture is complicated for whole life insurance coverage that involves a significant savings element, however.

Whole life insurance provides lifelong protection and the policy has cash value that grows at a pre-determined rate. The savings component in the early years of the policy can be used to help fund the benefit payable in later years. This enables the insurer to charge level premiums over the life of the policy for a guaranteed benefit. Each year, the proportion of the guaranteed benefit that would be paid from the pooled insurance fund reduces and the amount that is paid from the insured person's accumulated savings increases. At some point, the savings equal the benefit value of the policy, at which time there is no longer any benefit from paying premiums and the policy will be cashed in.

The premium for whole life insurance comprises four elements: a savings component, a pure insurance component, an intermediary service charge for risk pooling, and an intermediary service charge for savings management. The savings and pure insurance components involve no consumption and should not form part of the VAT base. The intermediary service charge for risk pooling should be subject to VAT. Whether the intermediary service charge for savings management should be taxed depends on the conceptual approach adopted: Auerbach and Gordon's view points to full taxation of the intermediary service charge, whereas Grubert and Krever's view implies that it should fall outside the VAT base.[57]

Due to the practical difficulty of separating the service charge from the savings element in the premium, the universal practice, even in countries that impose the VAT on intermediary pooling services for casualty insurance, is to simply exempt life insurance from the VAT. The exemption approach is an acceptable compromise in the case of life insurance. Since the vast majority of the policyholders are final consumers, the exemption does not create cascading problems in the VAT system. In addition, the government collects some VAT from life insurance as the insurers are denied input tax credits for their acquisitions related to exempt supplies. Input taxation on life insurance supplies effectively results in partial taxation of intermediary insurance services.

There are two proposals for bringing life insurance into the tax base. The first is the addition method, imposing the tax on the sum of wages and profit at the institutional level (which equals the value added by the insurer).[58] This requires the tax to be calculated on an accounts, rather than transactional, basis. The main criticism of applying the addition method to financial supplies is that it transforms the transaction-based VAT into an accounts-based tax and is therefore inconsistent with the invoice-credit VAT that is applied to all other supplies.[59] However, in the case of life insurance, the addition method could be integrated into the

[57] See the text above at nn 7 and 9–11.

[58] S Cnossen, 'A Proposal to Apply the Kiwi-VAT to Insurance Services in the European Union' (2013) 20 *International Tax and Public Finance* 867, 880; Bakker and Chronican (n 44) at 50.

[59] Gendron (n 1) at 409.

invoice-credit VAT by allowing insurers to deduct input tax on acquisitions used to provide life insurance services. As is the case with the exemption approach, the addition method is feasible for taxing life insurance because the policyholders are mostly final consumers, removing any need to allocate the VAT between the policyholders.

The second proposal largely replicates the approach used for general insurance discussed above.[60] Under this proposal, the VAT would be imposed on the full premium. The insurer's pay-out to the policyholder (either death benefits or savings) would be treated as payment for a deemed acquisition, attracting a notional input tax credit to the insurer. While the savings element in the premium would be subject to tax, the tax would correspond to the present value of the tax that would otherwise be paid in future years when the savings are applied to cover the actual cost of protection. This approach leaves the government with the same economic outcome as if the tax were imposed annually on the actual cost of protection over the life of the policy.[61]

Both approaches would result in the full taxation of intermediary services related to savings, an outcome that is conceptually problematic if one adopts the view of Grubert and Krever discussed earlier.[62] The second approach is perhaps a better option, as it is fully compatible with an invoice-credit VAT. Given its similarity to the method used for general insurance in jurisdictions where the VAT is applied to general insurance pooling services, it may not create additional administrative and compliance difficulties for these countries to adopt this approach for life insurance, especially where insurers operate in both life and general insurance sectors. Nevertheless, the exemption approach remains an appealing option for countries that do not include general insurance in their tax base.

# IV. Conclusion

The taxation of financial and insurance services under the VAT raises conceptual and practical challenges. While the conceptual inconsistencies remain as to the treatment of intermediary services related to savings and investment, these do not pose insurmountable obstacles for VAT design in practice, since the pursuit of conceptual purity will almost inevitably have to be compromised in favour of administrative feasibility.

Despite various reform efforts, no country has yet fully addressed the practical difficulties associated with taxing financial services, and there is considerable scope for improvement in most countries. The approaches adopted in the modern

[60] V Barham, SN Poddar and J Whalley, 'The Tax Treatment of Insurance Under a Consumption Type, Destination Basis VAT' (1987) 40 *National Tax Journal* 171.

[61] Bakker and Chronican (n 44) at 50.

[62] See text above at nn 9–11.

VAT systems that have departed from the traditional exemption model suggest that partial reforms are possible, though they entail different implications for efficiency, simplicity and revenue. Ultimately, the choice of VAT regimes for financial and insurance services reflects how a government balances different objectives, taking into consideration the specific characteristics of the financial and insurance sectors and the economy as a whole. In developed countries with advanced tax administrations, simplicity may not be a prime consideration. In contrast, in developing countries with more limited administrative capacity, considerations of simplicity and revenue generation may take precedence over the objective of achieving conceptual precision in tax design. This chapter presents viable options for taxing intermediary loan services, securities trading and insurance supplies. It demonstrates that, perhaps contrary to the common perception, the technical difficulties are no longer the principal barrier to reform in this area.

# 5

# International Cross-Border Issues

## I. Introduction

A fundamental principle of Value Added Tax (VAT) as a tax on final consumption is that, in the case of cross-border transactions, the VAT should operate as a destination-based tax that applies in the country where the final consumption takes place. This is achieved through two separate transactions: first, exports are zero-rated in the exporting country and, second, imports are subject to taxation on the same basis as domestic supplies in the importing country.

The destination-based regime is often compared with the 'origin basis' system in which the tax paid on a supply is the sum of the taxes that apply at the local rates on value added created in every country along the supply chain.[1] The origin basis system falls foul of the fundamental principle of VAT being a tax on final consumption, which requires that the tax applies at the rate specified by the country of consumption and that the tax revenue accrues to that country.[2] The destination principle ensures that neutrality in international trade is achieved by taxing imports and domestic supplies on the same basis. Owing to this advantage, the destination principle is widely accepted as the international norm for applying VAT to cross-border transactions.

Whilst desirable in principle, the destination principle raises practical difficulties in implementation. Three issues arise in the context of international cross-border sales. The first is how to determine when intangible supplies have been exported from one jurisdiction and when they are imported into another (tangible items can be traced relatively easily). This question is commonly answered by way of place of taxation rules. The second issue is how to remove the VAT on business expenses incurred by non-resident businesses. The third challenge is how to effectively collect the VAT on cross-border business-to-consumer (B2C) sales. Although the invoice-credit mechanism normally places the tax liability on business suppliers, it is administratively challenging to collect the tax on imports from overseas suppliers. This chapter examines these three main challenges.

[1] See, eg, L Ebrill and others, *The Modern VAT* (Washington, DC, International Monetary Fund, 2001) 179–84; M Keen and S Lahiri, 'The Comparison between Destination and Origin Principles under Imperfect Competition' (1998) 45 *Journal of International Economics* 323.

[2] The inefficiencies created by an origin-based VAT are explored in chapter six, in the context of inter-jurisdictional transactions within federations or large countries; see section II of chapter six.

# II. Place of Taxation Rules

There is remarkable divergence across countries in their legal approaches used to implement the destination principle, which subject cross-border supplies to taxation in the jurisdiction in which consumption takes place, in particular with regard to services. A common feature is that the intention of the legal approaches is not to identify the location where the consumption actually incurs.[3] Rather, a set of jurisdictional rules are used to predict the place of consumption. In other words, the destination principle is implemented through place of taxation rules which rely on proxies for the place of consumption.

## A. Goods

Place of taxation rules for goods normally include three components: place of supply rules that create a liability to domestic VAT if the supply is made within or from the jurisdiction; zero-rating rules that remove the tax on exports; and import rules that impose a VAT liability on goods imported from abroad into the jurisdiction.[4] Since the movement of goods can be easily tracked, the proxy used for predicting the place of consumption is normally the location of goods.[5] With effective border controls, goods are zero-rated when they leave a country and are taxed as imports when they enter a country. In the case of large goods arriving by rail, air or sea, the importers are required to pay the VAT at the point of importation. In the case of small goods sent by post or courier, collection from the importers, who are often private consumers, at the border could be very costly. Alternative approaches have been adopted in recent years, which are discussed later in this chapter.

## B. Services

The logic of identifying the place of taxation for services is essentially the same as for goods. The intangible nature of services, nevertheless, necessitates more complicated place of taxation rules because unlike goods, cross-border supplies of services do not move across borders and cannot be physically tracked. Where

[3] M Keen and W Hellerstein, 'Interjurisdictional Issues in the Design of a VAT' (2010) 63 *Tax Law Review* 359, 367.

[4] R Millar, 'Echoes of Source and Residence in VAT Jurisdictional Rules' in M Lang, P Melz and E Kristoffersson (eds), *Value Added Tax and Direct Taxation: Similarities and Differences* (The Netherlands, IBFD, 2009) 286.

[5] However, in particular cases, implicit or explicit rules are needed to deem deliveries of items such as airplanes, ships or trains to be made outside the country (as exports), where possession is handed over to the buyer's crew inside the country for the buyer to remove them from the jurisdiction. See, eg, (Australia) A New Tax System (Goods and Services Tax) Act 1999, s 38–185, item 3.

the consumption will most likely occur is thus far more difficult to ascertain in the case of services.

Place of taxation rules for services rely on a larger set of proxies, including the location of immovable property or goods to which the services relate, the place of physical performance, the location or residence of the supplier, the location or residence of the recipient and the place of effective use or enjoyment. The hierarchy given to the different proxies varies across countries but generally where services are attached to tangible proxies (for example, the locations of immovable property and goods), these proxies prevail over others. In contrast, the location or residence of the supplier or recipient is the least reliable proxy because it can be shifted easily.

The span of the legal drafting approaches used to identify the place of taxation is wide and it is difficult to segregate practices into different models. It can be seen, however, that the alternatives fall into two very broad camps, the schedular approach and the principle approach.[6]

Legislation using the schedular approach enumerates different types of supplies and sets out a place of taxation for each one based on the proxy chosen. VAT laws adopting a principle approach systematically apply a set of proxies to identify the broad circumstances in which consumption is assumed to take place within or outside the jurisdiction. In a principle-based system, a set of rules will be applied consecutively to determine the place of taxation, including rules on whether the supply is made in the jurisdiction[7] and whether the supply is an exported service,[8] or whether the supply is an imported service (in the case that the supply originates outside the jurisdiction).[9]

However, the distinctions between the two legislative approaches are not absolute and, in practice, most countries use a hybrid model that heavily relies on one of the two approaches but contains elements of both.[10] For example, the European Union (EU) uses the schedular approach, specifying the place of taxation (known as the 'place of supply' in EU legislation) for each category of supplies such as transport, restaurant and catering services, and services connected with immovable property.[11] These particular provisions fall back on the general rules, which provide the default position that the place of taxation of services is the customer's location or the supplier's location if the particular

[6] They were labelled the 'categorisation approach' and 'iterative approach' in Organisation for Economic Co-operation and Development (OECD), *International VAT/GST Guidelines* (Paris, OECD Publishing, 2017) 39.

[7] See, eg, (Australia) A New Tax System (Goods and Services Tax) Act 1999, s 9–25, paras (5)(a) and (b).

[8] See, eg, ibid, s 38–190.

[9] See, eg, ibid, s 9–25, para (5)(d).

[10] OECD, *International VAT/GST Guidelines* (n 6) at 39.

[11] Council Directive 2008/8/EC of 12 February 2008 amending Directive 2006/112/EC as regards the place of supply of services [2008] OJ L44/11. For a summary of the categories of services and the underlying proxy for each category, see R Millar, 'Jurisdictional Reach of VAT' in R Krever (ed), *VAT in Africa* (South Africa, Pretoria University Law Press, 2008) 191–92.

service in question is not explicitly covered by any of the specified categories.[12] In contrast, the place of taxation rules in the Australian Goods and Services Tax (GST) Act offer an example of the principle approach. The determination of the place of taxation is based on broad categories of proxies, including the location of property and the place of effective use or enjoyment,[13] without specifying particular types of supplies. However, the rules based on general principles are supplemented with implicit rules for specific types of supplies, such as GST-free (zero-rating) treatment of international passenger transport[14] and supplies of international roaming services.[15]

The two drafting approaches both give rise to interpretation difficulties. The difficulty associated with the schedular approach lies in the incapability of legislators to envisage every possibility and include a comprehensive list of supplies in the law. The United Kingdom (UK) and continental European courts, for example, regularly hear appeals concerning how particular supplies may fit into the enumerated lists.[16] However, the principle approach is not immune from uncertainty and litigation because the broad principles used are sometimes too general for the myriad of different configurations possible in ordinary commercial transactions.[17] Nevertheless, the principle approach may be more adaptable to unanticipated continual changes in the evolution of delivery of services, given that it will be increasingly challenging for legislators to divide modern services into strict categories.

## III. Foreign VAT Recovery

Under an invoice-credit VAT, business suppliers should be entitled to a full right to deduction of input tax. In the case that a business' input tax credits exceed its output tax due, the excess credits should be refunded to the business promptly. However, as noted in chapter two,[18] refunds have proven to be one of the most challenging aspects of VAT administration, with refund fraud remaining an enduring and intractable problem in many countries.[19] Developing countries with

[12] Directive 2008/8/EC, ibid, Arts 44 and 45.

[13] (Australia) A New Tax System (Goods and Services Tax) Act 1999, s 38–190, items 1 and 3.

[14] ibid, s 38–355, items 1 and 2.

[15] ibid, s 38–570.

[16] See, eg, Case C-327/94 *Jürgen Dudda v Finanzgericht Bergisch Gladbach* ECLI:EU:C:1996:355, [1996] ECR I-4595 (whether the provision of sound-engineering for concerts and similar events was artistic or entertainment services); *Adoum Tanjoukian v The Commissioners for Her Majesty's Revenue and Customs* [2012] UKUT 361 (TCC) (whether the sale of vehicle registration marks was a transfer or assignment of copyright, patents, licences, trademarks and similar rights).

[17] See, eg, *Fiduciary Ltd and Ors v Morningstar Research Pty Ltd and Ors* [2004] NSWSC 381 (Australia) (whether legal services made to a non-resident company with two directors and an employee presented in Australia at the time the thing was done were a supply connected with Australia).

[18] See the text at nn 78–79 in chapter two.

[19] For a review of various types of VAT refund fraud, see C Andrew and K Baer, 'How to Combat Value-Added Tax Refund Fraud' (IMF How to Notes 23/01, August 2023) 18–19.

weak auditing and control systems tend to be more concerned about the risks of fraudulent refund claims.[20] Some VAT systems, therefore, do not provide refunds and instead require businesses to carry excess credits forward to subsequent tax periods.

In cross-border circumstances, businesses may incur a significant amount of VAT on business expenditures abroad (in countries where they are not established or VAT-registered). In principle, the jurisdiction in which the input VAT is incurred should refund the VAT to the non-resident business so as to avoid the VAT to be embedded in the price of their taxable supplies. In practice, however, many countries do not provide an entitlement to refund to non-resident businesses,[21] with the result that the VAT charged on local supplies to non-resident enterprises becomes an irrecoverable cost to those businesses. This may give rise to compounding tax if subsequent supplies by the non-resident business and possibly its customers are subject to VAT. The absence of refund entitlements in the countries where the business expenses are incurred may discourage non-resident businesses from consuming services in these countries.[22]

In other countries where the entitlement to refunds is available, the systems in place are largely inconsistent in terms of the mechanism used, the scope of VAT recovery and the restrictions applied to refunds. Two main mechanisms are found to provide refunds to non-resident businesses:

1. Direct refund mechanism: Countries provide direct refunds for the VAT on business expenses incurred in their jurisdictions by non-resident businesses.
2. Registration mechanism: Countries have registration procedures in place that allow foreign businesses that do not make taxable supplies in the country to register and recover the input VAT paid.

While countries provide refunds on a unilateral basis, those using the direct refund mechanism tend to make refunds conditional upon the grant of reciprocal refund entitlements by the claimants' home countries to their resident businesses. The EU provides an example of the direct refund approach, allowing non-EU businesses to seek refunds by completing an application form.[23] Most of the Member States require a reciprocity agreement or reciprocal treatment for the recovery of VAT by non-resident businesses.[24] In contrast, New Zealand represents a jurisdiction that

[20] Ebrill and others (n 1) at 155–64.

[21] For example, in the OECD, five countries do not provide VAT refunds to non-resident businesses: Chile, Colombia, Costa Rica, Israel and Mexico. See, OECD, *Consumption Tax Trends 2024: VAT/GST and Excise, Core Design Features and Trends* (Paris, OECD Publishing, 2024) 54.

[22] P Dunne, 'GST: Business-to-Business Neutrality across Borders – A Government Discussion Document about GST on Cross-Border Supplies between Businesses' (New Zealand Policy Advice Division of Inland Revenue, August 2011).

[23] Thirteenth Council Directive 86/560/EEC of 17 November 1986 on the harmonization of the laws of the Member States relating to turnover taxes – Arrangements for the refund of value added tax to taxable persons not established in the Community territory [1986] OJ L326/40.

[24] For a summary of the rules and practices in the OECD countries, see OECD, *Consumption Tax Trends 2024* (n 21) at 128–38.

requires non-resident businesses to register for GST in order to recover the input tax paid.[25]

Both mechanisms have strengths and weaknesses. The registration system imposes higher compliance costs by requiring the non-resident businesses to register for VAT and file periodic returns.[26] These costs may deter non-registered businesses from seeking a refund. On the other hand, an increased number of registered persons will complicate the tax authority's administrative tasks. The direct refund system may be more susceptible to fraudulent refund claims compared to systems that require non-resident businesses to register for VAT.[27] Since the weaknesses of one system are in effect the strengths of the other, no definite conclusion can be drawn as to which system is superior. The implementation of either regime may be more administratively challenging for many developing and least developed countries.

# IV. Imports

The application of the destination principle in importing countries gives rise to distinct challenges in relation to different types of cross-border supplies – business-to-business (B2B) supplies of goods, B2B supplies of services, B2C digital supplies and B2C sales of low-value goods. The distinct challenges require policy responses tailored to each type of cross-border supplies.

## A. B2B

Generally, the importation of goods by registered businesses can be taxed at the border without difficulty. The VAT on imports is collected at the same time as customs duties (at the point of importation) by the customs authorities. Services, however, cannot be taxed in the same manner because they do not physically cross borders. The VAT on cross-border services imported by registered businesses is commonly collected via a reverse charge mechanism that shifts the VAT liability from foreign sellers to domestic purchasers.[28] The importer simultaneously accounts for VAT on the imported services and deducts the same amount as input

[25] (New Zealand) Goods and Services Tax Act 1985, s 54B.

[26] Dunne (n 22) at 12.

[27] ibid at 13.

[28] A variation of this system is used in China where the business customer remits the tax, as in the reverse charge mechanism, but the Chinese legislation places the liability to account for VAT on the non-resident supplier, not the customer. The tax is thus treated as a withholding tax and the non-resident supplier is barred by Chinese law from collecting the full contracted price for the supply. To overcome this, non-resident suppliers commonly negotiate a grossed-up price for the supply so that, after the VAT is withheld, the net amount received matches the tax-exclusive price that would be charged in a jurisdiction that uses the reverse charge mechanism.

tax in the same VAT return, as if it has supplied the services to itself. The VAT on the imported services is thus effectively self-assessed by the importer.

The reverse charge mechanism has proved to be an effective measure for taxing cross-border B2B services. However, it is unnecessary in situations where the importer uses the imported services to make taxable supplies, given that the deductible input tax cancels out the output tax due. Australia, for example, treats certain imported B2B services as out-of-scope supplies in circumstances where the importer would have been entitled to claim a full GST credit if they had been charged GST.[29] This approach, which suspends the tax on B2B supplies, in effect turns the import VAT into a retail sales tax.

A major advantage of the reverse charge mechanism, compared to the customs collection approach that applies to imported goods, is that it avoids a cash flow penalty on the importer. The customs collection model requires the VAT to be paid upfront upon importation and then recovered in normal VAT return, creating a time lag that places importers at a cash flow disadvantage relative to domestic suppliers.[30] To remove the negative impact on cash flow for importers of goods, some countries (such as the UK,[31] Australia[32] and Singapore[33]) introduced optional deferred payment schemes for B2B imported goods that allow importers to account for the import VAT due in their normal VAT return. Provided the enterprise is entitled to an input tax credit in respect of the acquisition of imported goods, the amount of import VAT deferred will simply be offset, as an input tax credit, against the output tax due in the same VAT return, which in practice removes the need for cash payment of VAT on imported goods.[34] The deferred payment scheme for imported goods aligns the timing of VAT payment on imported goods with that on goods obtained locally.[35]

However, the option to use deferred payment may expose the VAT system to a specific form of aggressive fraud, known as 'missing trader fraud'. This type of fraud typically involves a trader who charges VAT on sales but disappears without

[29] (Australia) A New Tax System (Goods and Services Tax) Act 1999, s 9-26(1), item 1. The reverse charge applies only in circumstances where, for example, the imported services are used to make exempt supplies (eg, financial supplies) or for personal consumption. See, ss 84-1, 84-5 and 84-10.

[30] (Australia) A New Tax System (Goods and Services Tax) Amendment Regulations 2000 (No 3) 2000 No 89 Explanatory Statement.

[31] The UK introduced postponed VAT accounting, effective from 1 January 2021, for all imports by VAT registered businesses, except for postal imports with a value of GBP 135 or less. See, The Value Added Tax (Accounting Procedures for Import VAT for VAT Registered Persons and Amendment) (EU Exit) Regulations 2019, SI 2019/60.

[32] Australia introduced the Deferred GST Scheme, at the time of the GST adoption in 2000, that allows eligible importers to defer payment of GST on all taxable imports into Australia. See, (Australia) A New Tax System (Goods and Services Tax) Amendment Regulations 2000 (No 3) 2000 No 89.

[33] Singapore introduced the Import GST Deferment Scheme (IGDS) in 2010. See, (Singapore) Goods and Services Tax Act 1993, s 27A.

[34] Editors, 'Deferred GST Scheme for Importers' (2000) 3 *Manifest: Journal of the Australian Customs Service* 17.

[35] (Australia) A New Tax System (Goods and Services Tax) Amendment Regulations 2000 (No 3) 2000 No 89 Explanatory Statement.

remitting the VAT to the tax authority. The deferred payment system (and the reverse charge mechanism) may facilitate this type of fraud in cross-border circumstances by allowing importers to exploit the timing window created by deferral. Specifically, importers could receive and resell the imported goods (and, though less commonly, services) before the VAT became due, and then go missing with the VAT collected.[36] Therefore, in countries where deferred payment is permitted for B2B imported goods, tax administrators should rigorously assess applications from taxable persons seeking to use the scheme.[37]

While the accounting procedures under the reverse charge mechanism for services and the deferred payment scheme for goods appear similar, the two mechanisms differ conceptually in terms of liability. Under the deferred payment scheme, the default position is that the importer is liable to pay VAT, and the deferred payment scheme acts as a timing mechanism by deferring the collection of VAT from the point of importation until the importer's next periodic return. In contrast, for services, the normal rule is that the foreign supplier has the inherent liability to pay VAT, but with the reverse charge mechanism, that liability is shifted to the importer, effectively deferring VAT collection to the importer's return.

## B. B2C

When VAT quickly spread around the world between the 1950s and 1990s,[38] internet commerce was in its infancy and the volume of cross-border sales of goods and services to private customers was relatively small, with customers predominantly purchasing goods or services from local stores or service providers. Until recently, imported goods of a value below a specified threshold were typically exempt from VAT, while imported digital products or services were left out of the VAT base in the importing country. The exemption that applies to imported low-value goods was justified on the basis that, if VAT were imposed on those goods, the collection costs would outweigh the revenue generated. Different challenges arise in the case of digital products or services, such as mobile apps, online video gaming and video and music streaming services. As noted, services cannot be physically stopped at the border. The solution many countries have used to tax imported B2B services – the reverse charge mechanism, which shifts the liability to pay VAT from the foreign supplier to the domestic purchaser – has proved unworkable for B2C supplies, where unregistered purchasers would be required to self-assess and pay VAT on their acquisitions.[39]

[36] This type of fraud poses a particularly significant threat to VAT revenues within the EU, as discussed in section III.A.i of chapter six.

[37] Fraud risks may also be addressed through the use of judicial or statutory anti-fraud rules, as discussed in the text at nn 43–45 in chapter six.

[38] Ebrill and others (n 1) at xiv–xv; and J Caragher, 'How Many Countries have VAT or GST? 175' (*VATCalc*, August 2024), available at www.vatcalc.com/global/how-many-countries-have-vat-or-gst-174/.

[39] J Brondolo and M Konza, 'Administering the Value-Added Tax on Imported Digital Services and Low-Value Imported Goods' (International Monetary Fund Technical Notes and Manuals, March 2021) 5.

The exclusion from the VAT base of imported digital supplies and imports of low-value goods had been an acceptable compromise for many years when the level of imports benefiting from the exemption was relatively small. However, over the past few decades, globalisation and technological advancements have dramatically increased the ability of private customers to acquire goods or services from suppliers located in other countries. As a result, the exemption approach has led to increasingly significant revenue losses. In the EU, for example, the VAT forgone due to the exemption of low-value imported goods was estimated to have risen from EUR 118 million in 1999 to EUR 640 million in 2011.[40] Non-collection of VAT on those goods has also incentivised consumers to shift their consumption from taxable domestic supplies to untaxed equivalents provided by overseas sellers, further eroding the tax base of the country of consumption.

In addition to the revenue implications, the tax relief for overseas sellers causes a number of distortions. First, it is a source of competitive distortion between domestic and overseas businesses making comparable supplies, as domestic suppliers are required to charge VAT on their sales. Domestic suppliers may have the incentives to restructure their affairs to make supplies from offshore locations.[41] Second, the exemption threshold for imported goods induces offshore suppliers to avoid paying VAT or evade the tax. It had been observed, for example, that overseas suppliers split the orders into consignments and shipped the items separately so that the declared value of each of the consignments fell below the exemption threshold.[42] The European Commission also reported that the exemption previously applied in the EU, known as low value consignment relief (LVCR),[43] was highly susceptible to fraud and abuse, as imported high-value goods were 'consistently undervalued or wrongly described' to benefit from the relief.[44] The revenue loss resulting from the fraud associated with the application of LVCR was estimated at EUR 7 billion per year.[45] The lack of compliance and effective enforcement at

[40] EY, 'Assessment of the Application and Impact of the VAT Exemption for Importation of Small Consignments' (European Commission, May 2015), available at taxation-customs.ec.europa.eu/document/download/b278411b-d701-4749-be9b-679b3ea549f1_en?filename=execsummary_lvcr-study.pdf.

[41] OECD, *Addressing the Tax Challenges of the Digital Economy, OECD/G20 Base Erosion and Profit Shifting Project Action 1 – 2015 Final Report* (Paris, OECD Publishing, 2015) 120.

[42] 'Collection Models for GST on Low Value Imported Goods: Productivity Commission Inquiry Report' ((Australia) Productivity Commission, 31 October 2017) 101.

[43] Under the LVCR regime, small consignments of a value up to EUR 22 imported into the EU were exempt from the import VAT. This exemption was abolished in 2021, when the EU implemented a new regime (the Import One Stop Shop (IOSS)) that requires non-EU suppliers to register and remit the VAT on their distance sales of goods to private customers in the EU. The IOSS is discussed below in the text at n 76.

[44] European Commission, 'Modernising VAT for E-Commerce: Question and Answer' (5 December 2017) MEMO/16/3746, available at ec.europa.eu/commission/presscorner/api/files/document/print/en/memo_16_3746/MEMO_16_3746_EN.pdf.

[45] European Commission, 'Questions and Answers: VAT Gap 2022 Report' (8 December 2022) QANDA/22/7519, available at ec.europa.eu/commission/presscorner/api/files/document/print/en/qanda_22_7519/QANDA_22_7519_EN.pdf.

the customs further undermined fair competition between domestic and overseas suppliers.

The exemption approach, adopted as a simplification measure, became increasingly controversial in light of the rapid increase in cross-border supplies of low-value goods and digital supplies on which no VAT was collected.[46] In addition, the COVID-19 pandemic has further shifted the tax base from the traditional bricks-and-mortar economy to the digital economy. There is a strong case for bringing imported B2C supplies into the scope of VAT in many countries. The challenge is to devise effective collection mechanisms.

### i. *Digital Services*

The common approach to taxing cross-border B2C digital services is to require non-resident suppliers to register and account for VAT in the jurisdiction in which private customers reside. The customer's location can be determined by reference to a range of indicators, including their billing address, bank account or credit card details, internet protocol address and mobile country code.[47] The approach has been adopted by more than 60 countries,[48] including South Africa, Japan, New Zealand, Russia, Australia, and all the EU Member States under harmonised EU legislation.

The main concern about this approach was that compliance is largely voluntary, in that the customer's jurisdiction has little enforcement capacity to audit, or sanction in the case of non-compliance, offshore suppliers.[49] Nevertheless, the experience of the countries that have adopted the approach suggests that high-profile suppliers with significant market share tend to be more tax-compliant, largely for reputational reasons.[50] Many countries introduced legislation to make digital platforms liable for the collection of VAT in respect of the supply of services or digital products they facilitate, thereby shifting the liability to pay VAT from a large number of small suppliers to fewer, and larger, digital platforms. This measure, which was later expanded to imported low-value goods, is discussed in greater detail below. However, the risk of revenue loss may persist if numerous small non-resident suppliers, who make supplies directly to final consumers rather than through digital platforms, fail to register in the customer's jurisdiction.[51] This may be less of a concern in countries where non-resident suppliers of digital services or products are only required to register if their total sales to final consumers in the country exceed the domestic registration threshold. The concern over

[46] OECD, *Consumption Tax Trends 2024* (n 21) at 54–55.
[47] See the list of indicators in New Zealand's GST legislation, for example, (New Zealand) Goods and Services Tax Act 1985, s 8B(2).
[48] Brondolo and Konza (n 39) at 2.
[49] OECD, *Addressing the Tax Challenges* (n 41) at 122.
[50] ibid.
[51] ibid.

non-compliance by small foreign suppliers diminishes further when that threshold is relatively high, as a high threshold is likely to exempt many of them from the obligation to register and account for VAT.

In addition, it is important to recognise that the requirements for registration and compliance with local rules may be particularly onerous for those who have taxable activities, and are faced with tax obligations, in multiple jurisdictions.[52] The risk of non-compliance may be further reduced by providing simplified registration and compliance procedures to ease the compliance difficulties for non-resident businesses. Many countries introduced optional simplified online registration procedures that aim to limit the compliance requirements to what is strictly necessary. An example is the 'pay-only' feature recommended by the OECD that limits the scope of the regime to the collection of VAT, without providing entitlements to input tax recovery to non-resident suppliers.[53] However, the compliance benefits of this feature are questionable, as most non-resident suppliers selling to private customers are unlikely to incur business expenses in the customers' jurisdiction. Moreover, simplified registration procedures typically do not permit non-resident suppliers to issue invoices. This restriction is often justified on the basis that the resident customers, being private consumers, do not require invoices since they are not eligible for input tax deductions.[54] A more compelling rationale for these features may be the need to protect the revenue interests of the taxing jurisdictions. Specifically, these features help prevent fraudulent claims by foreign suppliers and mitigate the risk of domestic businesses fabricating purchases from non-resident entities.

As a single economic bloc, the EU is well-positioned to design a simplification regime for non-EU businesses, given its capacity to harmonise rules across its 27 Member States. In 2003, the EU introduced a simplified registration scheme, the One Stop Shop (OSS) (also referred to as the 'non-Union scheme'), for non-EU businesses which make electronic supplies to EU customers.[55] This scheme aims to reduce compliance costs by enabling non-EU businesses to register in a single Member State of their choice (Member State of identification)

[52] JO Eloi, 'A Global VAT One Stop Shop: Boosting Development' (*Tax Adviser Magazine*, 21 August 2024), available at www.taxadvisermagazine.com/article/global-vat-one-stop-shop-boosting-development. In the EU context, it was estimated that the minimum one-off cost of VAT registration in another Member State is EUR 1,200. The minimum annual ongoing VAT compliance cost in another Member State is approximately EUR 8,000 for an average business, and EUR 2,400 for a small or medium-sized business. See, European Commission, 'Proposal for a Council Directive amending Directive 2006/112/EC as regards VAT rules for the digital age' COM/2022/701 final.

[53] OECD, *Mechanisms for the Effective Collection of VAT/GST: Where the Supplier is Not Located in the Jurisdiction of Taxation* (Paris, OECD Publishing, 2017) para 116. This approach has been adopted in countries such as New Zealand, Australia and Canada.

[54] ibid, para 141.

[55] Council Directive 2002/38/EC of 7 May 2002 amending and amending temporarily Directive 77/388/EEC as regards the value added tax arrangements applicable to radio and television broadcasting services and certain electronically supplied services [2002] OJ L128/41 (repealed by Council Directive 2006/112/EC of 28 November 2006 on the common system of value added tax [2006] OJ L347/1).

and to electronically submit VAT returns in that Member State for their EU-wide sales to private consumers. The VAT collected in the Member State of identification will be subsequently transferred to the respective Member States in which the customers reside (Member States of consumption). In 2021, the scope of the OSS was expanded to include all services supplied by non-EU businesses to private consumers within the EU.[56]

### *ii. Low-Value Goods*

Developments in taxing low-value goods followed the OECD and G20's initiative in addressing the tax challenges in the digital economy in 2015. The OECD identified four collection models that are distinguished by the party liable to account for VAT: the traditional customs collection model, the purchaser collection model, the vendor collection model and the intermediary collection model.[57]

The traditional customs collection model, under which customs authorities assess the value of imported goods and hold them until the recipient makes the VAT payment, is widely regarded as inefficient because of the administrative burden it imposes on the customs authorities.[58] This inefficiency is highlighted in an Australian study, which found that abolishing the exemption threshold altogether under the customs collection model would yield over AUD 600 million (approximately GBP 309 million) in GST revenue, but at the expense of raising the compliance and administrative costs for businesses, consumers and the Government by AUD 2 billion (approximately GBP 1.03 billion).[59]

The purchaser collection model requires domestic purchasers to self-assess and remit the VAT on imports. While the model does not impose compliance burden on offshore suppliers, the level of compliance by domestic purchasers is likely to be low, especially given that private consumers often have limited knowledge of their VAT obligations.[60]

The vendor collection model imposes the obligation to collect and remit the VAT on non-resident suppliers by requiring them to register in the customer's jurisdiction. Experience with digital services has shown that compliance with the

[56] Council Directive (EU) 2017/2455 of 5 December 2017 amending Directive 2006/112/EC and Directive 2009/132/EC as regards certain value added tax obligations for supplies of services and distance sales of goods [2017] OJ L348/7.

[57] OECD, *Addressing the Tax Challenges* (n 41) at 123–26.

[58] ibid at 123–24.

[59] (Australia) Productivity Commission, Collection Models (n 42) at 111.

[60] Prior to 2020, Canada required final consumers to self-assess and pay the GST/Harmonised Sales Tax (HST) on digital products or services acquired from non-resident vendors. The purchaser collection model proved ineffective in Canada, as GST/HST was often not collected on digital imports by final consumers. In response, Canada implemented a hybrid vendor/intermediary collection model in 2020 to replace the purchaser collection model. The application of this model is discussed below in the Australian context in the text following n 65. See, 'Supporting Canadians and Fighting Covid-19: Fall Economic Statement 2020' (Government of Canada, 2020) 189.

rules by non-resident suppliers could be difficult to enforce as they operate beyond the reach of the importing country's enforcement mechanisms.[61]

The intermediary collection model shifts the liability for the collection and payment of VAT due on online sales from non-resident vendors to intermediaries that facilitate these sales. Such intermediaries may include online marketplaces, couriers and postal operators. This model requires the introduction of a legal fiction in VAT legislation, whereby the intermediaries are deemed to be the suppliers, effectively shifting the obligation to account for VAT from the actual suppliers to the intermediaries. A major disadvantage of the model is that it would create additional compliance burdens for the intermediaries. However, at the same time, a large number of small suppliers would be relieved from the burden of complying with VAT rules in different jurisdictions.[62] In addition, placing the liability on the intermediaries, in particular digital platforms, could significantly reduce the number of new registrants that the tax authority has to administer. Previous studies indicate, for example, that approximately two-thirds of e-commerce supplies of goods were made via digital platforms.[63] Large intermediaries also tend to be more tax compliant than small retailers. For these reasons, the intermediary collection model is considered superior to the vendor collection model in terms of administration and enforcement efficiency.[64]

All four models available to impose the VAT on imported low-value goods have limitations. However, the weaknesses of individual models could be addressed, at least to some extent, with the selective application of different systems for different types of transactions. It is generally accepted that the traditional customs collection model operated effectively prior to the internet age, but proved wholly unsustainable with the exponential growth in online sales to private customers using web-based platforms to acquire goods from suppliers in other countries. Nevertheless, the efficiency of the collection of VAT from non-resident suppliers could be greatly increased if the vendor collection model is implemented along with the intermediary collection model.

Under the pressure of lobbying by domestic retailers,[65] Australia took the first move to implement a hybrid vendor/intermediary model, known as the Low Value Imported Goods (LVIG) regime, effective from July 2018.[66] Overseas suppliers, online marketplaces, and re-deliverers[67] are made liable for the GST on imported goods of a value of AUD 1,000 (approximately GBP 515) or less, which were

[61] See the text above at nn 49–51.

[62] OECD, *Consumption Tax Trends 2024* (n 21) at 50.

[63] OECD, *The Role of Digital Platforms in the Collection of VAT/GST on Online Sales* (Paris, OECD Publishing, 2019) 13.

[64] OECD, *Addressing the Tax Challenges* (n 41) at 125.

[65] 'Review of GST on Low Value Imported Goods' ((Australia) The Board of Taxation, December 2021) 11.

[66] (Australia) Treasury Laws Amendment (GST Low Value Goods) Act 2017.

[67] Re-deliverers are businesses that cater to the needs of Australian customers who purchase from overseas merchants that do not ship goods to Australia. These businesses create delivery addresses outside Australia and then forward the goods to Australia. Re-deliverers are deemed to be suppliers because the locations of final consumers are unknown to the actual overseas suppliers.

previously exempt from GST. Online marketplaces and re-deliverers are treated as the suppliers of the low-value goods and are required to register for, and collect, the GST if their turnovers, including the value of sales made through their platforms or redelivered by them, are above the GST registration threshold.

With no international experience to learn from, Australia largely replicated the design of the collection mechanism for low-value goods from that for imported digital services. The introduction of the LVIG regime initially encountered strong resistance from online marketplaces (such as Amazon and eBay) because of the additional compliance burden imposed on these businesses.[68] Three years after the implementation of the regime, the Australian Government reported that 'the LVIG regime has been successful in terms of revenue collections which have significantly exceeded the original estimates'.[69] In the first three years, the GST revenue collected under the regime was almost four and a half times the sum expected.[70] While the revenue authority was unable to measure the size of non-compliance with the LVIG regime, they were confident that the degree of compliance among larger businesses was high.[71] There were, however, some concerns about the compliance levels among smaller offshore businesses.[72]

The Australian regime serves as a useful template for other countries. The vendor/intermediary collection model has been implemented or is under consideration by a growing number of countries, most of which are developed countries, although the specific design details vary across jurisdictions.[73] The EU, for example, abolished the LVCR in 2021, while requiring non-EU suppliers and online marketplaces, which are deemed to be the suppliers,[74] to register and account for VAT on distance sales of low-value goods to private customers within the EU.[75] In the meantime, a new OSS regime, referred to as Import One Stop Shop (IOSS), was created, which allows non-EU businesses to register in a single Member State to declare and pay VAT on distance sales of goods of a value not exceeding EUR 150 to final consumers in the EU.[76] The introduction of the IOSS and the expansion of the non-Union scheme mentioned above[77] are

[68] 'Collection Models for GST on Low Value Imported Goods: Submissions' ((Australia) Productivity Commission), available at www.pc.gov.au/inquiries/completed/collection-models/submissions#initial.

[69] (Australia) The Board of Taxation (n 65) at 61.

[70] The regime generated GST revenue of AUD 760 million (approximately GBP 392 million), against the official forecast of AUD 170 million (approximately GBP 88 million). See (Australia) The Board of Taxation, ibid at 61.

[71] (Australia) The Board of Taxation, ibid at 12.

[72] (Australia) The Board of Taxation, ibid at 60.

[73] For example, New Zealand (2019), Norway (2020), the EU (2021) and Singapore (2023). Switzerland initially introduced the vendor collection model in 2019, before moving to a hybrid vendor/intermediary model in 2025. For a comparison of the schemes implemented in some of these jurisdictions, see (Australia) The Board of Taxation, ibid at 44–45.

[74] Council Directive 2006/112/EC of 28 November 2006 on the common system of value added tax [2006] OJ L347/1, Art 14a.

[75] Directive 2017/2455 (n 56).

[76] ibid.

[77] See the text above at n 56.

key components of the EU's 2021 VAT e-commerce package, a comprehensive set of measures aimed at modernising VAT rules in response to the exponential growth of the e-commerce market.[78] Similar to the experience in Australia, the implementation of the new rules in the EU has been regarded as successful based on revenues collected through the OSS schemes.[79]

A notable difference between the Australian and EU regimes is found in the application of registration threshold to non-resident suppliers. In Australia, the domestic registration threshold applies to non-resident suppliers making digital supplies and sales of low-value goods to Australian consumers, requiring them to register and pay the GST if their sales to Australian customers exceed the threshold. In contrast, the EU does not apply a threshold under the OSS regimes, requiring non-resident suppliers of both digital supplies and low-value goods to charge VAT from the first euro of sales to EU consumers. Owing to historical and policy alignment, the UK has followed the EU model, while many other non-EU countries have adopted the Australian approach.[80]

Singapore, however, offers an example of a third approach by applying a dual-threshold requirement to overseas suppliers. It requires overseas suppliers to register for GST only if they meet two conditions concurrently: 1) their annual global turnover exceeds the domestic registration threshold of SGD 1 million (approximately GBP 575,000); and 2) their B2C supplies of remote services and low-value goods to customers in Singapore exceed a separate, lower threshold of SGD 100,000 (approximately GBP 57,500).[81] The use of a distinct, lower threshold for supplies made to domestic customers may be necessary in Singapore's context,

[78] The package also extended the use of OSS schemes for intra-Community B2C sales of goods and services, as discussed in the text at n 59 in chapter six. The key legislative instruments forming part of the 2021 VAT e-commerce package are Directive 2017/2455 (n 56); Council Directive (EU) 2019/1995 of 21 November 2019 amending Directive 2006/112/EC as regards provisions relating to distance sales of goods and certain domestic supplies of goods [2019] OJ L310/1; and Council Implementing Regulation (EU) 2019/2026 of 21 November 2019 amending Implementing Regulation (EU) No 282/2011 as regards supplies of goods and services facilitated by electronic interfaces and the special schemes for taxable persons supplying services to non-taxable persons, making distance sales of goods and certain domestic supplies of goods [2019] OJ L313/14.

[79] The EU Member States collected EUR 20 billion in VAT revenues in 2022 via the new systems. See, Directorate-General for Taxation and Customs Union, European Commission, 'EU VAT Rules for E-commerce Two Years On: Updated Revenue Figures Point Again to a Successful Implementation' (*News*, 30 June 2023), available at taxation-customs.ec.europa.eu/news/eu-vat-rules-e-commerce-two-years-updated-revenue-figures-point-again-successful-implementation-2023-06-30_en#:~:text=30%20June%202023-,EU%20VAT%20rules%20for%20e%2Dcommerce%20two%20years%20on%3A%20Updated,playing%20field%20for%20all%20businesses.

[80] The OECD has observed that the application of registration thresholds remains typically limited to domestic businesses, and that such thresholds generally do not apply under the regimes that require non-resident suppliers to account for VAT on sales of low-value goods and digital services. However, this trend may largely reflect the fact that most OECD countries are also EU Member States, which are subject to harmonised VAT legislation that precludes the use of thresholds for non-EU suppliers. See, OECD, *Consumption Tax Trends 2024* (n 21) at 46. In contrast, a number of non-EU OECD countries such as New Zealand and Canada, as well as some other jurisdictions such as South Africa, have adopted the Australian approach, applying domestic registration thresholds to non-resident suppliers.

[81] (Singapore) Goods and Services Tax Act 1993, First Schedule para IA(1).

as its high domestic threshold may otherwise exclude a substantial number of foreign suppliers from GST obligations. However, considerable uncertainty may remain as to the practical enforceability of the global turnover threshold by local tax authorities. Nevertheless, Singapore's approach may serve as a model for countries with domestic thresholds that are markedly higher than those of other jurisdictions.

The rationale for applying a threshold to non-resident suppliers aligns with that used in a purely domestic context, as discussed in chapter three – namely, to strike a balance between administrative and compliance cost savings on the one hand, and revenue yields on the other.[82] In fact, the case for applying a threshold may be even stronger for non-resident sellers, who, unlike domestic suppliers, fall outside the direct reach of domestic enforcement mechanisms. However, the justification may carry less weight in the EU context, where the OSS regimes significantly reduce compliance costs for non-resident suppliers by allowing them to report and remit the VAT on their EU-wide sales through a single Member State. Outside the EU, there remains a good reason to exempt the smallest foreign suppliers, who are often not visible to domestic tax administrators, from the requirements of VAT registration and remittance by way of applying a threshold. Nevertheless, the question of threshold is less relevant to smaller suppliers operating via digital platforms that are deemed to be the suppliers, as any applicable threshold would apply at the platform level, thereby effectively removing the registration requirement for the underlying suppliers.

Despite initial opposition from some platforms to the intermediary collection model, international experience to date shows that digital platforms are playing an increasingly important role in enhancing the efficiency of the collection of VAT on cross-border supplies to final consumers. In effect, countries that have implemented the model, most notably Australia, have helped reduce the political resistance from platforms that other countries might otherwise face when considering similar reforms. As more countries adopt this approach, cross-border platforms are increasingly likely to accept the deemed supplier rules as the new global norm, thereby lessening their opposition to similar measures elsewhere. However, for the time being, in many non-OECD countries, the risks of revenue loss and competitive distortions may not yet be sufficiently significant to warrant policy actions on imported low-value goods and digital supplies, due to relatively lower customer demand for imported products.[83]

Table 5.1 below summarises the challenges and current approaches to applying the destination principle across different types of cross-border supplies.

[82] See the text at n 9 in chapter three.

[83] In China, for example, because of the strict internet censorship (known as the 'Great Firewall'), Chinese customers have very limited access to cross-border streaming services and advertising services, such as those provided by Netflix, Facebook and Google. See, Y Zu, 'China's VAT in the Digitalized Economy' in Y Xu (ed), *VAT in the Digital Era: Unilateral and Multilateral Options for Reform* (Oxford, Oxford University Press, 2023).

**Table 5.1** Challenges, Current Approaches and Weaknesses in Applying the Destination Principle to Cross-Border Supplies

<table>
<tr><th>Type of Cross-Border Supplies</th><th>Challenges</th><th>Current Approaches</th><th>Weaknesses</th></tr>
<tr><td rowspan="2">B2B goods</td><td rowspan="2">• no particular challenges</td><td>zero-rating exports in the exporting country, and taxation upon importation at the border</td><td>cash flow burden on the importer</td></tr>
<tr><td>some countries permit deferred payment of VAT on imports</td><td>risk of missing trader fraud</td></tr>
<tr><td>B2B services</td><td>• absence of physical borders<br>• suppliers who have liability to pay are outside the taxing jurisdiction</td><td>reverse charge mechanism</td><td>risk of missing trader fraud (less commonly)</td></tr>
<tr><td>B2C low-value goods</td><td>• high collection costs at the border<br>• foreign suppliers liable for VAT are outside the taxing jurisdiction<br>• domestic final consumers cannot be relied upon to self-assess VAT</td><td rowspan="2">vendor/ intermediary collection (deeming platforms to be the suppliers)</td><td rowspan="2">• possible non-compliance, particularly by small suppliers<br>• high compliance costs for foreign vendors/ intermediaries dealing with registration requirements in multiple jurisdictions</td></tr>
<tr><td>B2C digital supplies</td><td>• absence of physical borders<br>• foreign suppliers liable for VAT are outside the taxing jurisdiction<br>• domestic final consumers cannot be relied upon to self-assess VAT</td></tr>
</table>

# V. Towards a Coordinated Approach

## A. Weaknesses of the Unilateral Measures

So far countries have largely resorted to unilateral responses to international cross-border challenges. Meanwhile, the OECD has been playing its leadership role in developing an internationally agreed framework of principles in the form of soft law guidance, with a view to facilitating consistent and coherent application of domestic rules to cross-border transactions.[84]

Though unilateral actions based on OECD guidelines have achieved some success as stop-gap measures, where they have been adopted, they fall well short of providing effective, long-term solutions to the cross-border challenges. The destination principle assigns taxing rights exclusively to the jurisdiction in which consumption takes place. However, consistent application of the principle across jurisdictions requires a common understanding of the place of consumption, an objective not realised in practice where jurisdictions have adopted different, and sometimes inconsistent, statutory proxies for determining the place of consumption in relation to services.

For example, in a case that concerned the provision of clairvoyance and palmistry services by a palmist to non-resident clients, the UK VAT and Duties Tribunal, relying on the UK statutory rule that treats the residence of the supplier as the applicable proxy for the place of consumption, held that the supplies in question were taxable in the UK.[85] Under similar circumstances, in contrast, many non-EU countries would likely use the residence of the customer or the place of effective use or enjoyment as the proxy in their VAT legislation, resulting in the client's country of residence being treated as the place of taxation. Another example arises in the treatment of supplies of foreign currency intended for use outside the country. In such cases, the UK First-tier Tribunal, relying on domestic law aligned with EU law requirements, determined the place of taxation based on the customer's residence.[86] In contrast, the High Court of Australia, characterising the transaction as a supply made in relation to rights, applied a statutory place of use of rights test (a concept akin to the place of effective use or enjoyment) to determine the place of taxation as being outside Australia.[87]

[84] See, eg, OECD, *Addressing the Tax Challenges* (n 41); and OECD, *Mechanisms for the Effective Collection of VAT/GST* (n 53).

[85] *Mohammed (t/a The Indian Palmist) v Customs & Excise Commissioners* [2003] VAT Decision 18397. This is an example where the Tribunal decided that the supply in question does not fall within the scope of the specific category (services of a consultant), and therefore the fallback rule, based on the residence of the supplier, applies. See above, n 12 and the accompanying text.

[86] Directive 2006/112 (n 74) Art 59 provides that the place of supply of services to customers established outside the Community shall be the place where he has his permanent address or usually resides. In *1st Contact Ltd v Revenue and Customs Commissioners* [2012] UKFTT 84 (TC), the First-tier Tribunal considered whether the customers who came to the UK on a working holiday or for overseas experience from non-EU countries had their usual place of residence in the UK.

[87] (Australia) A New Tax System (Goods and Services Tax) Act 1999, s 38-190(1), item 4(a) provides that a supply that is made in relation to rights is GST-free if the rights are for use outside Australia. In

These examples demonstrate the differences in the approaches to the choice of proxies across countries, which may lead to problematic outcomes such as double taxation or unintended non-taxation. New Zealand's GST legislation clearly foresees the possibility of double taxation that might arise on supplies of remote services to a non-resident consumer in New Zealand that are physically performed in New Zealand.[88] This would be a circumstance under which two countries use different proxies to determine the place of taxation, with New Zealand relying on the place of effective use or enjoyment and the other country relying on the residence of the customer. The GST legislation provides a unilateral double taxation relief by allowing a New Zealand resident supplier a deduction that offsets their GST liability in New Zealand to the extent that the supply is subject to consumption tax in another jurisdiction.[89] Under this rule, the New Zealand supplier could claim an input tax credit up to the amount of New Zealand GST returned on the same supply. The allowable input tax credit is therefore limited to the lesser of the actual foreign VAT paid and the domestic GST payable on the supply.[90] To illustrate, assuming the before tax price is 100 and the GST rate in New Zealand is 15 per cent:

- If the foreign VAT rate were 20 per cent, the supplier would be entitled to an input tax credit of 15 (15 per cent x 100), capped at the amount of New Zealand GST payable.
- If the foreign VAT rate were 10 per cent, the supplier would be entitled to an input tax credit of 10 (10 per cent x 100), reflecting the actual amount of foreign tax incurred.

It is worth noting, however, that the different approaches to the choice of proxies do not necessarily raise concerns in practice. This is because, as discussed above,[91] many countries require non-resident businesses supplying remote services to their resident customers to register and remit VAT only if their total turnover from those supplies exceeds the domestic registration threshold (which varies across jurisdictions, as noted in chapter three).[92] The application of thresholds to non-resident suppliers thus limits the possibility of double taxation to some extent in practice.

*Travelex Ltd v Commissioner of Taxation* [2010] HCA 33 (Australia), the High Court of Australia held that the sale of foreign currency to a departing traveller was a supply of or in relation to rights for use outside Australia.

[88] For an example of the possible circumstances under which double taxation might arise, see 'GST on cross-border supplies of remote services' (Policy and Strategy, New Zealand Inland Revenue, May 2016) 26, available at www.taxpolicy.ird.govt.nz/-/media/project/ir/tp/publications/2016/2016-sr-gst-cross-border-supplies/2016-sr-gst-cross-border-supplies-pdf.pdf?modified=20200910084403&modified=20200910084403.

[89] (New Zealand) Goods and Services Tax Act 1985, s 20(3)(dc).

[90] This logic mirrors that of foreign tax credit commonly provided under income tax treaties, which is typically limited to the lessor of the actual foreign tax paid or the amount of domestic tax payable on the same income. For an explanation of the foreign tax credit in the income tax, see BJ Arnold, *International Tax Primer*, 5th edn (The Netherlands, Kluwer Law International, 2023) 62. See also below, the text preceding n 103.

[91] See n 80 above.

[92] See the text at n 1 in chapter three.

Conflicting jurisdictional claims may not always result from differences in the place of taxation rules between jurisdictions. Even where the identical place of taxation rules are in place, tax authorities and courts in different countries might disagree on the nature of the supply in question, resulting in divergent views on the applicable proxies to determine the place of taxation. *RCI Europe v Commissioners for Her Majesty's Revenue and Customs (RCI)* provides an example of the potential risk of double taxation.[93] This case concerned the place of taxation for supplies made by a UK-established business in facilitating and organising the exchange of timeshare usage rights held by its members in holiday accommodation outside the UK (mostly in Spain). The UK and Spanish tax authorities both assessed the taxpayer's transactions for VAT. Both countries relied on the EU VAT legislation, but they took different views on the applicable place of taxation rule. The UK authority claimed that the supplies should be taxed in the place where the supplier is located, whereas the Spanish authority argued that the place of taxation should be the place where the immovable property is situated. Both countries, therefore, considered themselves to have the jurisdiction to tax. The conflicting claims were eventually resolved with a preliminary ruling delivered by the Court of Justice of the European Union (CJEU). At the international level, however, no similar mechanism is available for resolving conflicting taxing claims.

The mechanisms used to provide refunds to non-resident businesses for expenses incurred in a country also reveal the limitations of unilateral actions in resolving cross-border conflicts. This is evidenced by the fact that many countries that adopted a direct refund system have already sought international cooperation by concluding reciprocal agreements.

The vendor/intermediary collection model has emerged as the preferred approach by OECD countries, and by an increasing number of non-OECD countries, for taxing both imported digital supplies and low-value goods. However, it is important to note that this model was initially chosen as the 'most feasible among the imperfect alternatives' for collecting VAT on imported low-value goods.[94] From a compliance perspective, the model raises concerns about the potentially high compliance burden resulting from registering for and reporting VAT (and possibly in different languages) faced by businesses selling to final consumers across multiple jurisdictions.[95] The compliance obligations may discourage small suppliers from engaging in cross-border B2C sales or increase the risk of non-compliance.[96] From an enforcement standpoint, the model's main vulnerability lies in its reliance on self-assessment by foreign suppliers, rendering compliance essentially voluntary. These problems could be alleviated by implementing simplified registration

[93] Case C-37/08 *RCI Europe v Commissioners for Her Majesty's Revenue and Customs* ECLI:EU:C:2009:507, [2009] ECR I-7533.

[94] (Australia) Productivity Commission, Collection Models (n 42) at 2.

[95] MCS Lamensch, 'Is There Any Future for the Vendor Collection Model in the 21st Century Economy?' (2016) 27 *International VAT Monitor* 182.

[96] OECD, *Mechanisms for the Effective Collection of VAT/GST* (n 53) para 33.

procedures to facilitate compliance, as well as by applying deemed supplier rules, which capture a significant share of cross-border B2C supplies made via digital platforms. Additionally, the OECD has recommended enhancing collection efficiency through increased international cooperation in tax administration, such as the exchange of information between jurisdictions.[97] The Australian tax authority, for example, relies on the Convention on Mutual Administrative Assistance in Tax Matters[98] to obtain information from non-residents.[99]

## B. A VAT Treaty

An alternative approach to addressing the cross-border VAT challenges might lie in the adoption of solutions based on international cooperation. For over a century, international cooperation has long been achieved in the field of income tax through a network of bilateral treaties designed to resolve double taxation and non-taxation arising from overlapping and conflicting jurisdictional claims. The extensive income tax treaty network now consists of over 3,000 bilateral treaties. In the field of VAT, however, international agreements are nearly absent. Over two decades ago, VAT treaties were considered unnecessary, as the relative uniformity of VAT systems and the single destination principle were believed to largely reduce the possibilities for jurisdictional conflicts.[100] This view no longer holds valid when globalisation, deregulation and digital transformation pose challenges to the application of the destination principle to cross-border sales. With the growth trajectory for digital supplies and imported low-value goods expected to continue, it is increasingly recognised that enhanced international cooperation is necessary to ensure fair and efficient collection of VAT in international trade. The possibility of introducing a VAT treaty has been explored in the literature in recent years.[101]

How could a VAT treaty address the cross-border VAT challenges? The experience with income tax treaties suggests that cooperation by way of treaty is possible only when such agreements interfere with domestic rules in the least possible manner, given that tax sovereignty remains a core aspect of state sovereignty. Thus, while countries could agree, in principle, that the place of taxation under the VAT is the country where consumption takes place, they may prefer to retain the autonomy to implement this principle in their preferred manner through domestic

[97] OECD, *Addressing the Tax Challenges* (n 41) at 205.

[98] OECD and Council of Europe, *The Multilateral Convention on Mutual Administrative Assistance in Tax Matters: Amended by the 2010 Protocol* (Paris, OECD Publishing, 2011).

[99] (Australia) The Board of Taxation (n 65) at 63.

[100] BJ Arnold, J Sasseville and E Zolt, 'Summary of the Proceedings of an Invitational Seminar on Tax Treaties in the 21st Century' (2002) 50 *Canadian Tax Journal* 65, 68.

[101] See, eg, NP Eriksen, 'Should Tax Treaties Play a Role for Consumption Taxes?' (2005) 33 *Intertax* 166; T Ecker, *A VAT/GST Model Convention* (The Netherlands, International Bureau of Fiscal Documentation, 2013); Y Zu, 'Developing VAT Treaties: International Tax Cooperation in Times of Global Recovery' (2022) 42 *Legal Studies* 159; Y Xu, 'A Multilateral Option for VAT in International Trade?' (2022) 71 *International and Comparative Law Quarterly* 857.

legislation, free from external constraints. Consequently, a common set of place of taxation rules is arguably more difficult to achieve at the international level unless states are willing to cede a degree of sovereignty to a supranational body, as seen in the EU.[102] However, it may still be possible for countries to agree on a common set of proxies to determine the place of consumption, as well as the hierarchy of proxies in their application.

In addition, the *RCI* case discussed above shows that inconsistent application of place of taxation rules can occur even when identical rules are used. It is, therefore, necessary to incorporate dispute resolution mechanisms and, where appropriate, methods for providing double tax relief in a VAT treaty. New Zealand's unilateral double taxation relief, which allows resident businesses to deduct the foreign tax paid from their domestic tax liability, is essentially the VAT equivalent of the foreign tax credit in the income tax.[103] Although its application is limited in scope in New Zealand's context, it could serve as a model for designing double tax relief methods in a VAT treaty. The provisions of double tax relief methods in a VAT treaty could be adapted from those in the income tax model treaty,[104] substituting input tax credits in the VAT for foreign tax credits in the income tax. This approach would require the country of establishment to provide double tax relief if dispute resolution fails.

A VAT treaty also offers a potential solution to the inefficiencies associated with one of the unilateral approaches to providing refunds to foreign businesses incurring business expenses in a country. The direct refund system can be easily implemented by a treaty in which two countries agree to refund the input tax collected on expenses incurred by the businesses registered in the other country. The effective implementation of the system would require an information exchange provision, under which the non-resident business' home country confirms the registration status of the business to minimise the risks of fraudulent refund claims in the country that grants the refund.

One possible response to the collection difficulties that arise from taxing cross-border digital supplies and low-value goods is to replicate the OSS system used in the EU for intra-Community B2C supplies (as discussed in chapter six)[105] at the international level, facilitated by a treaty.[106] The treaty would place the obligation for collecting the VAT on B2C sales of digital supplies and low-value goods on the exporting country. The tax would be collected at the rate applicable in the customer's jurisdiction by the exporting jurisdiction, which would then transfer the revenue collected to the customer's jurisdiction via a clearing house mechanism. Revenue inflows and outflows would be netted against each other, with only the net balance transferred between each pair of countries. Although the tax

[102] Ecker proposed a VAT model treaty that harmonises domestic place of taxation rules in Ecker, ibid.
[103] See above n 90.
[104] OECD, *Model Tax Convention on Income and on Capital* (Paris, OECD Publishing, 2017), Art 23B.
[105] Refer to section III.B of chapter six.
[106] The idea was first explored in Zu (n 101), and subsequently discussed by Eloi in Eloi (n 52).

would be collected on an origin basis, the allocation outcomes would be entirely consistent with the destination principle.

Compared with the current unilateral approach based on the vendor/ intermediary collection model, the treaty arrangement offers the advantage of significantly reducing compliance costs for overseas suppliers. It removes the obligations for those businesses to register and file tax returns in every country where they have private customers (subject to threshold requirements). The reduction in compliance burden would, in turn, reduce the tax barriers to cross-border trade, in particular for relatively small businesses making direct sales to overseas customers, which are disproportionately impacted by the existing unilateral measures.

One caveat is that the proposed model would require closer cooperation in terms of mutual assistance in the collection of taxes than in the existing income tax treaties. The income tax provision on mutual assistance aims to establish a mechanism for states to lend assistance in recovering unpaid taxes in other states upon request.[107] The proposed VAT treaty would make it automatically obligatory for states to collect the current tax applied to certain supplies by other countries. A potential obstacle to the proposed cooperative regime could be that countries, in particular developed countries equipped with strong tax administrations, may be reluctant to rely on foreign tax administrations for the collection of their own taxes due to concerns over disparities in administrative capacities. However, current unilateral measures that rely on foreign business suppliers for the collection of VAT may be even less effective than the collection by relatively weaker tax administrations under a coordinated framework.

Moreover, the proposed VAT treaties may attribute additional benefits to developing countries where treaties are concluded between developed and developing countries. The continued growth of consumer demand for cross-border B2C supplies driven by rising incomes in the developing world creates new opportunities for e-commerce market players in developed countries. However, weaker administrative capacity in developing countries places constraints on their ability to effectively capture cross-border sales. The OSS arrangement facilitated by treaties would enable developing countries to piggy-back off the administrative capacity of countries hosting enterprises that sell into their territories while increasing the competitiveness of their domestic exporters.

## VI. Conclusion

While there is a broad consensus among countries on applying the destination principle to cross-border transactions, the implementation of the principle in the era of globalisation presents challenges in three main areas. First, the determination of the place of consumption for services relies on complex place of taxation

[107] OECD, *Model Tax Convention on Income and on Capital* (n 104), Art 27.

rules. Second, there is no consistent approach to refunding the VAT incurred on business expenses by non-resident businesses. Third, the collection of VAT on imported goods and services requires effective mechanisms, which may vary depending on the types of supplies or suppliers involved.

To date, countries have largely relied on unilateral measures, guided by OECD recommendations, to address the cross-border challenges. Although the unilateral measures have achieved temporary success, they face important limitations in resolving conflicts and bridging gaps in cross-border circumstances. Enhanced international cooperation by way of treaties offers the potential for more sustainable and effective solutions, especially in light of the ever-expanding global market driven by the rapid acceleration of technological advancements.

# 6

# VAT in Federations

## I. Introduction

The operation of Value Added Tax (VAT) presents unique challenges in federations. Two issues arise in federal countries, economic communities, or large countries with subnational governments faced with expenditure responsibilities. The first is whether there should be a vertical allocation of taxing rights in a jurisdiction with multiple tiers of government, that is, should sub-central jurisdictions have the fiscal autonomy to levy the VAT (for example, determine the base and rate) in addition to or without a central VAT? The European Union (EU) provides an example of a jurisdiction with separate subordinate jurisdictions and no central (EU) tax. Canada and India provide examples of a jurisdiction in which national and subordinate jurisdictions levy parallel VATs. Australia and China are examples of jurisdictions with a national VAT only.

Inevitably, the legal basis for a vertical allocation of taxing rights rests on constitutional authority, a subject outside the scope of this book. However, distinct from the question of whether sub-central governments can levy separate VATs, the central government may agree to share the VAT revenue with subordinate jurisdictions. Whether this is the case and the extent of revenue-sharing are political decisions that are also beyond the scope of the book. China and Ethiopia provide examples of a national VAT, with the revenue shared between the national and subnational governments. Sitting at the far end of the sharing spectrum is Australia, where the central government holds exclusive power to levy a Goods and Services Tax (GST) but distributes all the revenue collected to subnational governments.

Whether subnational governments levy their own VATs or the central government has exclusive taxing rights but agrees to share some or all of its revenue with lower tier governments, a second question arises as to how the VAT should be shared between subnational jurisdictions. This is the central question to be examined in this chapter. While there are a range of systems in operation and theoretical models advocated by experts, the options fall into three categories. Allocation regimes in the first category assigns the VAT revenue on an origin basis, that is, to the sub-central jurisdiction from which a supply is made. Systems in the second category, with many variations, allocate the VAT revenue to subordinate jurisdictions on a destination basis. These systems must address many of the conceptual and practical issues discussed in the previous chapter, albeit in a somewhat different context. Systems in the third category disregards both the origin of supplies and their destination, instead allocating the VAT revenue on the basis of a fiscal equalisation formula. The formula may look at other revenue sources available to subordinate jurisdictions or allocate on a per capita basis or use some combination of these factors. This chapter reviews models that are currently in use to allocate the VAT revenue among subordinate jurisdictions.

## II. Allocation on the Basis of Origin

An origin-based VAT applies the tax to inter-jurisdictional supplies at the rate applicable in the jurisdiction of origin, with the revenue accruing to that jurisdiction. Two proxies are used to determine the origin for sharing the tax bases among subnational jurisdictions in practice: the jurisdiction of production (as is the case in Brazil), and the place at which the supplier is registered (as is the case in China and Ethiopia).

The origin basis system might be used in countries with a national VAT only and countries where subnational VATs co-exist with a central VAT. China and Ethiopia provide examples of the former, with a share of the VAT revenue collected under the national VAT allocated between the local governments (provinces in China and states in Ethiopia) on an origin basis. Suppliers do not need to distinguish between inter- and intra-jurisdictional sales. With no need for border adjustments, applying the VAT on the basis of origin in VAT systems that operate at a subordinate level does not create administrative and compliance difficulties for tax authorities and businesses. In Brazil, the state-level VAT, known as ICMS, is levied on goods and certain services on an origin basis, whereas a federal tax (the IPI) functions more as a selective excise and import tax than as a broad-based federal VAT.[1]

However, the use of origin-based VAT in a federal country or large country with multi-tiered governments may lead to a range of serious distortions. First, an origin-based tax without uniform rates and base alters the relative prices of supplies across jurisdictions, distorting consumption and production decisions.[2] Second, one inherent problem associated with the origin-based allocation of tax revenue is that local governments have an interest in seeing the tax operating as if it were a set of regional VATs, leading to horizontal tax competition among local governments. In countries where local governments have the autonomy in terms of base- and rate-setting and administration, local governments may attract mobile tax bases (for example, investment in the production of goods or services)

[1] VJ Perry, 'International Experience in Implementing VATs in Federal Jurisdictions: A Summary' (2010) 63 *Tax Law Review* 623, 628–29.

[2] R Hill and M Rushton, 'Harmonizing Provincial Sales Taxes with the GST: The Problem of Interprovincial Trade' (1993) 41 *Canadian Tax Journal* 101.

by adjusting the VAT rates or bases. The tax competition between Brazilian states – the so called 'tax war' – has long been a problem in Brazil's tax system, resulting in erosion of the VAT base and undermining economic performance by distorting business behaviours.[3] To address the long-standing inefficiencies, Brazil has eventually legislated to move from an origin- to a destination-based VAT over the next few years (2026–33).[4]

The horizontal tax competition could also occur in a country where the subnational governments do not have the autonomy over rates and base. In China, for example, although provinces have no legal power to alter VAT rates or base, they were found to have indirectly granted tax preferences, either illegally or by circumventing the formal rules, to attract enterprises to register in their jurisdictions.[5] A common approach used is to grant 'tax refunds' of the local share of the corporate income tax or VAT or both to enterprises newly registered in the jurisdiction for the initial three to five years.

A third issue is that an origin-based VAT gives rise to cross-subsidies between states, possibly intensifying regional inequality. In the case of inter-jurisdictional business-to-business (B2B) sales, the tax remitted by the seller in the exporting jurisdiction will be recovered by the purchaser in the importing jurisdiction. In effect, the exporting jurisdiction retains the revenue that is foregone by the importing jurisdiction, amounting to a subsidy from the latter to the former. The cross-subsidies arise whether the rates are harmonised or not. In addition, it is often the case that net exporting jurisdictions are wealthier states, while net importing jurisdictions tend to be poorer.[6] Consequently, the origin-based VAT may disproportionately benefit wealthier states, creating economic and fiscal imbalances to the detriment of the destination jurisdictions.

## III. Allocation on the Basis of Consumption

As noted in the international context in the previous chapter, in theory the VAT revenue should accrue to the jurisdiction where consumption takes place. A destination-based VAT achieves this by imposing tax as supplies enter the

[3] L de Mello, 'The Brazilian "Tax War": The Case of Value-Added Tax Competition among the States' (2008) 36 *Public Finance Review* 169.

[4] MR Lukic, 'Tax Reform in Brazil and the Unique Federal Arrangement to Implement Its Dual-VAT' (*Kluwer International Tax Blog*, 26 February 2024).

[5] Where the local governments offer preferential tax treatment illegally, taxpayers' rights to receive the concessions are not legally protected. In a case that concerned the non-performance of a municipal government's administrative promise (in the form of administrative documents) to offer tax preferences to enterprises, the taxpayer's claim for unpaid tax refunds was dismissed by the court on the grounds that the administrative promise by the municipal government violates the probative provisions in the legislation. See, Administrative Ruling of the Intermediate People's Court of Leshan City, Sichuan Province (2016) Chuan 11 Xing Zhong No 56 (in Chinese).

[6] WA Yesegat and R Krever, 'Value Added Tax and Fiscal Federalism in Ethiopia' (2020) 28 *African Journal of International and Comparative Law* 147, 159.

jurisdiction, while zero-rating, and providing full input tax credits for, supplies exported from the jurisdiction. Border points, where the import tax can be collected and the exports confirmed for zero-rating purposes, are typically absent from a country with multiple levels of government or a single economic community composed of different countries. The challenge, therefore, is to devise feasible alternative measures to allocate the revenue to the destination jurisdiction without incurring significant administrative costs. The nature of the issue involved is not dissimilar to that of taxing intangible supplies in the international context discussed in chapter five. The set of solutions available to federations or economic unions is nevertheless different and is largely confined to domestic or regional political factors, including whether there is an overarching fiscal authority and the extent to which subnational governments have autonomy in setting the rates and base. Four main models are currently in use in different jurisdictions: the international zero-rating model, clearing house, Compensating VAT (CVAT) and consumption statistics model.[7]

## A. The International Zero-Rating Model

### *i. EU*

As discussed in the international context in chapter five,[8] the reverse charge mechanism for services offers a practical solution for taxing cross-border B2B supplies in circumstances where physical border controls are absent. The widely adopted model for taxing cross-border B2B services has the jurisdiction from which the supplies are made zero-rating exports and the importing jurisdiction imposing tax on imported services via a reverse charge mechanism. A parallel system for goods, the deferred payment system, has been used in the EU for taxing intra-Community supplies of goods between registered enterprises in different Member States, following the removal of physical borders between the Member States at the end of 1992. Under the deferred payment system, the collection of the VAT on imports is deferred until the first sales of the importer within the importing jurisdiction.[9] The EU system was intended to be temporary at the time when the common system of VAT was established (hence referred to as the 'transitional VAT system'), but still remains in place today.[10] A general system of reverse charge

[7] A model that received some attention in the literature but is omitted from the discussion in this chapter is VIVAT ('viable integrated VAT'). This model was proposed for the EU, but was not adopted. See M Keen and S Smith, 'The Future of Value Added Tax in the European Union' (1996) 11 *Economic Policy* 373.

[8] See the text accompanying and preceding n 28 in chapter five.

[9] Council Directive 2006/112/EC of 28 November 2006 on the common system of value added tax (VAT Directive) [2006] OJ L347/1, Art 211. See also, RM Bird and P-P Gendron, *The VAT in Developing and Transitional Countries* (Cambridge, Cambridge University Press, 2007) 146.

[10] European Commission, 'Commission Staff Working Document Impact Assessment: Generalised reverse charge mechanism – Accompanying the document Proposal for a Council Directive amending Directive 2006/112/EC on the common system of value added tax as regards the temporary application

for B2B services was introduced in 2010 through what is commonly referred to as the 2010 VAT Package,[11] alongside a change of the general place of taxation (referred to as the 'place of supply' in the EU) rules for B2B services that aligns the rules with the destination principle.[12]

Nevertheless, the deferred payment and reverse charge systems, which introduced important changes in the way that VAT is charged and accounted for on goods and services moving between the EU Member States, have been exploited through a notorious and widespread form of cross-border fraud in the EU, known as 'missing trader intra-Community' (MTIC) fraud.[13] MTIC fraud schemes are typically complex, large-scale operations involving organised crime networks.[14] In its basic form, the scheme involves a fraudulent importer acquiring goods VAT-free (as zero-rated exports in the exporting country), and charging VAT on its onward domestic supply. The importer then 'disappears'[15] (hence the term 'missing trader') before remitting the collected VAT to the tax authority.[16] Meanwhile, the business customer could rely on the invoice issued by the missing trader to claim an input tax credit, despite the fact that the corresponding output tax on the sale was never paid to the government. As a result, the government incurs a revenue loss.

A MTIC fraud scheme exploits two features of the intra-Community cross-border B2B rules.[17] The first is zero-rating of exports, which removes the VAT in the exporting country. The second is the deferred payment (or reverse charge) system, creating a time lag between the point of importation and the VAT due date and, thus, allowing importers to receive goods without paying the (import) VAT but at the same time charge the (domestic) VAT on their resale. The treatment of a single intra-Community supply as two distinct transactions creates a 'break' at a particularly weak point in the VAT payment chain – namely, the interface between domestic and foreign tax administrations.[18] The intra-Community

of the generalised reverse charge mechanism in relation to supplies of goods and services above a certain threshold' (21 December 2016) SWD (2016) 457 final.

[11] Council Directive 2008/8/EC of 12 February 2008 amending Directive 2006/112/EC as regards the place of supply of services [2008] OJ L44/11; VAT Directive (n 9) Art 196. Previously, there was also a mandatory reverse charge under Art 196 for certain services. In addition, Art 194 already included an optional reverse charge at the Member State level.

[12] The general place of taxation was shifted from the place where the supplier is established to the place where the customer is established.

[13] C Andrew and K Baer, 'How to Combat Value-Added Tax Refund Fraud'(IMF How to Notes 23/01, August 2023) 10.

[14] P Baert, 'Filling the Gap: The EU's Fight against VAT Fraud' (European Parliament Briefing, 29 January 2025), available at www.europarl.europa.eu/RegData/etudes/BRIE/2025/767221/EPRS_BRI(2025)767221_EN.pdf.

[15] Possible ways in which companies can 'disappear' are explained in J Malan and I Bosch Chen, 'Possible Solutions for Missing Trader Intra-Community Fraud' (Committee on Budgetary Control, European Parliament, 2022) 18.

[16] For a graphical illustration of the basic form of the MTIC fraud, see European Union Committee (House of Lords), '20th Report of Session 2006-07: Stopping the Carousel: Missing Trader Fraud in the EU' (2006-07, HL 101) 9.

[17] S Smith, 'VAT Fraud and Evasion' in R Chote and others (eds), *The IFS Green Budget: January 2007* (London, The Institute for Fiscal Studies, 2007) 170.

[18] Baert (n 14) at 4.

cross-border arrangements are therefore considered 'a fundamental flaw in the design of the VAT system'.[19] The most severe form of the MTIC is the well-known carousel fraud. As the name implies, this scheme operates like a carousel, with the same consignment of goods being repeatedly exported and re-imported by companies set up for the specific purpose of committing the fraud. The MTIC fraud schemes give rise to significant revenue loss,[20] and have plagued EU legislators and the Member States since the removal of fiscal frontiers. MTIC fraud in the EU is significantly more prevalent than the general missing trader fraud schemes that might arise from the use of the reverse charge mechanism for services or from the exploitation of deferred payment for goods at international borders, as discussed in chapter five.[21] This higher prevalence can be largely attributed to the less stringent border controls within the EU compared to those at international borders, as well as the historical and still common requirement for upfront payment of VAT and import duties in many jurisdictions outside the EU, limiting the scope for this type of fraud at the border.

Over the past two decades, the EU has actively taken measures to close the VAT loopholes in relation to MTIC fraud.[22] One solution is to allow the Member States to introduce a reverse charge mechanism for domestic supplies between registered businesses in relation to specific goods or services in the pre-defined areas that are identified as particularly sensitive to MTIC fraud. The operation of the domestic reverse charge mechanism mirrors that of the reverse charge applied to imported B2B services in the international context, that is, the VAT is accounted for by the customer rather than the supplier. Where suppliers are obliged to use the reverse charge mechanism for domestic supplies, they would not charge VAT on their sales, thereby removing their opportunity to disappear with the amount of VAT charged on the domestic supplies.

However, the rationales for using the reverse charge mechanism in the cross-border and domestic contexts are different. In the cross-border context, reverse charge serves as a practical solution for taxing cross-border supplies in situations where physical border controls are absent and it is administratively burdensome to collect the tax from foreign suppliers. In the domestic context, in contrast, reverse charge is used as an anti-fraud measure, aimed at reducing VAT evasion in high-risk sectors.[23] Ironically, the reverse charge mechanism introduced in the EU based on the

[19] European Union Committee (House of Lords) (n 16) at 7.

[20] The estimated EU-wide foregone revenue from the MTIC fraud ranged from EUR 12.5 billion to EUR 32.8 billion between 2010 and 2023, representing 1.2–3.1% of the actual VAT revenue. See, European Commission, 'VAT Compliance Gap due to Missing Trader Intracommunity (MTIC) Fraud – Final Report. Phase II' (2024) 57, available at op.europa.eu/en/publication-detail/-/publication/dd40080c-bd27-11ef-91ed-01aa75ed71a1/language-en.

[21] See the text at n 36 in chapter five.

[22] European Commission, 'VAT Compliance Gap Report' (n 20) at 38–66.

[23] The reverse charge mechanism is also used in some countries to combat wholly domestic missing trader fraud arising in specific industries, such as gold (eg, the UK, Australia and South Africa) and construction (the UK). See the UK rules, eg, Value Added Tax Act 1994 c 23, s 55, and Value Added Tax (Section 55A) (Specified Services and Excepted Supplies) Order 2019/892. This type of fraud scheme is perpetrated by traders who have acquired goods free of tax (gold in certain forms) or who provide personal services with few or no taxable inputs (construction sub-contractors). These traders then charge output tax on their supplies without filing the VAT return or paying the tax to the

first rationale has contributed to the very type of fraud it is intended to combat in the latter context. In effect, the reverse charge mechanism has become a countermeasure to a problem it inadvertently facilitated. This process is illustrated in Figure 6.1 below. However, it is important to point out that the reverse charge mechanism is not inherently facilitative of the missing trader element of the MTIC fraud, in which the fraudster collects the VAT on sales and then disappears. Rather, it is the deferral of VAT payment involved in the reverse charge or deferred payment systems in the context of cross-border transactions that creates the vulnerability.

**Figure 6.1** Reverse Charge Mechanism: Both a Problem and a Solution

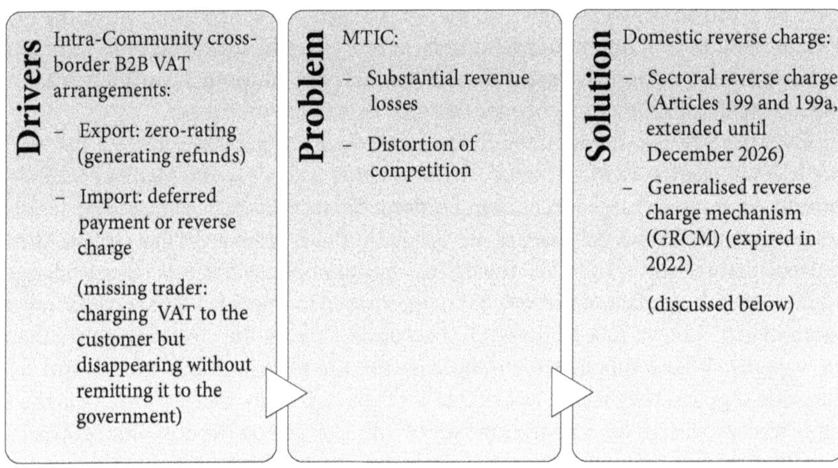


The domestic reverse charge mechanism was initially introduced in the EU in 2006 as a temporary measure, pending the development of more robust longer term solutions. However, its application, both in terms of scope and duration, has since been expanded over the following decade.[24] The Member States may opt to apply the reverse charge mechanism to a predetermined list of supplies of goods and services.[25] Additionally, they may submit a special request to apply the reverse charge mechanism to specific sectors beyond the list, which must be authorised by the European Council.[26]

tax authority. The fraud is well documented in the case law. For example, in the Australian context, see *ACN 154 520 199 Pty Ltd (in liquidation) and Commissioner of Taxation* [2019] AATA 5981 (Australia).

[24] For a summary of the legislative history of the reverse charge mechanism, see R de la Feria, 'Editorial: The New VAT General Reverse-Charge Mechanism' (2019) 28 *EC Tax Review* 172, 174.

[25] VAT Directive (n 9) Arts 199 and 199a. Article 199 allows the Member States to apply a reverse charge mechanism for certain transactions such as construction works, immovable property supplies, used material or waste supplies. Article 199a allows the Member States to apply the reverse charge mechanism on a temporary basis for listed supplies such as the transfer of allowances to emit greenhouse gases, mobile phones, integrated circuits, game consoles or cereal supplies.

[26] The specific derogations can be granted on the basis of Art 395 of the VAT Directive. In addition, Art 199b of the VAT Directive offers a faster procedure, known as the Quick Reaction Mechanism (QRM), for the introduction of the reverse charge mechanism for sudden and massive fraud. See, VAT Directive (n 9), Arts 395 and 199b.

Despite the availability of the sectoral reverse charge mechanism, certain Member States requested authorisation to implement a temporary generalised reverse charge mechanism (GRCM) that would apply more broadly and not be restricted to any specific sector.[27] New rules were subsequently adopted in 2018 to allow individual Member States to apply, on a voluntary basis, a GRCM to all domestic supplies above a threshold of EUR 17,500 per transaction.[28] The optional GRCM was introduced as an exceptional measure, which was limited in time (until 30 June 2022) and could only be applied under very strict technical conditions. Under a GRCM, the payment of the VAT that would be due on the supplies made between businesses is suspended all the way until the supplies are made to a non-taxable person. This approach deviates from a core feature of the VAT – the invoice-credit mechanism – and, in effect, temporarily transformed the VAT into a retail sales tax (RST). Following the expiry of the temporary GRCM in 2022, the application period for the optional sectoral reverse charge mechanism was further extended until 31 December 2026.[29]

The European Commission reported that 'the Member States generally considered the reverse charge mechanism an effective and efficient tool in fighting VAT fraud, and the fraud decreased significantly or disappeared in the defined sectors'.[30] However, the use of the reverse charge mechanism gave rise to several concerns. First, the limited and sector-specific application of the reverse charge mechanism increases the complexity of the VAT rules and is likely to raise the compliance costs for all businesses subject to the measure, including those that are fully compliant.[31] These increased costs may result from businesses having to simultaneously navigate two different regimes, applying the reverse charge mechanism to certain supplies while continuing to follow standard VAT rules for others. However, the additional compliance burden for legitimate businesses may be considered justifiable if the introduction of the reverse charge mechanism succeeds in creating a level playing field for these businesses by effectively reducing fraud.[32]

[27] For example, Austria and Czech Republic.

[28] Council Directive (EU) 2018/2057 of 20 December 2018 amending Directive 2006/112/EC on the common system of value added tax as regards the temporary application of a generalised reverse charge mechanism in relation to supplies of goods and services above a certain threshold [2018] OJ L329/3 (no longer in force).

[29] Council Directive (EU) 2022/890 of 3 June 2022 amending Directive 2006/112/EC as regards the extension of the application period of the optional reverse charge mechanism in relation to supplies of certain goods and services susceptible to fraud and of the Quick Reaction Mechanism against VAT fraud [2022] OJ L155/1.

[30] European Commission, 'Report from the Commission to the Council and the European Parliament on the effects of Articles 199a and 199b of the Council Directive 2006/112/EC on combatting fraud' (8 March 2018) COM (2018) 118 final.

[31] A study on the impact of the optional sectoral reverse charge mechanism concluded that the mechanism increases compliance costs by 43% for businesses. See EY, 'Assessment of the Application and Impact of the Optional 'Reverse Charge Mechanism' within the EU VAT System' (Final Report, November 2014) 62.

[32] European Commission, COM (2018) 118 final (n 30).

Second, the optional sectoral reverse charge may simply shift the fraudulent activities to suppliers of goods and services that are not subject to a reverse charge rule or to other Member States that did not introduce the mechanism.[33] The potential migration of MTIC fraud has led to increased pressure to broaden the scope of the sectoral reverse charge. As a result, the continuing expansion of the sectoral reverse charge may merge in time into a de facto generalised reverse charge or an RST.[34]

Third, in the case of the GRCM that applies only to supplies of a value exceeding a certain threshold, the reverse charge rules may be easily circumvented by businesses artificially splitting the taxable value of transactions.[35] Finally, the use of a reverse charge mechanism may lead to a concentration of fraud at the retail level, which becomes the single point of VAT collection.[36] As noted in chapter one,[37] this risk is one of the key reasons the RST has long been regarded as inferior to a VAT. However, it may not be straightforward to identify where the weakest administrative controls lie within the supply chain. While the MTIC fraud exploits a vulnerable point where responsibility shifts between domestic and foreign tax administrations, the retail stage, where there is no paper trail, also presents a significant control weakness.[38] Nevertheless, it has been suggested that the risk of this new type of fraud could be reduced if the use of the reverse charge mechanism is limited to commodities that are not typically sold to unregistered persons, such as emission allowance and semi-finished products.[39]

In justifying the necessity to extend the application of the optional sectoral reverse charge as a set of 'temporary and targeted ad-hoc measures', the European Commission concluded that these risks and costs are outweighed by the potential benefits in the absence of alternative and more effective longer term solutions.[40] However, it is important to recognise that the use of the domestic reverse charge mechanism essentially places governments in a reactive position, playing catch-up with fraudsters.[41] The distortions the reverse charge mechanism introduces into the functioning of an invoice-credit VAT system highlight the need for a more fundamental and forward-looking policy response.[42]

[33] ibid.

[34] European Union Committee (House of Lords) (n 16) at 24.

[35] European Commission, SWD (2016) 457 final (n 10) at 33.

[36] Commission of the European Communities, 'Commission staff working paper on measures to change the VAT system to fight fraud' COM (2008) 109 final.

[37] See the text at nn 23–25 in chapter one.

[38] The European Commission took the view that the potential loss of revenue could be greater in absolute terms at the retail stage, due to the larger number of smaller economic operators, which complicates audit and enforcement efforts. See, European Commission COM (2008) 109 final (n 36).

[39] B Mattauschová, 'Implementation of the Reverse Charge Regime' in 'Closing VAT GAP through Reverse Charge Mechanism: Collection of the tax conference of the Ministry of Finance with the support of International Fiscal Association, CR' (December 2015, Prague) 47.

[40] European Commission, COM (2018) 118 final (n 30).

[41] Andrew and Baer (n 13) at 22.

[42] ibid.

In addition to the use of the reverse charge mechanism, MTIC fraud is also addressed by tax authorities by applying what is known as the 'knowledge principle' developed by the judiciary through case law. This principle allows the tax authority to deny a taxable person's right to deduction where they 'knew or should have known' that their acquisitions were connected with fraudulent evasion of VAT.[43] The case law from the United Kingdom (UK) demonstrates that HM Revenue & Customs (HMRC) has successfully relied on this principle to combat MTIC fraud.[44] Outside the EU and the UK, this approach is also adopted in Singapore, where a statutory anti-fraud rule based on the knowledge principle was introduced in 2021 to address missing trader fraud and other fraudulent activities.[45]

To further strengthen anti-fraud measures, the EU has recently enacted legislation mandating the adoption of a harmonised, real-time digital reporting system based on e-invoicing for intra-EU cross-border B2B transactions by 2030.[46] The system, known as the Digital Reporting Requirements (DRRs), will require businesses to transmit transaction data in real time to a centralised EU database, enabling automated cross-checking of cross-border VAT compliance among the Member States. While the DRRs are not expected to eradicate fraud entirely, they will provide tax administrations with immediate access to transactional data. This facilitates earlier detection and intervention compared to the traditional approach, which relies on monthly and quarterly VAT returns. The effectiveness of real-time reporting has already been demonstrated in several Member States in the past decade, with notable reductions in non-compliance and increases in VAT revenue.[47] The EU anticipated that the transition to mandatory e-invoicing could reduce VAT fraud by an estimated EUR 11 billion annually, while at the same time lowering compliance costs for businesses by EUR 4.1 billion per year.[48] Globally, the adoption of real-time reporting based on e-invoicing is gaining momentum as governments seek to modernise tax administration and strengthen enforcement capacities.[49]

[43] The Court of Justice of the EU (CJEU) laid down the principle (also known as the 'Kittel principle') in Joined Cases C-439/04 and C-440/04 *Axel Kittel v Belgian State and Belgian State v Recolta Recycling SPRL* ECLI:EU:C:2006:446, [2006] ECR I-06161.

[44] See, eg, Joined Cases *Mobilx Ltd (in Administration) v The Commissioners for Her Majesty's Revenue & Customs, The Commissioners for Her Majesty's Revenue & Customs v Blue Sphere Global Ltd, Calltel Telecom Ltd & Anr v The Commissioners for Her Majesty's Revenue & Customs* [2010] EWCA Civ 517; and *POWA (Jersey) Limited v The Commissioners for Her Majesty's Revenue and Customs* [2012] UKUT 50 (TCC).

[45] (Singapore) Goods and Services Tax Act 1993, s 20(2A). The missing trader fraud is explicitly listed (Ninth Schedule, Illustration 1) as an arrangement that was intended to be caught by section 20(2A).

[46] Council Directive (EU) 2025/516 of 11 March 2025 amending Directive 2006/112/EC as regards VAT rules for the digital age [2025] OJ L2025/516.

[47] G Luchetta and others, 'VAT in the Digital Age: Final Report. Volume 1, Digital Reporting Requirements' (European Commission, March 2022) 36–39. For evidence from Italy, see M Heinemann and W Stiller, 'Digitalization and Cross-Border Tax Fraud: Evidence from E-Invoicing in Italy' (2025) 32 *International Tax and Public Finance* 195.

[48] European Commission, 'Questions and Answers: VAT in the Digital Age' (Brussels, 8 December 2022) QANDA/22/7518, available at https://ec.europa.eu/commission/presscorner/detail/es/qanda_22_7518.

[49] See nn 14 and 15 in chapter three.

### *ii. Canada's GST-QST System ('Dual VAT' System)*

An alternative to the EU system of zero-rating exports and subjecting imports to a reverse charge rule is to treat B2B imports as out-of-scope supplies, thereby effectively disregarding these supplies in the importing jurisdiction, provided that they are zero-rated in the exporting jurisdiction. The out-of-scope treatment should be subject to the exceptions for imports for which input tax credits are unavailable (for example, imports used in making exempt supplies). As discussed in chapter five, Australia has adopted this approach in the international context in relation to B2B imported services.[50] Treating B2B imports as out-of-scope supplies has the advantage of simplifying compliance in relation to transactions that are revenue neutral. However, it is important to recognise that this advantage is achieved by effectively converting the VAT into an RST.

This approach is used in Canada in what is called a 'dual VAT' system.[51] The federal government and the province of Québec impose separate VATs, the former known as the GST and the latter the Québec Sales Tax (QST). The rates and bases of the GST and QST are set independently by the federal and provincial governments, but the bases are largely harmonised. Both the GST and QST are administered and collected by the province, which hands over the federal share of the revenue to the federal government. In terms of inter-jurisdictional sales, exports from Québec are zero-rated for QST purposes and B2B imports from another province to Québec are treated as out-of-scope supplies, not subject to import VAT unless the importer is a registered business and no input tax credit could be claimed if the tax were paid on imports. It is believed that the cross-border evasion problem seen in the EU is mitigated in Québec, as the federal GST audit can serve as a cross-checking mechanism for inter-jurisdictional sales.[52] Notionally, final consumers are liable for the QST on inter-provincial imports they receive. However, because final consumers are not registered, there is no effective way of enforcing this liability.

## B. Clearing House

The simplest response to the elimination or absence of border controls within economically integrated areas or federations entailing the lowest administration and compliance costs would be the adoption of an origin-based VAT, with the tax imposed on the seller at the time of sale without regard to the location of the customer. A traditional destination basis VAT, in contrast, would require suppliers to register in every subordinate jurisdiction in the federation or common market,

[50] See the text at n 29 in chapter five.

[51] For a description of the system, see RM Bird and PP Gendron, 'Dual VATs and Cross-Border Trade: Two Problems, One Solution?' (1998) 5 *International Tax and Public Finance* 429.

[52] ibid at 434.

calculate the VAT separately for customers in each jurisdiction and remit the tax to the jurisdiction in which the customers are based.

While an origin basis VAT offers the advantage of simplicity and low compliance costs, it violates the fundamental principle of VAT as a tax on final consumption. A solution to the conundrum is the establishment of a clearing house system that would allow suppliers to declare and pay tax on an origin basis, with the clearing house transferring the VAT collected on inter-jurisdictional supplies to the tax authority of the customer's country. This system allows the local collection of tax with local auditing and enforcement for all sales, whether local or inter-jurisdictional.

A clearing house system for B2B sales was proposed by the European Commission for the European Community, the forerunner to the EU, in 1985 as an arrangement for VAT collection on intra-Community sales following the proposed elimination of internal customs borders.[53] However, the proposal based on an origin-based collection system supplemented by a clearing house was opposed by the Member States,[54] and the EU instead introduced the deferred payment system for goods when customs border controls were removed eight years later.[55] Deferred payment works on a self-assessment basis and can only be used to tax B2B supplies, necessitating alternative arrangements for inter-jurisdictional business-to-consumer (B2C) sales.

The growth of internet usage and e-commerce over the following decades prompted the EU to consider a clearing house mechanism as a simplification measure, ultimately leading to the introduction of the One Stop Shop (OSS) non-Union scheme in 2003. As noted in chapter five,[56] the system facilitated the distribution of VAT revenue collected from non-EU suppliers making supplies of electronic services to private customers within the EU to the respective Member States of consumption. In 2015, the system was extended to cover intra-Community B2C digital supplies, including telecommunications, broadcasting and electronically supplied services, under what became known as the mini One Stop Shop (MOSS).[57] This scheme allows EU-established businesses to opt to declare and remit, in a single Member State, the VAT due on all their EU-wide B2C digital supplies. Due to the perceived success of the system,[58] the scheme was further

[53] Commission of the European Communities, 'Completing the Internal Market' COM (85) 310 final.

[54] European Union Committee (House of Lords) (n 16) at 27.

[55] See the text preceding n 9 above.

[56] See the text at n 55 in chapter five.

[57] Council Regulation (EU) No 967/2012 of 9 October 2012 amending Implementing Regulation (EU) No 282/2011 as regards the special schemes for non-established taxable persons supplying telecommunications services, broadcasting services or electronic services to non-taxable persons [2012] OJ L290/1.

[58] European Commission, 'Commission Proposes New Tax Rules to Support E-commerce and Online Businesses in the EU' (Press release, 1 December 2016); Directorate-General for Taxation and Customs Union, European Commission, 'EU VAT Rules for E-commerce Two Years On: Updated Revenue Figures Point Again to a Successful Implementation' (*News*, 30 June 2023).

extended in 2021 to become an enlarged OSS, covering all B2C services and intra-Community distance sales of goods.[59]

The clearing house system is not a panacea to the challenges of reallocating VAT revenue in a federation or common market in which each jurisdiction levies its own VAT. A key benefit of an origin basis tax is the simplicity achieved by applying origin-basis rules to both local and inter-jurisdictional sales. Difficulty arises, however, where different rates are imposed by different states, in which case the VAT revenue transmitted to the importing state would be determined by applying the rate imposed by the exporting state. The EU's solution to this problem was to adopt a hybrid system that combines features of both origin- and destination-basis systems – origin-based collection and destination-based allocation of VAT revenue. Under the EU's OSS scheme, registered businesses charge VAT at the rate applicable in the country where the customer is located (the destination country) and remit the VAT to the country in which they are registered (the origin country). Accounts are filed with the clearing house which calculates the net VAT revenue to be transferred between each pair of countries.

The outcome is consistent with the destination principle – VAT is charged at the rate in the jurisdiction in which consumption takes place and the revenue accrues to that country – but comes at the cost of losing some of the benefits of a pure origin basis taxation. Compared to the alternative of direct registration in each country in which businesses operate under a traditional destination basis system, the OSS system reduces compliance costs as it removes the need for businesses to register in each of the Member States in which they have customers. At the same time, the OSS leads to lower administrative costs by significantly reducing the number of registrants in the destination country. However, businesses are still required to track every sale, identify the location of their customers and keep track of the current rate in that country applicable to each type of supply they make. These obligations may have to be accepted as the unavoidable costs of achieving the benefits of the destination-based allocation of VAT revenue. On the whole, the EU's OSS system has been considered a success in respect of both the revenue yields and the reduction of administrative and compliance costs.

The most severe difficulty with the clearing house approach might be that of collection incentives.[60] Two methods can be used to calculate the net amount of VAT revenue for clearing. The first method, used in the EU, relies on information

[59] Council Implementing Regulation (EU) 2019/2026 of 21 November 2019 amending Implementing Regulation (EU) No 282/2011 as regards supplies of goods and services facilitated by electronic interfaces and the special schemes for taxable persons supplying services to non-taxable persons, making distance sales of goods and certain domestic supplies of goods [2019] OJ L313/14. At the same time, the scope of the non-Union scheme was extended, whereas the Import One Stop Shop (IOSS) was newly introduced. These are part of the 2021 EU VAT e-commerce package discussed in the text at nn 56 and 75–76 in chapter five.

[60] M Keen, 'VIVAT, CVAT and All That: New Forms of Value-Added Tax for Federal Systems' (IMF Working Paper WP/00/83, April 2000).

gathered from invoices by the supplier's country. The second is to reallocate revenue on the basis of aggregate consumption statistics discussed below.[61] Both methods, however, may weaken incentives for effective collection and enforcement. Under the first method, there might be little incentive for the tax authority in the supplier's jurisdiction to detect unreported or underreported sales if any missing revenue recovered will flow to the customer's country.[62] Similarly, tax administrators may lack the motivation to strengthen collection efforts under the second method if the additional revenue generated is to be shared with other countries.[63] Therefore, the proper functioning of a clearing house system requires strong trusts among tax administrations in different jurisdictions. In the EU, the risk inherent in having to trust other Member States' revenue authorities was considered reasonably low because of the deeply integrated nature of the European economy.[64]

## C. CVAT

A model designed for a country with both central and local VATs has inter-jurisdictional sales zero-rated in the state VATs but instead subject to an additional tax called the CVAT, which operates at the central level and is administered by the central government.[65] The system is therefore comprised of a central VAT applying to all sales within the country, local VATs applying only to intra-state sales, and a CVAT imposing only on inter-state sales. This approach would require a uniform tax base for the central VAT and the local VATs, to some extent compromising the fiscal autonomy of the state governments.

The CVAT is applied to inter-state sales made to both registered and unregistered customers. To avoid excess CVAT credits and refunds, the CVAT could be made creditable against both central and local VATs.[66] However, this would result in substantial transfers of tax credits and liabilities between the central and local governments, in order to ensure that revenue collected on exports from one state can be used to finance input tax credits or refunds claimed in another state. From the taxpayers' perspective, the net outcome of the CVAT approach would be that registered

[61] Refer to section III.D below. This method was proposed by the European Commission in 1996, but it was not adopted due to political resistance from the Member States. See, Commission of the European Communities, 'A Common System of VAT: A Program for the Single Market' COM (1996) 328 final.

[62] This concern was raised in the context of B2B supplies. See, European Union Committee (House of Lords) (n 16) at 27 and 99.

[63] L Ebrill and others, *The Modern VAT* (Washington, DC, International Monetary Fund, 2001) 190–91.

[64] European Union Committee (House of Lords) (n 16) at 27.

[65] The CVAT approach was originally proposed by Ricardo Varsano in 1995 and was modified by McLure in 2000 in CE McLure, 'Implementing Subnational Value Added Taxes on Internal Trade: The Compensating VAT (CVAT)' (2000) 7 *International Tax and Public Finance* 723.

[66] ibid, at 731.

businesses are entitled to credits for the CVAT they paid on inter-state acquisitions, while unregistered purchasers bear the costs of the CVAT on their final consumption. The CVAT, therefore, has no revenue implications for inter-state B2B sales. However, some CVAT revenue would be raised from inter-state imports by final consumers, which would need to be distributed to the states of consumption.

The CVAT approach is often compared with the dual VAT system discussed above.[67] The CVAT, if it works as intended, offers a clear advantage over the dual VAT system in terms of its ability to capture inter-state sales to unregistered customers. The CVAT with an overarching central administration could reduce the risk of revenue loss from inter-state B2B and B2C sales. Therefore, from the perspective of enforcing tax compliance, the main advocate of the CVAT considers it to be a better choice for countries with relatively weak administrative capacity.[68] The benefits, however, come at the cost of more complicated mechanisms and increased administrative and compliance burdens.[69] Registered sellers must distinguish between two types of domestic supplies (which is not required under a deferred payment system): intra-state sales (taxed at the central and local VAT rates) and inter-state sales (taxed at the central and CVAT rates, but zero-rated for local VAT purposes).[70]

The approach was adopted with modifications in India when its GST came into effect in 2017.[71] The Integrated GST (IGST), which functions in a similar way to the CVAT, is imposed on inter-state supplies of goods and services. The Central GST (CGST) applies to all taxable supplies within the country. In addition, the State GSTs (SGSTs), levied by the state governments, apply to intra-state sales. Both the IGST and CGST are administered by the central government, but the IGST revenue is shared between the central government and the destination states. The tax bases and rates are harmonised across the CGST and SGSTs, and the IGST rate equals the sum of the CGST and SGST rates. The IGST credits can be used to offset the CGST or SGST liabilities in a prescribed order.[72] Moreover, both the CGST and SGST credits can be used to offset the IGST liability, but cross-utilisation between the CGST and the SGST is not permitted.[73] These arrangements necessitate complex, and sometimes highly intricate, rules for the cross-utilisation of credits by businesses and for the transfer of funds between the central and state governments.

[67] Refer to section III.A.ii above. On the comparison between the CVAT and the dual VAT, see, eg, RM Bird and P-P Gendron, 'CVAT, VIVAT, and Dual VAT: Vertical "Sharing" and Interstate Trade' (2000) 7 *International Tax and Public Finance* 753.

[68] McLure (n 65) at 724.

[69] HH Zee, 'Inter-jurisdictional Sharing of the VAT' in R Krever (ed), *VAT in Africa* (South Africa, Pretoria University Law Press, 2008).

[70] McLure (n 65) at 730.

[71] For a more detailed description of the Indian arrangements, see S Mukherjee, 'India: The Challenges of Implementing VAT in a Federal State' in RF van Brederode (ed), *Virtues and Fallacies of VAT: An Evaluation after 50 Years* (The Netherlands, Kluwer Law International, 2021) 594–95.

[72] (India) The Central Goods and Services Tax Act 2017, s 49(5).

[73] ibid.

The Indian experience with the CVAT structure has revealed significant challenges during the initial years of implementation. The complex design of the GST system, involving multiple components, has made the tracking and reconciliation of input tax credits particularly difficult.[74] The settlement of IGST to states has faced persistent difficulties because of mismatches between returns submitted by suppliers and purchasers, leading to inaccuracies in the determination of the destination states. These issues have been further compounded by limited coordination between the central and state tax authorities. In addition, concerns have emerged regarding the cash flow burden on businesses, particularly those operating across state borders, which may accumulate excess credit in one tax component (such as the SGST) but still face liabilities in another (such as the CGST), due to the restrictions on cross-utilisation of input tax credits.[75] It remains to be seen whether the challenges can be effectively addressed over time through accumulated experience and refinements in policy design.

## D. Consumption Statistics

The VAT revenue can also be distributed among the subordinate jurisdictions on the basis of the proportion of national consumption that takes place in each jurisdiction as revealed by national accounts data. The Harmonised Sales Tax (HST) in Canada provides an example of this approach. The HST is applied in five provinces, operating in parallel with the federal GST. The bases of the HST and the federal GST are harmonised into a single, joint central-provincial GST/HST, which is administered solely by the federal government. The applicable HST rates vary across provinces, ranging between 13 and 15 per cent. The HST revenues are shared among the participating provinces by the federal government through a complex formula based on estimated taxable consumption in each HST province using the proportion of national consumption as a surrogate foundation for the formula.[76]

Allocation based on consumption statistics could be used either in countries with a central VAT only or in countries where there are centrally administered subnational VATs. Compared to the other approaches discussed above, the allocation of revenue on the basis of consumption statistics achieves administrative and compliance cost savings by avoiding the need to track individual transactions. However, this method may compromise accuracy if the VAT system involves the

[74] D Mehta and S Mukherjee, 'Emerging Issues in GST Law and Procedures: An Assessment' (NIPFP Working Paper Series No 347, 24 August 2021) 12, available at nipfp.org.in/media/medialibrary/2021/08/WP_347_2021.pdf.

[75] A Sinhal, 'The Atrocity of Section 49(5), Clause (e) & (f): When GST Credit Utilization Becomes a Trap' (Tax Management India, 9 May 2025), available at www.taxmanagementindia.com/visitor/detail_article.asp?ArticleID=14371.

[76] For details of the allocation of HST revenues, see RM Bird and P-P Gendron, 'Sales Taxes in Canada: The GST-HST-QST-RST "System"' (2010) 63 *Tax Law Review* 517, 554–59.

use of multiple rates and widespread exemptions, particularly when it is assumed that the relative proportions of taxable consumption at each rate, as well as exempt supplies, are consistent across jurisdictions. A further consideration for developing countries would be the challenges of sharing VAT revenue in this manner in the absence of accurate consumption statistics.

## IV. Fiscal Equalisation Formula

A common feature of federations is their reliance on horizontal fiscal equalisation (HFE) to transfer financial resources between sub-central jurisdictions, aiming to reduce disparities in their revenue-raising capacities and expenditure needs. While HFE elements are unrelated to how the VAT functions, they could be incorporated into formulas used to distribute the VAT revenue among subnational jurisdictions. For example, although the Australian GST is a national tax administered by the federal government, its revenue is fully distributed to the states on the basis of an HFE formula. While German VAT revenue is vertically allocated among three levels of government, the share allocated to the Länder (states) is further distributed among them through a fiscal equalisation mechanism.

The aim of Australia's HFE system is to give states broadly similar fiscal capacities to provide services and infrastructure at comparable standards. The formula distributes the GST revenue unequally to raise the capacity of the fiscally weaker states to match that of the stronger ones. In addition, a relativity floor was recently introduced to ensure that each state receives at least 75 per cent of its per capita share of GST revenue, based on its share of Australia's population. Since the poorer states are effectively subsidised by the rich ones, it is argued that the HFE system creates disincentives for states to develop new revenue sources or make efficient spending decisions, potentially hindering the country's economic growth.[77]

In Germany, approximately 45 per cent of the VAT revenue is allocated to the Länder, at which level the horizontal equalisation occurs. The Länder with a below average per capita fiscal capacity receive surcharges to their population-based VAT shares, whereas the Länder with an above average per capita fiscal capacity face deductions from per capita equally distributed VAT revenue.[78] The equalisation rate, based on the portion of difference from the average fiscal capacity per capita compensated, is capped at 63 per cent. The German system shares a similar incentive problem with the Australian system – both the

[77] 'Horizontal Fiscal Equalisation: Productivity Commission Inquiry Report' ((Australia) Productivity Commission, 15 May 2018).

[78] Y Bury, LP Feld and HT Burret, 'Skimming the Achieved? Quantifying the Fiscal Incentives of the German Fiscal Equalization Scheme and Its Reforms since 1970' (2024) 25 *Economics of Governance* 291.

Länder that face deductions and those that receive surcharges might lose incentives to increase their fiscal capacity due to the fiscal equalisation.[79] The central dilemma in designing a fiscal equalisation scheme in a federal country appears to be finding the optimal trade-off between reducing disparities in fiscal capacity, on the one hand, and mitigating disincentives to increase that capacity, on the other.[80]

## V. Possible Options

As discussed in the previous sections, VAT revenue could be shared among subnational jurisdictions on the basis of the place of origin, the place of consumption, or fiscal equalisation needs. Allocation based on origin is the least desirable option because it contradicts the fundamental logic of a consumption tax and leads to significant economic distortions. Therefore, the discussion on possible options for federal countries or large countries with multi-tiered governments focuses on the destination-based approaches and fiscal equalisation mechanisms.

### A. National VAT Only

As noted by Bird and Gendron, particularly in a developing economy context but equally true in developed countries as illustrated by Australia, the simplest and administratively most efficient system is a single national VAT, with the revenue distributed among subordinate jurisdictions.[81] Allocation on the basis of fiscal equalisation is a viable option in countries where local governments lack fiscal autonomy over the base and rates. Nevertheless, such systems must be carefully designed to achieve equalisation goals without creating excessive disincentives for subnational governments to strengthen their revenue bases from other sources. However, if destination-based allocation is considered desirable, both the consumption statistics approach and the clearing house mechanism can be applied in countries with a national VAT only. Where reliable consumption data are available, allocation based on consumption statistics could offer significantly greater simplicity compared to a clearing house system.

[79] Concerns about the adverse incentives were raised in relation to Germany's pre-2020 equalisation system. See, eg, J Werner, 'Fiscal Equalisation among the States in Germany' (Institute of Local Public Finance Working Paper 02-2008, January 2008).

[80] 'Some International Themes in Fiscal Equalisation: An Australian Perspective' (Australian Government Commonwealth Grants Commission, April 2022).

[81] Bird and Gendron (n 9) at 149.

## B. Subnational VATs Only

In the case of subnational VATs operating without a central VAT, the key design challenge is to find ways to allocate the revenue to the jurisdiction of consumption in the absence of border controls, while allowing local governments to retain autonomy over base- and rate-setting. Possible options include the zero-rating model and the clearing house mechanism. The EU experience has shown that the zero-rating model, which is highly susceptible to the missing trader fraud, is wholly unsustainable when applied to inter-jurisdictional B2B supplies. In addition, it does not provide an effective solution for taxing inter-jurisdictional B2C sales, with the collection of VAT largely relying on self-compliance by private customers.

In contrast, the origin-based collection, combined with a clearing house mechanism, could address the inefficiencies of the zero-rating model in relation to inter-jurisdictional B2C supplies. The clearing house system may also be extended to B2B supplies. As noted earlier,[82] an origin-based VAT creates a problem of cross-subsidies between subnational jurisdictions – the exporting jurisdiction collects the output tax from the exporter, while the importing jurisdiction bears the cost of financing the input tax credits provided to the importer. A clearing house could be relied on to resolve this mismatch by transferring the VAT revenue collected from the exporting jurisdiction to the importing jurisdiction.

Taxation at origin with a clearing mechanism has the advantage of preserving the invoice-credit chain in cross-border trade, thereby offering an effective solution to cross-border missing trader fraud, as the importer would no longer receive supplies VAT-free.[83] However, revenue losses may still arise due to errors or fraud in the jurisdiction of supply (for example, a supply not correctly classified as an inter-jurisdictional supply, or a supplier becoming insolvent or acting as a missing trader domestically) or in the jurisdiction of acquisition (for example, false or inflated input tax claims).[84] This implies that risks beyond the control or visibility of the jurisdiction of acquisition that is responsible for paying input tax credits may be transferred to it, along with the transfer of revenue.[85] Nevertheless, it has also been noted that the potential disincentives for tax authorities to enforce the VAT due through the clearing house (as discussed above)[86] may pose a lower risk than the more systemic threat of cross-border missing trader fraud.[87]

[82] See the text above preceding n 6.

[83] RF van Brederode and S Pfeiffer, 'Combating Carousel Fraud: The General Reverse Charge VAT' (2015) 26 *International VAT Monitor* 146, 148.

[84] These risks were noted in the EU context when a clearing system for B2B supplies was under consideration. See, European Commission COM (2008) 109 final (n 36).

[85] ibid.

[86] See the text above at n 62.

[87] European Union Committee (House of Lords) (n 16) at 27.

## C. National VAT Co-Exists with Subnational VATs

The co-existence of a national VAT and subnational VATs presents the most complex scenario for VAT design in a federal context. Both the clearing house and CVAT models may be employed in countries where a central VAT operates along-side subnational VATs. The incentive issues inherent in the clearing house approach could be mitigated if there is an overarching fiscal authority administering a separate national VAT, while also managing the clearing house for subnational VATs. The national VAT could serve as a parallel data source for cross-checking inter-jurisdictional transactions reported under the subnational VATs. However, this approach requires a broadly harmonised base, thereby limiting local fiscal autonomy. In such a configuration, the cleaning house mechanism becomes a variation of the CVAT model, especially given that the CVAT model involves the clearing of input tax credits among national and subnational governments. Although the CVAT architecture appears complex and does pose significant administrative and compliance challenges, a certain degree of complexity may be inherent, and thus unavoidable, when adapting an invoice-credit VAT to the political realities of a federal system. The success of such a regime hinges on the careful design of the cross-utilisation of credits across different tax components and the transfer of credits among governments to ensure that administrative and compliance costs remain manageable.

Table 6.1 below presents a comparative overview of the principal features and challenges associated with the three destination-based models.

**Table 6.1** Comparison of the Destination-Based Models in a Federal Context

| | **Local autonomy over base and rate setting** | **Requirement for a central VAT** | **Administrative and compliance difficulties** | **Effectiveness in achieving the destination principle (subnational level)** |
|---|---|---|---|---|
| **zero-rating** | full (requires harmonised base under the dual VAT model) | not required (but may operate alongside a central VAT, as under the dual VAT model) | • administration: requires significant resources for combatting cross-border missing trader fraud<br>• compliance: no added compliance burden for businesses | • ineffective for B2C sales<br>• vulnerable to fraud in B2B transactions (though possibly less so under the dual VAT model) |

*(continued)*

**Table 6.1** ***(Continued)***

| | **Local autonomy over base and rate setting** | **Requirement for a central VAT** | **Administrative and compliance difficulties** | **Effectiveness in achieving the destination principle (subnational level)** |
|---|---|---|---|---|
| **clearing house** | full | not required | • administration: risk of weakened enforcement across jurisdictions<br>• compliance: suppliers must identify customers' locations and applicable rates in the customers' jurisdictions | • effective for B2C supplies (as evidenced by EU experience)<br>• potentially applicable to B2B transactions (with additional complexity similar to that noted for the CVAT) |
| **CVAT** | requires harmonised base | required | • administration: complex revenue apportionment and clearing of credits between central and local governments; burdensome tracking where transaction volumes are high<br>• compliance: businesses must distinguish between intra- and inter-jurisdictional sales; complicated rules for cross-utilisation of input tax credits | • dependent on administrative and compliance capacities<br>• Indian experience shows challenges due to complexity and coordination deficits |

# VI. Conclusion

The allocation of VAT among subordinate jurisdictions in a federal system, a large country with multiple tiers of government or an economic union remains a complex area of VAT design, for which no single optimal model exists. The ultimate choice is often shaped by political considerations, including, in some cases, constitutional constraints, as well as the administrative capacity of relevant institutions and the degree of coordination among them. Notably, the available options may vary, depending on whether subordinate jurisdictions levy separate VAT systems, with or without a central VAT, or receive a portion of VAT revenue collected by a higher level jurisdiction. A comparative analysis of the existing models offers valuable insights into the relative strengths and weaknesses of various approaches, which can be evaluated in light of specific political and institutional contexts.

The review presented in this chapter suggests that the key challenge is to preserve the neutrality of the VAT in cross-border situations, without giving rise to unreasonably high administrative and compliance costs. It follows that the destination principle remains a valid design norm for applying VAT to cross-border transactions in both international and federal contexts. Nevertheless, additional complexity in the design and implementation of an invoice-credit VAT may be unavoidable for it to function effectively within the specific parameters of a given federal context. The complexity may be particularly pronounced where both the central and subnational governments levy their own VATs. Although none of the solutions discussed in this chapter is entirely satisfactory, workable destination-based mechanisms are available for a wide range of scenarios and are clearly preferable to origin-based systems. Countries that are currently using an origin-based approach to allocate the VAT among subnational governments are therefore encouraged to consider transitioning to a destination-based or fiscal equalisation system.

# 7

# The Sharing Economy

## I. Introduction

Recent years have seen the remarkable expansion of the sharing economy, propelled by digital platforms, which has transformed the way goods and services are supplied and consumed, allowing businesses and individuals to connect with consumers on a far larger scale than previously possible. There is no universal definition of the 'sharing economy' but the term broadly refers to an emerging model of business that has enabled labour and assets to be shared among individuals and businesses for either monetary or non-monetary[1] benefits or a combination of both.[2] Common examples of sharing economy activities include the provision of ride-sharing services through apps like Uber and short-stay accommodation through sites like Airbnb. The possibilities brought by the sharing economy are unlimited. While measurement of the true size of the sharing economy has proven challenging (due to the complexity of the activities involved, for example), available evidence suggests that it has expanded globally within a short period of time and has significant potential for further growth in the years to come.[3]

The exponential growth of the sharing economy has revolutionised the commercial reality and created a pressing need for governments to evaluate its implications for Value Added Tax (VAT) policy and administration. The underlying activities carried out in the sharing economy are generally not new. What is new is the use of technology to facilitate the occurrence of activities on a much more widespread and intermittent basis, allowing many thousands of new economic actors, most of whom operate below the VAT registration threshold, to generate income with relative ease and flexibility. This emerging economic phenomenon potentially creates significant risks to the VAT base and tax administration, while also disrupting traditional business models. At the same time, the new technology

[1] A challenge of taxing sharing economy activities performed for non-monetary consideration, as is the case with other supplies made for non-monetary consideration, is to determine the value of consideration. This issue is not discussed in this chapter.

[2] For the working definition provided by the Organisation for Economic Co-operation and Development (OECD), see, OECD, *The Impact of the Growth of the Sharing and Gig Economy on VAT/GST Policy and Administration* (Paris, OECD Publishing, 2021) 15. The term 'sharing economy' is sometimes used interchangeably, or in conjunction with, 'gig economy', with the latter placing greater emphasis on the sharing of labour (and/or assets) by freelancers. This chapter uses the term 'sharing economy' to cover both the concepts of sharing and gig economy.

[3] ibid, at 16.

that gives rise to the problems may hold the solution to these problems. The reliance of the new economic actors on digital platforms opens the door to comprehensive withholding regimes aimed at the platform operators. Over the past few years, a few jurisdictions have pioneered policy innovations to address the VAT challenges in the sharing economy. This chapter examines these challenges and explores the effective approaches to taxing sharing economy activities under the VAT, drawing on international practices.

## II. Sharing Economy Challenges

Although sharing economy activities are, in principle, captured by standard VAT rules, the new business model does not fit neatly within existing tax frameworks and administrative practices. In countries that have adopted registration thresholds, many sellers operating through digital platforms are likely to be small suppliers who have a turnover below the VAT threshold and, thus, do not charge VAT on their sales. Viewed collectively, however, these new sellers generate hundreds of millions of pounds sterling in sales through digital platforms that may not be fully subject to VAT.

The proliferation of sharing economy activities gives rise to two main policy concerns. The first is competitive distortions that might arise between the new economic actors operating below the threshold and their traditional counterparts who are required to charge VAT on similar supplies. Before the rise of the sharing economy, small suppliers below the threshold were not seen as posing a significant competitive threat to VAT-registered businesses.[4] But the situation has changed, with the sharing economy introducing new business models that allow large groups of small suppliers to access a substantial customer base and, collectively, compete with larger traditional businesses.[5] The second concern is potential long-term erosion of the VAT base resulting from a shift in activities from a relatively small number of large, more tax compliant businesses in traditional business sectors to a large number of small sellers, whose activities are generally not subject to VAT, in the sharing economy.[6] These two concerns tend to be more significant in countries with relatively high registration thresholds.

The initial question arising from these two concerns is whether VAT should apply to the sharing economy supplies that are not adequately captured by existing VAT laws. The main drivers of potential policy responses to the rise of the sharing economy are likely to vary across countries, making a jurisdiction-by-jurisdiction evaluation necessary. Concerns over competitive distortions and base erosion are, to a large extent, premised on the assumption that the

[4] The relative competitive advantages enjoyed by small businesses below the threshold, compared to businesses within the VAT system, are discussed in chapter three, in the text preceding n 20.

[5] European Commission, 'Proposal for a Council Directive amending Directive 2006/112/EC as regards VAT rules for the digital age' COM/2022/701 final.

[6] HM Treasury, 'VAT and the Sharing Economy: Call for Evidence' (December 2020) 6.

under-taxed sharing economy activities are substitutions of, and consequently in direct competition with, traditional business activities that fall within the scope of VAT in the same economic sectors. A relevant question to be considered is, therefore, whether the fundamental economic activities of these new businesses are economically equivalent to existing activities, or whether the sharing economy is growing its respective markets and sectors, without encroaching on the businesses in the traditional industries.[7] There does not seem to be a clear answer to this question, and the likely impact of the sharing economy growth on the traditional businesses may vary by sector and evolve over time. Yet, by and large, countries see a few dominant sharing economy sectors, in particular ride-sharing and short-term accommodation sectors, as creating a distortive impact on the traditional industries, such as taxi and hotel industries.[8] A further concern raised in some countries is that the growing popularity of short-term accommodation has led to an increasing number of properties being re-purposed from long-term into short-term accommodation, causing broader disruptions in housing markets (for example, reducing supply for long-term renting and putting upward pressure on rents).[9]

In countries with low or no registration thresholds, the growth of the sharing economy may create new pressures on tax administration, as a large number of small businesses, which most likely have limited compliance capacity and knowledge of their tax obligations, enter the VAT system.[10]

In sum, the key challenge in the sharing economy is determining whether, and how, the VAT can be collected efficiently to minimise the risks of competitive distortions and base erosion. In light of the challenges, the Organisation for Economic Co-operation and Development (OECD) published a report in 2021 outlining a range of options that countries could consider implementing.[11]

## III. Current Practices

Current country practices fall within three broad categories. The first is determination of tax liability on a case-by-case basis, using common law principal and agent tests to identify the supplier for VAT purposes.[12] In the context of the sharing economy, the key question to be determined is whether the supply of services is

[7] Some within the business and professional communities argue that the sharing economy expands the overall market, rather than taking market share away from the traditional economy. See, eg, HM Treasury, 'VAT and the Sharing Economy: Summary of Responses to the Call for Evidence' (July 2021) 3; and PwC, 'Sharing or Pairing? Growth of the Sharing Economy' (2015) 25.

[8] Evidence suggests that accommodation and transportation are the two largest sharing economy sectors globally in terms of market value. See OECD (n 2) at 17.

[9] This appeared to be a reason behind the adoption of the deemed supplier rules in Canada in 2021 (discussed below in the text at nn 50–53). See, 'Supporting Canadians and Fighting Covid-19: Fall Economic Statement 2020' (Government of Canada, 2020) 112.

[10] OECD (n 2) at 36.

[11] ibid.

[12] Civil law countries have similar tests but are governed by civil codes.

being made by the platform or by the individual or entity providing the underlying service. The second involves the removal of the registration threshold for suppliers of certain sharing economy services. The third establishes mechanisms for the digital platforms to collect or withhold the VAT on behalf of the underlying suppliers.

## A. Common Law Agent and Principal Rules

A fundamental question in the determination of the tax status of platforms and underlying suppliers is who is making the supply to the final customers. There are three possible legal relationships, each with different tax implications:[13]

1. Employment relationship:

   The platform employs the service providers under contracts of service. In this case, the platform makes the supplies directly to the customers.

2. Independent contractors – platform as principal:

   The platform engages the underlying suppliers as independent contractors under contracts for services. The platform acts as the principal, in which case the underlying providers supply their services to the platform, and the platform then makes an onward supply of those services to the customers.

3. Independent contractors – platform as agent:

   The platform acts as an agent for the self-employed contractors, who supply the services directly to the customers, while the platform merely facilitates the transactions.

The question of whether there exists an employment relationship between the two parties for tax purposes matters because VAT laws impose a tax on supplies made by taxable persons in the course of a business. Thus, an individual providing services as an employee is not liable for VAT. It is important to note that the application of labour laws related to the employee and independent contractor distinction is underpinned by different policy considerations than those of tax law. As such, the labour law definition of employment status does not determine, although it may be relevant to, the characterisation of employment relationship for tax purposes. It has been suggested, in the European Union (EU) context, that individual providers operating via digital platforms are typically regarded as independent contractors for VAT purposes.[14]

[13] The legal relationships are outlined by HM Revenue & Customs (HMRC) in the context of traditional economic sectors. See, HMRC, 'VTAXPER68600 – Particular trades: Hairdressing: Who is Making the Supply? – the Three Possibilities' (HMRC internal manual: VAT Taxable Person Manual, Updated 13 October 2022), available at www.gov.uk/hmrc-internal-manuals/vat-taxable-person/vtaxper68600.

[14] G Luchetta and others, 'VAT in the Digital Age: Final Report. Volume 2, The VAT Treatment of the Platform Economy' (European Commission, March 2022) 63.

If it is concluded that the underlying supplier is an independent contractor, the common law relationship between the principal and the agent prescribes the VAT consequences of the legal relationships among the three parties typically involved in sharing economy transactions – the platform, the underlying supplier and the final customer. This is the approach currently used in the United Kingdom (UK). The key question is whether the platform acts as a principal or an agent in relation to the underlying supply, which is examined on a case-by-case basis in light of specific facts and circumstances.

The categorisation of the platform as a principal or an agent gives rise to vastly different VAT implications. Where the platform acts as an agent, it will be treated as an intermediary that connects the underlying suppliers with their customers and facilitates their interaction. The platform will be considered as supplying intermediation (or facilitation) services to the underlying suppliers.[15] The fees or commissions charged by the platform will be subject to VAT. The underlying supplier, if registered for VAT, would be liable for remitting the tax on the underlying supply made to the final consumer. In contrast, where the platform acts as a principal, it will be considered as first acquiring the supply from the underlying suppliers and then providing the procured supplies to the final consumers. The platform will be responsible for accounting for the VAT on the supplies it makes to the final consumers. The facilitation services it provides are not treated as separate taxable supplies; instead, the platform's commission is embedded in the price it charged to the final consumers.

A large proportion of sellers operating on sharing economy platforms are likely to be individuals whose turnover falls below the VAT registration threshold. The agent and principal distinction is more significant in the circumstances where the underlying sellers are not registered for the VAT, given that the platform's liability varies substantially depending on which role it falls under. Figures 7.1 and 7.2 below illustrate the VAT consequences of the transactions among a VAT-registered platform, an unregistered underlying supplier and a final consumer, with the platform acting as an agent and a principal, respectively. Suppose that the platform charges the underlying supplier GBP 20 (VAT-exclusive) for the intermediation services, and the final consumer is charged GBP 100 (VAT-exclusive) for the underlying supply. The applicable VAT rate is 20 per cent. The arrows represent the directions of financial and tax flows. Figure 7.1 shows that, where the platform acts as an agent, the VAT collected by the tax authority is the VAT on the intermediary services (GBP 4). Figure 7.2 shows that, where the platform acts as a principal, the VAT collected by the tax authority is the VAT on the entire underlying supply provided to the final consumer (GBP 20). The difference in terms of the platform's VAT liability between the two roles is the VAT that applies to the amount passed on by the platform to the underlying seller. Therefore, sharing economy platforms would generally prefer to be treated as agents from a VAT perspective, since output tax is accounted for on a much reduced value.

[15] In an economic sense, the facilitation services will be provided to both the underlying supplier and the recipient of the supply, although, under many platform business models, the facilitation fee will be charged to the supplier or the recipient only. See, ibid, at 20.

**Figure 7.1** Platform Acting as an Agent (Assumes the Platform is VAT-Registered and the Underlying Supplier is Unregistered)

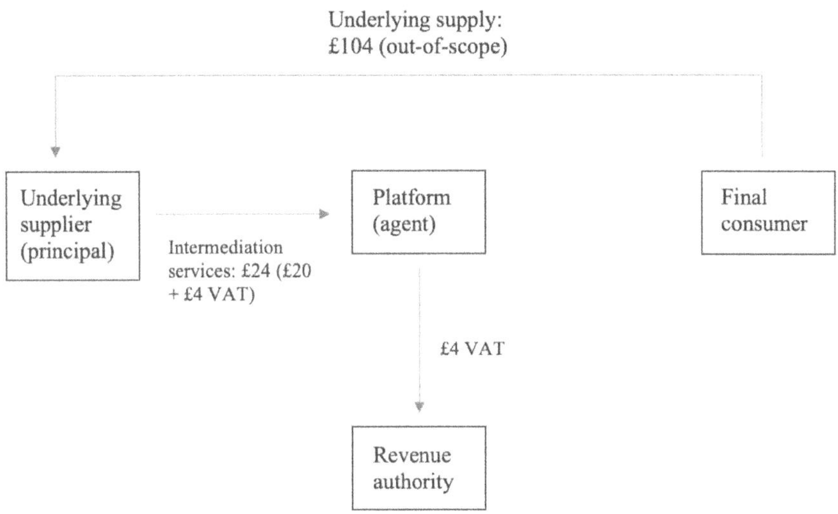


**Figure 7.2** Platform Acting as a Principal (Assumes the Platform is VAT-Registered and the Underlying Supplier is Unregistered)

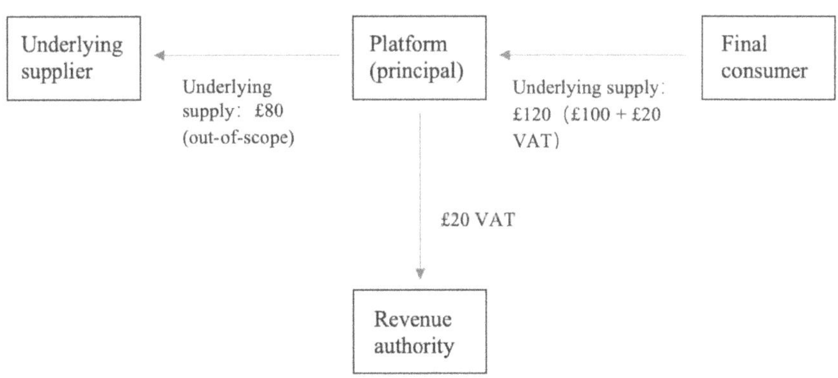


The UK courts generally, in their case law on agent and principal relationships, uphold the contractual relationship between the relevant parties, unless the 'contractual terms constitute a purely artificial arrangement which does not correspond with the economic and commercial reality of the transactions'.[16]

[16] *Commissioners for Her Majesty's Revenue and Customs (HMRC) v Secret Hotels2 Ltd* [2014] UKSC 16, at para 29, quoting Case C-653/11 *Her Majesty's Commissioners of Revenue and Customs v Paul Newey* ECLI:EU:C:2013:409, [2013] OJ C225/19; HM Treasury (n 6) 12.

A landmark judgment delivered by the Supreme Court of the United Kingdom (UKSC), *HM Revenue and Customs v Secret Hotels2 Ltd*,[17] emphasises the importance of the contractual terms in characterising the relationship between the parties for VAT purposes. In that case, the UKSC, relying on a strict interpretation of the written agreements between the parties, held that a company that marketed and arranged hotel accommodation through an online website was acting as an agent for the hoteliers, rather than a principal in the supply of hotel accommodation to customers. There is a substantial body of case law on agent and principal relationships, although not specifically in the context of the sharing economy, with varying outcomes as to whether a taxpayer is acting as a principal or an agent.[18]

The tax advantages associated with agency arrangements can pose revenue risks. Litigation in this area often involves artificial business splitting to avoid VAT registration, an issue discussed in chapter three.[19] In such cases, businesses seek to act as an agent for a number of traders, each with a turnover below the registration threshold, to reduce their overall tax liability. HM Revenue & Customs (HMRC) has found that these schemes are particularly common in hairdressing salons (which seek to act as agents for individual hair stylists) and driving schools (which seek to act as agents for self-employed driving instructors).[20]

Furthermore, reliance on agent and principal relationships in the determination of tax consequences runs the risk of tax administrators or adjudicators applying inappropriate concepts, definitions or rules that had been developed by courts or legislators for other areas of law. Uber, for example, has fought intricate legal battles in the UK over employment[21] and licensing regulations[22] in recent years. While these cases did not directly concern the VAT, they had knock-on effects on the VAT consequences for not only Uber, but also the entire private hire vehicle (PHV)[23] sector, affecting both traditional and sharing economy operators. In particular, Uber's lawsuits over licensing regulations resulted

[17] *HMRC v Secret Hotels2 Ltd*, ibid.

[18] See, eg, *Williams v Revenue and Customs Commissioners* [2019] UKFTT 79 (TC) (taxi firm was not acting as an agent for the drivers when contracting with local authorities); *Gibbs Travel (A Firm) v Customs & Excise* [2004] UKVAT V18472 (04 February 2004) (taxi firm was acting as an agent for the drivers, not as a principal).

[19] See the text at n 37 in chapter three.

[20] HMRC, 'VTAXPER36000 – Issues to Consider: Agency and Disbursements: Revenue Risks Associated with Agency' (HMRC internal manual: VAT Taxable Person Manual, Updated 13 October 2022), available at www.gov.uk/hmrc-internal-manuals/vat-taxable-person/vtaxper36000.

[21] *Uber BV and others v Aslam and others* [2021] UKSC 5.

[22] *Uber London Ltd v Transport for London* [2020] 9 WLUK 518 (High Court ruled that a PHV operator licenced in London must operate as a principal); *Uber Britannia Ltd v Sefton Metropolitan Borough Council* [2023] EWHC 1975 (KB) (High Court ruled that a PHV operator licenced in the rest of England (except Plymouth) and Wales must act as a principal), overturned by *DELTA Merseyside Ltd and another v Uber Britannia Ltd* [2024] EWCA Civ 802 (Court of Appeal ruled that PHV operators in England (except London and Plymouth) and Wales are not required to operate as principals).

[23] Taxi and PHV services are two distinct types of services based on how passengers are engaged with the services. Taxis can pick up passengers at ranks, be hailed on the street, and undertake pre-booked journeys. In contrast, PHVs can only be booked in advance through a licensed operator.

in court rulings that required PHV operators to enter into contracts as principals with passengers. The implication of these decisions was that VAT became chargeable on fares for PHV travel booked through certain operators who had previously acted as agents for the PHV drivers with turnovers below the registration threshold.[24] The series of cases led to a somewhat bizarre outcome that the VAT treatment of PHV operators is effectively determined by the licensing regulations, whose primary purpose is to protect public safety.

The UK experience shows that the agent and principal rules, operating along with a registration threshold, have brought significant uncertainties in determining VAT liability. The problem existed well before the arrival of the sharing economy, but it has undoubtedly become more acute in that context, with sharing economy players vigorously testing alternative legal characterisations in courts in an effort to minimise their tax liabilities.[25] The only sensible solution is to use legislative interventions to address the underlying tax issues, thereby rendering the agent and principal distinction irrelevant. The UK Government, however, does not appear particularly concerned about the potential competitive distortions arising from the growth of the sharing economy in the PHV sector, possibly because PHV operators have not been treated consistently for VAT purposes, with some operating as agents while others as principals, even within the traditional economy.[26]

## B. Sector-Specific Thresholds

One possible approach to address the VAT challenges created by the ever-expanding sharing economy is to modify the registration threshold. However, lowering or removing the threshold across the board may not be the most appropriate response. As discussed in chapter three,[27] the registration threshold is adopted for a reason, which is to balance the compliance and administrative cost savings of excluding small businesses from the VAT against the relatively limited revenue that would otherwise be collected from them. A general adjustment of the threshold would have significant spillover effects across all sectors of the economy and lead to unduly increased pressure on tax administration and

[24] This outcome is still relevant in London, following the decision in *Uber London Ltd v Transport for London* [2020] 9 WLUK 518.

[25] See, eg, *The Commissioners for His Majesty's Revenue and Customs v Bolt Services UK Ltd* [2025] UKUT 00100 (TCC). In this case, the Upper Tribunal upheld the First-tier Tribunal's decision that the taxpayer's on-demand ride-hailing services fell within the scope of the Tour Operators Margin Scheme (TOMS). TOMS is a simplification scheme mandated by EU law that allows tour operators to account for VAT on their margin (the sales price less the purchase price), without the right to deduct input tax. The implication of the case, therefore, is that the taxpayer is liable to account for VAT only on the facilitation fees it charges drivers.

[26] Government analysis suggests that approximately one-third of the PHV market currently operates under the agency model. See, HM Treasury, HMRC and Department for Transport, 'VAT Treatment of Private Hire Vehicles: Consultation' (April 2024) 16.

[27] See the text at n 9 in chapter three.

compliance burden for small businesses in more traditional sectors.[28] A more appropriate response may be the adoption of sector-specific policies targeting the sectors where the application of current VAT laws to sharing economy activities presents the greatest challenges, such as the accommodation and transportation sectors.

A few countries have taken measures to bring specific sharing economy activities into the scope of VAT. Australia and Canada, for example, adopted a special threshold rule for taxi businesses at the time of Goods and Services Tax (GST) adoption, requiring them to register for the GST regardless of their turnover.[29] This special rule operates as an exception to the otherwise universal rule that only businesses with a turnover exceeding the registration threshold are required to register for GST.[30] The policy rationale underlying the special rule is to avoid customers' confusion over pricing if some taxi drivers charged GST-inclusive prices but others charged GST-exclusive prices, depending on whether they are registered or not.[31] This might, in particular, be a concern for business passengers, as they would prefer acquiring the taxi services from registered drivers to be entitled to input tax credits.[32]

The special rule that applies to taxi services was later applied to ride-sharing services in both countries – by judicial interpretation of existing law in Australia and by legislative intervention in Canada – so as to ensure that the GST applies consistently to taxi and ride-sharing services. The Australian Taxation Office (ATO), the revenue authority in Australia, issued guidance in 2015, which requires ride-sourcing drivers to register and account for GST on the grounds that ride-sourcing services fall within the definition of 'taxi travel'[33] under the GST legislation. A legal challenge to the ATO's guidance brought by Uber had subsequently failed, following the Federal Court of Australia decision, which held that UberX services constitute supplies of 'taxi travel' within the meaning of the GST Act.[34] Canada, in 2017, removed the registration threshold for ride-sharing services arranged through online platforms by amending the definition of 'taxi business' in the GST/Harmonised Sales Tax (HST) legislation to include a self-employed commercial ride-sharing driver.[35] The meaning of 'taxi business' was narrowly tied to the regulation of fares by federal or provincial governments before

[28] 'The Role of Digital Platforms in the Taxation of the Gig and Sharing Economy: A Government Discussion Document' (New Zealand Government, March 2022) 29.

[29] (Australia) A New Tax System (Goods and Services Tax) Act 1999, s 144–5; (Canada) Excise Tax Act (R.S.C., 1985, c. E-15), s 240 (1.1).

[30] The standard registration thresholds in Australia and Canada are AUD 75,000 (approximately GBP 38,124) and CAD 30,000 (approximately GBP 17,004), respectively.

[31] (Australia) Explanatory Memorandum to A New Tax System (Goods and Services Tax) Bill 1998, at para 6.267.

[32] ibid, at para 6.268.

[33] (Australia) A New Tax System (Goods and Services Tax) Act 1999, s 195-1.

[34] *Uber B.V. v Commissioner of Taxation* [2017] FCA 110 (Australia).

[35] (Canada) Excise Tax Act (R.S.C., 1985, c. E-15), s 123(1), amended by the 2017 Canadian Federal Budget.

the 2017 amendment, making it impossible to be interpreted in a way that captures ride-sharing services without changing the legislation.

An inevitable complexity arising from the use of multiple thresholds is that some sharing economy providers engage in different activities that are subject to different threshold rules. A common example is a driver who provides both ride-sharing (for example, Uber) and food delivery (for example, Uber Eats) services. Australia and Canada have adopted different approaches in such a situation. In Australia, the specific threshold rule for ride-sharing services takes priority over the general GST registration threshold rule. In other words, drivers that provide ride-sharing services are required to register and account for GST on all their supplies, not limited to their ride-sharing activities. In Canada, in contrast, the sector-specific threshold and the general threshold rules are applied in parallel. In cases where an individual has taxable sales from both ride-sharing and other services, and the total turnover is below the general registration threshold, they are required to collect and remit GST/HST only on their ride-sharing services. However, they must return GST/HST on all their supplies if their total sales from ride-sharing and other services exceeds the general threshold.

The Australian approach may distort business choices and discourage drivers' participation in ride-sharing or food delivery activities. It also raises equity concerns, as drivers with a turnover below the standard registration threshold who provide only food delivery services are treated favourably compared to drivers of similar business size who offer both food delivery and ride-sharing services. In contrast, the Canadian approach does not give rise to these issues. However, the Canadian approach to thresholds may be considered inconsistent with international practice. Under the Canadian rules, a driver who provides both ride-sharing and other services is effectively treated as separate enterprises for different activities, whereas in other countries, a registered person is required to account for VAT on all taxable supplies, regardless of the type of service.

A further complexity arises in relation to input tax deduction for the GST paid by drivers on their business inputs such as fuel and vehicle maintenance. One distinct feature of the sharing economy is that many individual providers use their assets for both business and private purposes. However, the deduction of input GST is allowed only to the extent that the expenditure can be attributed to a taxable person's business activities that fall within the scope of the GST. Drivers who incur expenses partly for business and partly for private purposes would need to apply input tax apportionment rules to adjust for their private use of acquisitions, which are often complex and costly to comply with. This would exacerbate existing issues with tax compliance, placing ride-sharing drivers at a disadvantage compared to small businesses operating below the threshold in non-taxi sectors. The equity considerations make the removal of threshold for sharing economy providers more difficult to justify. However, this problem may be mitigated to some extent in Canada, as ride-sharing drivers have the option to use the quick method of accounting (discussed in chapter three)[36] that removes the need to accurately track their expenses.

## C. Deemed Supplier

It has been suggested that an approach based on sector-specific thresholds fails to recognise the advantages digital platforms have in managing VAT collection more efficiently at an aggregate level, given that they are already collecting and processing a large amount of data on an ongoing basis.[37] In recognition of the increasingly important role platforms could play in collecting the VAT on behalf of the underlying suppliers, a few jurisdictions have introduced a legal fiction in their VAT legislation that deems the digital platform to be the supplier of the goods or services provided by the underlying seller. As such, the determination of the application of registration threshold applies at the level of the platform, rather than the level of the individual seller. The platform would be obliged to account for VAT on all supplies made through it, regardless of each individual seller's turnover. This approach effectively removes the registration threshold for small businesses by the backdoor, by making small supplies from businesses that would not ordinarily be required to register for VAT part of the platform's turnover.

New Zealand adopted the deemed supplier approach, effective from 1 April 2024. The new rules require online platforms[38] – rather than the sellers on the platforms – to collect and return the GST on the sales of three categories of 'listed services' facilitated by the platforms, namely ride-sharing and ride-hailing, food and beverage delivery, and short-stay and visitor accommodation.[39] Certain large underlying sellers are allowed to opt out of the deemed supplier rules.[40]

The GST law treats a supply from an underlying seller to a customer as two separate deemed supplies that occur consecutively: a supply from the underlying seller to the platform, followed by the same supply from the platform to the customer.[41] The supply from a GST-registered seller to the platform is deemed to be a zero-rated supply.[42] This ensures that the registered seller could recover the input tax related to the underlying supply. The deemed supply made by a non-GST registered seller to the platform is not subject to GST. The platform is treated as

[36] See the text immediately preceding and following n 92 in chapter three.

[37] New Zealand Government (n 28) 29.

[38] The term used in the New Zealand legislation is 'marketplace'.

[39] (New Zealand) Taxation (Annual Rates for 2022-23, Multinational Tax, and Remedial Matters) Act 2023; Taxation (Annual Rates for 2023-24, Multinational Tax, and Remedial Matters) Act 2024.

[40] (New Zealand) Goods and Services Tax Act 1985, ss 60C(2BB) – (2BF), (3D) and 85D. These sellers include, for example, registered businesses that make taxable supplies of more than NZD 500,000 (approximately GBP 227,678) in a 12-month period.

[41] (New Zealand) Goods and Services Tax Act 1985, s 60(1C).

[42] ibid, s 11A(1)(jc).

making this same supply at the standard rate of 15 per cent to the buyer. As noted earlier,[43] the platform may charge a fee to the seller for the facilitation services it provides. The facilitation services are subject to the ordinary GST rules, regardless of the seller's registration status.

Figure 7.3 illustrates an example of how the new rules for digital platforms operate where the supplies they facilitate are provided by GST-registered sellers. Suppose that the GST-exclusive prices for the underlying supply and the facilitation services are NZD 100 and NZD 20, respectively, and the GST rate is 15 per cent.

**Figure 7.3** New Zealand: Underlying Supplier (Seller) is GST-Registered

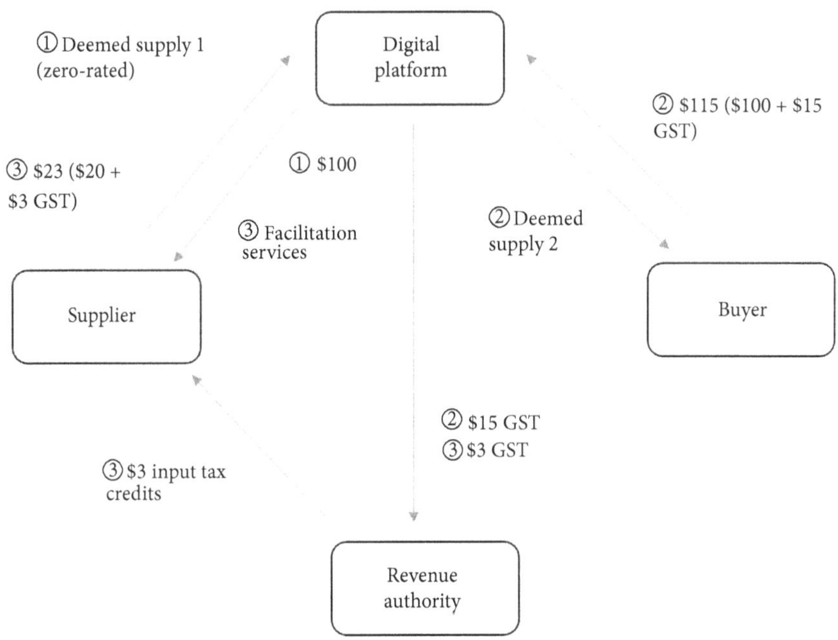


Table 7.1 below details the implications of the deemed supplier rules for the platform and the registered supplier. The platform's net cash balance is NZD 20, corresponding to the GST-exclusive fee it charges the supplier for the facilitation services. The supplier's net cash balance is NZD 80, correctly reflecting the value added by the supplier (after deducting the expenses from the sale prices).[44] The revenue authority collects NZD 15 GST, which represents the tax on the value of the underlying supply. The outcomes are correct for all the parties.

[43] See the text above accompanying and following n 15.

[44] For simplicity, other expenses incurred by the seller in making the supply through the platform are ignored in the example.

**Table 7.1** New Zealand: Implications of the Deemed Supplier Rules for Platforms and Registered Suppliers

| Party | Implications |
|---|---|
| **platform** | 1. acquires a deemed zero-rated supply from the supplier (Deemed supply 1) for \$100: – \$100<br>2. makes a deemed supply to the customer (Deemed supply 2) for \$115 (\$100 + \$15 GST): + \$115<br>3. provides facilitation services to the supplier for \$23 (\$20 + \$3 GST): + \$23<br>4. remits the GST of \$18 (\$15 on the deemed supply + \$3 on the facilitation services) to the revenue authority: – \$18 |
| **registered supplier** | 1. makes a deemed zero-rated supply (Deemed supply 1) to the platform for \$100: + \$100<br>2. acquires the facilitation services from the platform for \$23 (\$20 + \$3 GST): – \$23<br>3. claims the input tax credits of \$3 (in respect of the facilitation fee) from the revenue authority: + \$3 |

The legal fiction makes platforms fully liable for GST on the activities provided by the sellers through the platforms. An important design challenge is to develop a mechanism that enables the sellers to recover their GST costs associated with supplies provided through the platform. Registered sellers can recover the GST incurred on expense items in their GST returns. However, many individual sellers operating on sharing economy platforms are not registered for GST, thereby having no means of recovering the GST on their inputs. The complexity is compounded by the mixed business and private uses of assets by sharing economy sellers.

A presumptive input tax entitlement regime can be a useful mechanism to enable unregistered sellers to recover the GST costs without imposing a significant compliance burden. An important feature of the deemed supplier model in New Zealand is the application of a flat rate scheme. Under this approach, digital platforms are required to charge GST at the standard rate and remit only a proportion of that amount to the revenue authority, with the remainder being passed on to the seller in recognition of the fact that there will be unrecoverable GST included in their input costs.[45] The special regime is largely modelled on the presumptive input tax entitlement regime discussed in chapter three (for example, the flat rate scheme used in the UK).[46] The application of a flat rate scheme inevitably introduces additional complexity in the context of the sharing economy, as the scheme is essentially applied to suppliers who are not registered for GST. This necessitates an additional step that requires the platform to pass on to the underlying supplier

[45] New Zealand Government (n 28) 36.
[46] See section V.C in chapter three.

the amount of GST that represents the input tax credits the supplier would have been entitled to if they were GST-registered.

More specifically, digital platforms collect the GST at the standard rate of 15 per cent on the listed services, passing on 8.5 per cent to sellers who are not GST-registered and remitting the remaining 6.5 per cent to the Government.[47] The 8.5 per cent passed on to unregistered sellers is known as the 'flat-rate credit' and was calculated based on the average amount of input tax typically claimed by GST-registered suppliers of the listed services (including the GST incurred on facilitation services).[48] Digital platforms must identify sellers that are GST-registered from those who are not, as only unregistered sellers are eligible to receive the flat-rate credit.[49]

Figure 7.4 illustrates how the flat rate scheme operates in circumstances where the seller is not registered for GST, with all other factors remaining the same as in Figure 7.3.

**Figure 7.4** New Zealand: Flat-Rate Credit Where Underlying Supplier (Seller) is Unregistered

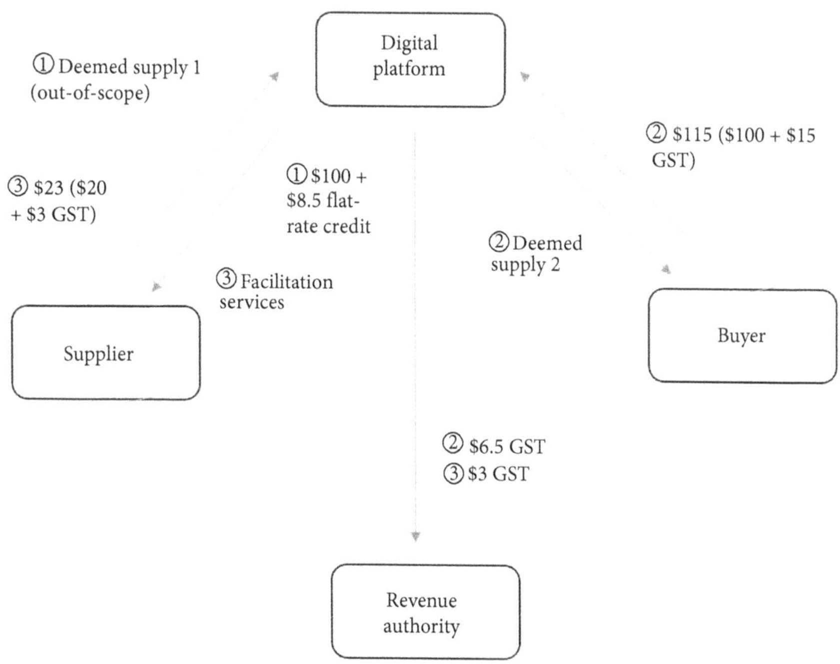


[47] (New Zealand) Goods and Services Tax Act 1985, s 20(3N).

[48] 'GST on accommodation and transportation services supplied through online marketplaces' (New Zealand Inland Revenue, Updated 1 April 2025) 26.

[49] (New Zealand) Goods and Services Tax Act 1985, s 60H(1) requires underlying suppliers to notify the marketplace of their GST registration status.

Table 7.2 below outlines the implications of the deemed supplier rules for the platform and the non-GST registered supplier. As in Table 7.1, the platform's net cash balance remains NZD 20, which represents the GST-exclusive facilitation fee charged to the supplier. The unregistered supplier's net cash balance is NZD 85.5, which consists of the price of the underlying services after deducting the facilitation fee, plus a tax credit of NZD 5.5 (NZD 8.5 flat-rate credit received, less NZD 3 GST paid on the facilitation services). This NZD 5.5 approximates the unrecoverable input tax incurred by the unregistered supplier on expenses unrelated to the use of the platform. The revenue authority collects NZD 9.5 in GST from the platform. However, it would already have collected NZD 5.5 in GST from the underlying supplier at the point the latter incurred the irrecoverable input tax on their purchases. In total, therefore, the revenue authority receives the full NZD 15 GST due on the underlying supply.

**Table 7.2** New Zealand: Implications of the Deemed Supplier Rules for Platforms and Unregistered Suppliers

| Party | Implications |
|---|---|
| **platform** | 1. acquires a deemed out-of-scope supply from the seller (Deemed supply 1) for \$100: – \$100<br>2. makes a deemed supply to the customer (Deemed supply 2) for \$115 (\$100 + \$15 GST): + \$115<br>3. passes on the flat-rate credit of \$8.5 (\$100 x 8.5%) to the supplier: – \$8.5<br>4. provides facilitation services to the supplier for \$23 (\$20 + \$3 GST): + \$23<br>5. remits the GST of \$9.5 (\$6.5 on the deemed supply + \$3 on the facilitation services) to the revenue authority: – \$9.5 |
| **unregistered supplier** | 1. makes a deemed zero-rated supply (Deemed supply 1) to the platform for \$100: + \$100<br>2. acquires the facilitation services from the platform for \$23 (\$20 + \$3 GST): – \$23<br>3. receives the flat-rate credit of \$8.5 (in respect of the underlying supply) from the platform: + \$8.5 |

Canada implemented the deemed supplier approach for platform-based short-term accommodation in 2021. Supplies of short-term accommodation, defined as rentals with a period of continuous occupancy of less than one month,[50] by GST/HST-registered property owners remain subject to the ordinary GST/HST rules. Under the newly introduced deemed supplier rules, accommodation platform operators are deemed to be the suppliers of, and are responsible for returning the

[50] (Canada) Excise Tax Act (R.S.C., 1985, c. E-15), s 123 (1).

GST/HST on, the short-term accommodation supplies they facilitate, where the property owners are not registered for the GST/HST.[51] The facilitation services provided by accommodation platforms to property owners are deemed to be out-of-scope supplies.[52] This deeming rule for facilitation services recognises the fact that unregistered property owners are unable to claim input tax credits in respect of the underlying supplies of short-term renting.[53]

The EU also legislated to introduce a deemed supplier regime, to be implemented by the Member States between July 2028 and January 2030, as part of its VAT in the Digital Age (ViDA) package.[54] The new rules target only short-term accommodation rental services and passenger transport services by road that are facilitated by platforms. A short-term accommodation rental service will be 'considered as having a similar function to the hotel sector if it is uninterrupted, provided to the same person and for a maximum of 30 nights'.[55] The platform will be deemed to be the supplier of the underlying supply where no VAT is charged by the underlying seller (for example, because the seller is not registered for VAT).[56] The deemed supply by the underlying seller to the platform will be treated as an exempt supply, with no entitlement to input tax deduction for the seller.[57] However, registered business suppliers will have the option to account for VAT on their own supplies made through the platform, which would enable them to recover the input VAT related to their platform-facilitated supplies.[58]

The Canadian and EU regimes are broadly similar in design. With the intended outcome of bringing all platform-facilitated supplies within the scope of VAT, the two regimes, in essence, represent codifications of the principal model for platform-facilitated supplies by unregistered suppliers and of the agent model for supplies made by registered suppliers.[59] The only notable difference between the two regimes is the treatment of facilitation services. Under the EU regime, facilitation services will be treated as ordinary taxable supplies, with the VAT on these services becoming an additional element of irrecoverable VAT for underlying sellers.

[51] ibid, s 211.13(3)(a).

[52] ibid, s 211.13(3)(b).

[53] Government of Canada (n 9) at 196.

[54] Council Directive (EU) 2025/516 of 11 March 2025 amending Directive 2006/112/EC as regards VAT rules for the digital age [2025] OJ L, Art 3(1).

[55] ibid Recital (30).

[56] ibid Recital (23).

[57] European Commission (n 5) at 17.

[58] Directive 2025/516 (n 54) Recital (28).

[59] The principal model and agent model refer to the VAT treatment based on the common law rules governing principals and agents, as discussed above in section III.A.

# IV. Lessons from Current Practices

While approaches to taxing sharing economy activities vary across countries, some general lessons could be drawn from the existing practices. The UK experience illustrates the uneasy coexistence between the application of agent and principal rules and the VAT registration threshold in the context of the sharing economy. This tension arises from the significant differences in VAT consequences depending on whether platforms act as principals or agents, particularly if the underlying suppliers are not required to register for VAT (which is a common feature of sharing economy business models).

Where legislative interventions have been adopted, countries have favoured a targeted strategy, focusing policy actions on the dominant sharing economy sectors, notably short-term accommodation and ride-sharing services, that are considered as creating the most immediate risks to VAT revenue and raising concerns about competitive distortions.[60] Both the legislative schemes discussed involve removing the registration threshold for sharing economy providers to bring their supplies into the scope of VAT, although the deemed supplier approach does so indirectly.

## A. Addressing Equity Concerns

The decision as to whether to adopt special regimes for the sharing economy requires consideration of a number of equity concerns. The legislative measures introduced in New Zealand, Canada and the EU were intended to level the playing field between sharing economy suppliers and their traditional economy competitors. However, these measures may themselves give rise to new equity concerns. Small businesses that operate through digital platforms may be placed at a competitive disadvantage compared to similarly sized businesses in the broader economy that remain below the registration threshold.[61] This disparity may be more pronounced in countries with a high registration threshold. It is important to distinguish the two dimensions of equity that are under discussion. The first concerns competition at the aggregate level – between sharing economy providers as a group and larger businesses, which operate above the threshold, in the corresponding traditional markets. The second relates to competition at the individual

[60] The EU estimated that the adoption of the deemed supplier model could generate up to EUR 6.6 billion per year in additional VAT revenue for the Member States over the first ten years of implementation. See, European Commission, 'Questions and Answers: VAT in the Digital Age' (8 December 2022) QANDA/22/7518 available at ec.europa.eu/commission/presscorner/detail/en/qanda_22_7518; New Zealand estimated that the new deemed supplier measure is expected to raise approximately NZD 47 million per annum (author's own calculation: roughly equivalent to 0.17% of the total GST receipts). See, 'Regulatory Impact Statement: Taxation of the Gig and Sharing Economy: GST: Coversheet' (New Zealand Inland Revenue, 25 May 2022).

[61] New Zealand Government (n 28) 28.

level – among individual businesses of similar sizes, whose turnovers are below the threshold, across different sectors of the economy.

Whether rules that deem a platform to be the supplier promote or undermine equity depends on the basis of comparison. This can be illustrated using the example of short-term accommodation services. In countries that have adopted deemed supplier rules for platform-facilitated short-term accommodation services, property owners who provide short-term accommodation services through platforms are required to charge VAT from the first dollar earned. In contrast, those who offer the same services through traditional channels are not required to charge VAT unless their turnover exceeds the registration threshold. When the focus is on the underlying service, it seems inequitable that short-term accommodation services provided via different channels (platform vs traditional) are treated differently for VAT purposes.

However, if the full economic picture is considered, the comparison is not between like-for-like providers. One person may be advertising their services with a note pinned on a local bulletin board, reaching the tiniest fraction of the market, while another is offering the same services through a giant multinational firm with a global reach of customers. It would be peculiar if the person selling through a global enterprise were considered to be operating the same way as the person who advertises on their own, thereby justifying the comparison at the aggregate level. In this light, the two aspects of equity that are prima facie contradictory – aggregate-level competition and individual-level fairness – could, at least in theory, be reconciled by taking into account the economics of scale and the extensive user base of sharing economy platforms. Nonetheless, it remains practically challenging to strike an appropriate balance between these two dimensions of equity in the design of the special regimes. This challenge tends to be greater in countries with higher registration thresholds, where concerns about both types of equity are often more pronounced.

## B. Sector-Specific Thresholds

The threshold for ride-sharing services was removed in both Australia and Canada to align the GST treatment of these services with that of traditional taxi services. The primary policy objective in these contexts was to achieve equity between suppliers of similar services. However, the removal of threshold may lead to an unreasonably high compliance burden on sharing economy providers who engage only occasionally in sharing economy activities to earn small and sporadic income, often using assets for both business and private purposes. This could be less of a concern in countries like Canada, where a presumptive input tax entitlement scheme is available to small businesses. Furthermore, differentiated thresholds may create new issues of uncertainty and unfairness, notably given the constantly evolving nature of sharing economy sectors and their convergence across sectors. The Australian approach, under which drivers engaged in both ride-sharing and food delivery face a tougher threshold rule than those providing food delivery alone, illustrates these challenges. For these reasons, sector-specific thresholds may not be an ideal solution in jurisdictions where standard threshold rules continue to apply to comparable services in traditional sectors.

## C. Deemed Supplier

### *i. Platform as Deemed Supplier*

The deemed supplier model can be seen as an extension of the electronic marketplace rules that apply VAT to supplies of remote services and low-value imported goods provided to domestic customers (discussed in chapter five),[62] by making digital platforms liable for the collection of VAT. The common feature of the two regimes is the recognition of the role digital platforms could play in facilitating the collection of VAT on behalf of underlying sellers. This approach helps reduce compliance costs for small underlying sellers by shifting the obligation to collect and remit the VAT onto the digital platforms.[63] In this regard, the deemed supplier model could go some way towards addressing the concern that sharing economy providers, whose activities are brought within the scope of VAT, are placed at a disadvantage.

However, small businesses, especially those who are approaching the threshold, have to continue to monitor their turnover to determine if they are required to register. In both Canada and the EU, the deemed supplier rules only apply to services provided by underlying suppliers who are not registered for VAT. This means small suppliers that grow beyond the threshold and are, consequently, required to register for VAT must leave the deemed supplier regime and begin accounting for VAT on their platform-facilitated supplies under the standard VAT rules. New Zealand's deemed supplier regime, by contrast, applies to services provided by both GST-registered and unregistered suppliers, while still maintaining a distinction between the two groups. In all three regimes, the distinction between VAT-registered and unregistered suppliers for the purpose of applying the deemed supplier rules also increases compliance costs for platforms, which must identify the VAT status of each underlying supplier.

In the EU, the perceived unfairness of the deemed supplier model emerged as the most controversial aspect of the ViDA proposal. In May 2024, the adoption of ViDA was blocked by Estonia, using its veto power and expressing concern that the proposed deemed supplier rules would impose an undue burden on small businesses and distort competition. Consequently, a significant amendment was made to the original proposal in order to secure political consensus. This amendment allows the Member States to exclude underlying suppliers benefiting from small

[62] See the text preceding n 64 in chapter five.
[63] New Zealand Government (n 28) at 28.

business regimes, including those below the threshold who have not voluntarily registered for VAT, from the application of the deemed supplier rules.[64] Following prolonged negotiations among the Member States, an agreement was reached in November 2024, two years after the European Commission proposed the ViDA package. The deemed supplier model was subsequently adopted in March 2025, with implementation scheduled between July 2028 and January 2030.

In the Member States where the option to exclude small businesses below the registration threshold were to be exercised, the scope of the deemed supplier regime would be significantly narrowed. This might defeat the purpose of the regime, while creating additional complexity. Whilst the policy choice of allowing the Member States to exclude small businesses from the regime was made within the EU's unique political context, the negotiation process in the EU illustrates that in practice, perceptions of which aspect of the equity should take priority are heavily shaped by country-specific factors, including the structure of the economy and the level of the VAT registration threshold. Interestingly, Spain, one of the only two EU Member States without a VAT threshold, has declared its intention to apply the deemed supplier model prior to the earliest implementation date in 2028.[65] As noted earlier,[66] in countries with no or very low thresholds, the challenge is how to collect the VAT efficiently from a large number of individual suppliers. In these countries, the adoption of the deemed supplier model would not create equity concerns at the individual level. Indeed, both New Zealand and Canada have relatively low GST thresholds (approximately GBP 27,369 and GBP 16,861, respectively). The adoption of the deemed supplier regime in these countries suggests that countries with a low threshold are less likely to be concerned about the perceived unfairness at the individual supplier level.

### *ii. Input Tax Entitlements for Underlying Suppliers*

One important distinction between the deemed supplier model applied in the sharing economy and the electronic marketplace rules in the context of cross-border business-to-consumer sales is that, under the latter, there is generally no question of input tax deduction for (foreign) underlying suppliers. However, the deemed supplier rules, which shift the tax liability from the underlying supplier to the platform, create a mismatch between output tax and input tax in relation to the underlying supply. While the platform is liable for the output tax on the underlying supply, the underlying supplier, who is not registered for VAT, bears the VAT on the inputs used in making the supply.

[64] Directive 2025/516 (n 54) Recital (29).

[65] Council of the European Union, 'VAT in the Digital Age Package: = Statements' (30 October 2024) 3. Spain's preference for early adoption of the regime appeared to have been driven by the concern that the rapid expansion of the short-term accommodation sector has led to a sharp decline in long-term rental supply in major cities such as Madrid and Barcelona.

[66] See the text at n 10 above.

Approaches to input tax entitlements for underlying suppliers vary across countries. New Zealand is the only country that allows full input tax deduction within the regime. Canada partly addresses the inability of property owners to claim input tax credits by treating their acquisition of facilitation services from the platform as an out-of-scope supply, thereby avoiding an element of input tax for property owners. However, Canada does not provide property owners with an entitlement to input tax deduction for expenses unrelated to the use of the platform (such as electricity, maintenance and cleaning expenses). The EU regime also does not provide a mechanism for input tax recovery for underlying suppliers. The unrecoverable input tax includes the VAT on facilitation services acquired by underlying suppliers, given that these services will be taxed under the ordinary VAT rules.

The entitlement to input tax deduction for taxable persons is a fundamental feature of an invoice-credit VAT system, which ensures that tax is levied only on final consumption and not on business inputs. The unavailability of input tax credits in the EU, and to a lesser extent in Canada, may result in embedded tax being included in the final price of the underlying supply. This effectively reverts the VAT to a turnover tax, albeit with limited application. This approach places sharing economy providers at a competitive disadvantage compared to taxable persons within the VAT system. Furthermore, if the sharing economy activities are acquired by business customers, the denial of input tax credits to underlying suppliers would lead to cascading in the VAT system. The EU could have, at least, learned from the Canadian experience by deeming facilitation services as out-of-scope, or zero-rated, supplies.

The approach to input tax entitlements, to some extent, determines whether participation in the regime is mandatory for underlying suppliers. Due to the unavailability of input tax recovery for underlying suppliers in Canada and the EU, suppliers are allowed to leave the deemed supplier regime by voluntarily registering for VAT to be able to claim input tax credits. Depending on how widely underlying suppliers take up this option, this approach risks undermining one of the main advantages of the deemed supplier model, that is, to shift the obligation to account for VAT, and the associated compliance burden, from small underlying suppliers to digital platforms. In practice, this opt-out option is likely to be most appealing to suppliers operating near the registration threshold and anticipating further growth. By contrast, for small suppliers with very low turnover, the compliance costs associated with VAT registration may outweigh the benefit of input tax recovery. These suppliers face a difficult choice between disproportionally high compliance costs and the denial of input tax recovery. Worse still, the unfavourable tax treatment may ultimately discourage their participation in the sharing economy.[67]

In contrast, New Zealand's deemed supplier rules demonstrate how a flat rate scheme can be employed to enable underlying suppliers to recover their input

[67] Some general tax-related reasons that might defer future sharing economy involvement are noted in N Rahim and others, 'Research on the Sharing Economy' (HMRC Report 453, 05 May 2017) 57.

taxes. This makes it feasible to apply a mandatory regime to underlying suppliers, in particular those not registered for GST, without placing them at a disadvantage. As discussed in chapter three,[68] however, the inherent nature of a presumptive input tax entitlement scheme is that it compromises accuracy in favour of simplicity. By way of comparison, the registration approach (removal of threshold) adopted in Australia and Canada for taxi and ride-sharing drivers has the advantage of offering the highest degree of accuracy, as it allows drivers to claim credits for the actual input tax incurred. However, in the specific context of the sharing economy, where suppliers are often less capable of accurately keeping track of expenses, the gains in terms of simplicity offered by a presumptive regime may justify a limited degree of inaccuracy in determining the deductible input tax.

It is noteworthy that the flat rate scheme was considered but discarded by the EU at an early stage on the grounds that the scheme creates additional complexity that would outweigh the benefits of allowing input tax recovery for underlying suppliers.[69] However, in navigating the trade-offs between simplicity and accuracy, it is important to recognise that the expansion of the sharing economy is still in its early days. The deemed supplier model, combined with the use of a flat rate scheme to provide input tax deduction, in New Zealand appears to achieve a better balance between simplicity and neutrality. As such, it is likely to be more future proof should the deemed supplier model be extended to additional sharing economy sectors in the coming years.

The flat rate scheme may be well-suited for implementation in the UK where such a scheme is already in place for small businesses that cross the registration threshold (as discussed in chapter three),[70] if the UK Government decided to apply VAT to sharing economy activities. The challenge for the UK might be that its high threshold makes it harder to justify the removal of the threshold for small underlying suppliers indirectly by virtue of the deemed supplier rules. In countries with a high threshold, one option is to build an additional concessional element into the presumptive input tax credit to recognise the sudden increase in tax burden for small suppliers below the threshold. For example, the presumptive input tax credit could include one per cent concessional credit, in addition to the presumptive input tax calculated on the basis of industry averages. The quick method of accounting in Canada, discussed in chapter three,[71] offers an example of this approach, although it is not specifically applied in the context of the sharing economy.

Sharing economy activities also have cross-border dimensions. Thus, the application of the deemed supplier rules in the cross-border context requires thorough consideration. New Zealand's rules may present a few challenges when applied to cross-border circumstances. First, as noted, unlike the Canadian and EU regimes,

[68] See the text following n 85 in chapter three.

[69] Luchetta and others (n 14) at 108. It was also noted that the option was not welcomed by platform operators and tax authorities.

[70] See the text preceding n 86 in chapter three.

[71] See the text following n 91 in chapter three.

New Zealand's deemed supplier rules also apply to GST-registered underlying suppliers. This policy choice appears to have been driven by the concern that allowing GST-registered sellers to opt out of the regime may give rise to compliance risks.[72] For example, unregistered sellers could purport to be registered for GST to the platform to stay out of the regime.[73] However, where the platform is a non-resident and the registered seller and the customer are residents, the application of the deemed supplier rules effectively splits a single domestic supply into two cross-border supplies and shifts the tax liability from a resident to a non-resident. Whether this approach mitigates or exacerbates compliance risks and the related burden on registered suppliers requires careful evaluation.

Second, under the flat rate scheme, where the platform is a non-resident and both the unregistered supplier and the final consumer are residents, the non-resident platform would be required to collect 15 per cent GST from the domestic customer and then pass on 8.5 per cent to the resident supplier, and remit the remaining 6.5 per cent to the government. In this scenario, the efficiency of GST collection relies almost entirely on a non-resident platform, technically outside the reach of domestic enforcement mechanisms, with the GST payment effectively circulating through the non-resident platform before returning to the country. The reliance on offshore platforms to accurately determine the registration status of underlying suppliers, correctly split the GST and transfer the flat rate credit to unregistered suppliers, may introduce considerable enforcement challenges, as domestic authorities have limited capacity to monitor compliance or take corrective action when obligations are not fulfilled. Nevertheless, given that New Zealand's regime is both innovative and relatively new, it may still be too early for a comprehensive evaluation of the model.

An alternative to New Zealand's flat rate scheme for unregistered suppliers, which could to some extent reduce the reliance on foreign platforms for VAT collection, is a mechanism that operates as a margin scheme. Instead of charging VAT at the full standard rate on the underlying supply, the platform would be required to charge VAT at a reduced rate, remitting the resulting VAT to the government. This reduced rate is calibrated to approximate the net VAT that would have been collected if the supplier were registered and entitled to input VAT deduction. Unlike New Zealand's model, this approach would remove the need for platforms to pass on part of VAT (specifically, the difference between the standard rate and the reduced rate applied to the value of the supply) to the underlying supplier.

The scheme functions as a margin scheme in substance, because applying a reduced rate to the full value of the underlying supply would, in theory, yield the same outcome as applying the standard rate to the underlying supplier's margin (that is, the final price charged to the consumer minus the supplier's expenses).

[72] New Zealand Government (n 28) 33.

[73] ibid.

Given that the government would have already collected the VAT on the underlying supplier's expenses (which is unrecoverable by the underlying supplier), the margin scheme would, in effect, ensure the total VAT remitted to the government aligns with the amount that would have been collected at the standard rate on the final price of the underlying supply.

Applying the margin scheme to the scenario illustrated above in Table 7.2, the GST-exclusive price of the underlying supply would need to be increased to NZD 108.5 to reflect the irrecoverable input tax borne by the underlying supplier, which is assumed to be embedded in the price and passed on to the consumer. This amount (NZD 108.5) consists of the original NZD 100 plus the irrecoverable input tax components totalling NZD 8.5, namely NZD 5.5 in GST on expenses unrelated to the use of the platform and NZD 3 on the facilitation services. The NZD 8.5 corresponds to the flat rate credit transferred to the underlying supplier by the platform under New Zealand's model. To ensure the government collects a total of NZD 15 in GST, the reduced VAT rate applied to the underlying supply should be set at six per cent. The total GST collected by the government comprises NZD 6.5 on the underlying supply (calculated as NZD 108.5 x 6%), NZD 3 on the facilitation services, and NZD 5.5 on the underlying supplier's other input purchases.

The margin scheme has the advantage of offering simplicity compared to New Zealand's flat rate scheme, while achieving the intended outcome when the customers are final consumers. However, an important limitation of the approach is that, where the supply is made to a business customer, tax cascading might occur. Specifically, the input tax embedded in the price (NZD 8.5 in the example discussed above) becomes subject to VAT again if the business customer uses the acquired sharing economy supply to make taxable supplies.

This scenario is comparable to that discussed in chapter three, where an unregistered trader sells directly to a registered business.[74] As such, the extent of cascading would be no greater than under the agent model, in which underlying suppliers are treated as making direct supplies to (business) customers. Nonetheless, it is still possible that business customers will simply refrain from acquiring the platform-facilitated supplies altogether because of the higher VAT-exclusive prices. To minimise the potential distortions, underlying suppliers could be allowed to opt out of the margin scheme if they prefer to voluntarily register for VAT and account for it under the ordinary rules. Designed in this way, a margin scheme with an opt-out option can be seen as a middle-ground approach between the New Zealand model and the approaches adopted in the EU and Canada. Notably, the margin scheme extends input tax deduction entitlements to unregistered suppliers, while the opt-out option allows them to exit the scheme if they find it disadvantageous. This approach may offer a more effective trade-off between simplicity and the accurate determination of tax liability than existing models.

[74] See the text preceding n 20 in chapter three.

Table 7.3 below offers a summary of the key design features of the special schemes designed for sharing economy activities discussed in this chapter.

**Table 7.3** Summary of the Existing Approaches to Taxing Sharing Economy Activities

| **Jurisdiction** | **Scheme** | **Sharing economy activities** | **Liability to account for VAT** | **Input tax deduction for underlying suppliers** | **Small business regime for underlying suppliers within the scheme** |
|---|---|---|---|---|---|
| **Australia** | removal of threshold | ride-sharing | underlying supplier | yes (actual) | none |
| **New Zealand** | deemed supplier | ride-sharing, food delivery, short-term accommodation | platform | yes (presumptive for unregistered suppliers) | flat rate scheme (mandatory for unregistered suppliers) |
| **Canada** | removal of threshold | ride-sharing | underlying supplier | yes (actual/ presumptive) | quick method accounting (optional) |
| **Canada** | deemed supplier | short-term accommodation | platform | limited (the tax on facilitation services is removed) | none |
| **The EU** | deemed supplier | short-term accommodation, passenger transport by road | platform | no | none |

## V. Conclusion

There is little doubt that the rapid expansion of the sharing economy has fundamentally transformed a number of sectors. This new economic reality has presented challenges for VAT systems around the world that were designed for a traditional economy dominated by brick-and-mortar business models. The VAT implications are likely to vary across jurisdictions, depending on the nature and scale of the sharing economy and the specific design of VAT registration thresholds. Nevertheless, two common concerns are the distortion of competition between sharing economy participants and traditional businesses, and the potential long-term erosion of the tax base. A few jurisdictions have adopted measures to address these concerns.

There are several key design criteria that need to be considered once it is decided that VAT should be applied to sharing economy activities. First, it may be sensible to target specific sectors where the sharing economy creates the most urgent pressures, whilst continuing to monitor the growth and evolution of the sharing economy. Second, ideally a balance should be sought between two aspects of equity – between sharing economy providers as a group and large traditional businesses, on the one hand, and between individual sharing economy providers and small businesses in the broader economy, on the other. Third, a related point is that any special regimes that bring sharing economy activities within the scope of VAT to level the playing field with traditional businesses should avoid placing sharing economy providers at a disadvantage. What this implies is that sharing economy providers should be entitled to input tax deductions for supplies made through platforms that are deemed to be the supplier, aligning with the treatment of VAT-registered businesses generally. Moreover, simplification measures for sharing economy providers to claim input taxes should be considered. Assessed against this set of criteria, New Zealand's deemed supplier model stands out as the strongest existing model. This chapter proposes a margin scheme as a preferable alternative to New Zealand's model.

The sharing economy is still in the early stages of growth, and it will become increasingly difficult to draw clear distinctions between sharing economy activities and those in the broader economy. Over time, the sharing economy could grow to such an extent that policymakers may be compelled to revisit the longstanding trade-offs and see them in a new light, particularly regarding the setting of VAT registration thresholds and the use of small business regimes. This chapter suggests that the use of simplification schemes may become more justifiable given this evolving economic landscape. Furthermore, as digital platforms take on a more prominent role in the collection of VAT on behalf of underlying suppliers across a wider range of sectors, countries with high VAT thresholds may eventually find it feasible to lower their thresholds.

# 8

# The Future of the VAT

The world has had over 70 years' experience with the Value Added Tax (VAT) since France introduced the first VAT in 1954. What lessons can be drawn from decades of policy design and implementation? To what extent do real-world VAT systems deviate from the theoretical design norms of an ideal VAT? Do these deviations call for a reassessment of the established design norms, and do they signal a need for reform? How might the accumulated experience help shape the future of the VAT?

These questions are answered in this chapter by drawing on the analysis of a range of VAT issues, which present common challenges in VAT design and implementation, in the previous chapters.

## I. Deviations from the Design Norms

As set out at the beginning of the book (in chapter one),[1] the established design norms of a good VAT in theory have three limbs: a single rate and a broad base; invoice-credit mechanism; and the destination principle in cross-border trade.

As discussed in chapter two, almost all VAT systems, apart from New Zealand's, deviate from the first norm to varying degrees, applying reduced rates, zero-rate and exemptions to a range of goods and services to pursue various redistribution, social and economic objectives. The VAT concessions should be properly treated as equivalents of direct spending programmes. Over the decades, VAT experts have argued persuasively that VAT concessions are an inefficient and unfair instrument for achieving redistributive goals, while at the same time, leading to significant legal and economic distortions and high administrative and compliance costs. In particular, the use of exemptions, which breaks the invoice-credit chain of the VAT, is perhaps the most serious deviation from the invoice-credit mechanism in a majority of VAT jurisdictions.

Ideally, the concessions should be replaced with fairer and better targeted direct spending programmes. However, experience with attempts to broaden the VAT base has shown that such reforms can be politically challenging. This is, therefore, an area of VAT in which the options for reform may appear conceptually

[1] See the text at n 6 in chapter one.

straightforward, but the practicalities of implementing effective solutions are considerably more complex. The key to successful reform may lie in the simultaneous adoption of targeted spending programmes to compensate the poor as part of base broadening reforms. If this still proves politically unattainable, efforts should be made to redesign concessions to enhance targeting efficiency and reduce collateral negative consequences.

Apart from being used as subsidies, exemptions are also applied broadly to financial supplies and insurance services in most countries, in particular traditional VAT jurisdictions (discussed in chapter four). The rationale for applying exemptions to these supplies was based on the practical difficulty of applying an invoice-credit VAT, on a transaction-by-transaction basis, to supplies for which no explicit price charged can be identified, such as intermediary loan services and insurance services. A few modern VAT jurisdictions, however, departed from the exemption approach, with modifications introduced to mitigate the economic distortions associated with exemptions of intermediary loan services. It is worth noting that New Zealand's approach of zero-rating business-to-business (B2B) financial services essentially replicates the operating mechanism of a retail sales tax (RST). It, thus, represents a deviation from the invoice-credit mechanism of VAT. An alternative approach proposed in this book is to apply a reduced rate (the separate rate approach)[2] to gross interest on loans, with the resulting tax liability serving as a proxy for the tax that would arise under the full taxation of intermediary services.

Moreover, New Zealand and Australia have successfully introduced models for taxing general insurance services that are entirely consistent with the invoice-credit mechanism of VAT. Over time, therefore, the rationale for incomplete taxation for financial and insurance supplies, based on the practical difficulties, is becoming increasingly difficult to justify. An exception to this conclusion, however, is the application of exemptions to life insurance services. The use of exemptions is likely to be less harmful in the case of life insurance because the recipients of the supplies are predominantly private customers, thereby avoiding the cascading effects arising from applying exemptions to intermediary stages of the supply chain.

Most countries use a registration threshold to relieve small businesses with turnovers below a specified level from the obligation to register for and remit VAT. The use of a threshold, therefore, as is the case with exemptions, creates exclusions from the VAT base and breaks the VAT chain when unregistered businesses trade with VAT-registered businesses. It therefore deviates from both the first and second norms – namely, a broad base and the invoice-credit mechanism. The adoption of thresholds is justified on the basis of administrative considerations – small businesses are typically associated with disproportionately high administrative and compliance costs, while contributing a small proportion of VAT revenue. Therefore, the neutral benchmark VAT, which applies uniformly to all

[2] See the text following n 44 in chapter four.

types of supplies made by all categories of suppliers, fails to adequately account for constraints on administrative and compliance capacities, that often impede the effective implementation of economically sound policy. The use of thresholds should be more appropriately viewed as an integral component of the design norms of a good VAT, rather than a deviation from the norm. This conclusion holds true not only in the domestic context, but also when the scope of VAT is extended to cover supplies made by non-resident suppliers, as is the case with cross-border business-to-consumer (B2C) supplies of digital services and low-value goods.

However, a registration threshold that creates a boundary between businesses above the threshold and those below it inevitably gives rise to distortions. In particular, small businesses excluded from the VAT by a threshold may enjoy a competitive advantage over their competitors within the VAT system. A phenomenon observed in an increasing number of countries in recent years is business bunching just below the threshold to avoid the sudden increase in VAT liability and compliance costs that would result from crossing the threshold. Thus far, no clear or desirable policy response to the bunching problem has emerged, especially given the lack of empirical evidence that reveals the extent of the exact causes of business bunching. Nevertheless, the presence of bunching unambiguously demonstrates the sensitivity of business behaviour to VAT design. A good starting point for addressing the problem may be to explore opportunities to achieve simplifications in the VAT system, which might include, by way of an example, removing some poorly targeted concessions.

Many countries responded to the disproportionately high compliance costs faced by small businesses within the VAT system with the adoption of simplification regimes. The purported simplification benefits of most small business regimes are questionable, and the use of these regimes quite often creates new problems. In particular, the presumptive input tax entitlement regime, discussed in chapter three,[3] aims to provide simplified calculation at the expense of accurate determination of tax liability. Under a presumptive regime, a lower flat rate, which incorporates a predetermined allowance for input tax credits, is applied to business turnover with no entitlements to input tax deduction for the trader. This serves as a proxy for the application of the standard rate under ordinary VAT rules. Although the presumptive regimes aim to replicate the outcomes of the standard invoice-credit VAT system, the presumptive nature of the regime inevitably introduces inaccuracies in individual cases, as evidenced by the United Kingdom (UK)'s experience with the flat rate scheme (FRS). The use of presumptive input tax entitlement regimes could be seen as a deviation from the invoice-credit mechanism.

The relative competitive advantage enjoyed by small businesses excluded by a registration threshold, which was not previously considered to be a serious concern, has been exacerbated by the rapid expansion of the sharing economy in recent years. The new business models in the sharing economy allow large groups

[3] Refer to section V.C of chapter three.

of small suppliers, typically with turnovers below the registration threshold, to operate via platforms and collectively compete with VAT-registered businesses. Developed countries that are concerned about the distortion of competition and revenue loss in certain sharing economy sectors, in particular ride-sharing and short-term accommodation, have introduced new targeted rules (the deemed supplier rules) that deem platforms facilitating the sharing economy activities to be the suppliers. As a result, the platforms are required to remit VAT on behalf of the underlying suppliers. These deeming rules represent a de facto removal of the threshold for individuals supplying services through platforms in the sharing economy. At the same time, the involvement of platforms in the collection of VAT reduces compliance burden for underlying suppliers and administrative costs for tax administrators. This will result in a rebalancing of revenue yields against administrative and compliance cost savings. The increasingly rapid spread of the sharing economy models across various economic sectors may eventually motivate countries to lower the general registration threshold, thereby broadening the VAT base in the long run.

Nevertheless, the use of the deemed supplier model in the sharing economy creates a new problem of mismatch between the output VAT paid by platforms (on behalf of underlying service providers) and the input VAT incurred by the unregistered service providers. The deemed supplier model adopted without measures to grant input tax credits to unregistered service providers, as seen in the European Union (EU) and Canada, deviates from the invoice-credit mechanism and effectively reverts the VAT into a turnover tax. In contrast, New Zealand uses a presumptive input tax entitlement regime to provide input tax credits to unregistered suppliers. The use of a presumptive regime is more justifiable in this context than as a general simplification regime (discussed in chapter three). This is because the presumptive scheme that applies to sharing economy activities is limited in scope, and any inaccuracies in input tax entitlements are therefore likely to be insignificant. Moreover, the simplification benefits the scheme delivers are likely to be greater when the scheme applies to unregistered suppliers (as opposed to small businesses already within the VAT system), since it allows unregistered suppliers to remain outside the formal VAT system.

In cross-border situations, the operation of the invoice-credit mechanism and the destination principle can give rise to frictions among countries. One prominent issue, discussed in chapter five,[4] concerns the right of businesses to obtain refunds from the country where they are not established for the business expenses incurred in that country. The absence of refund entitlements for non-resident businesses, or the restricted application of refund mechanisms, may be driven by administrative concerns, such as the risk of fraudulent claims, or by the lack of reciprocal refund treatment for a country's resident businesses in the non-resident's home jurisdiction. However, this approach can lead to an element of

[4] Refer to section III of chapter five.

business expense being taxed twice – once in the country where the expenses are incurred, and again in the country in which the foreign business inputs that bear irrecoverable input VAT are used to make taxable supplies. The failure to provide an effective refund mechanism in such circumstances constitutes a deviation from both the invoice-credit mechanism and the destination principle. Although many countries grant refunds to non-resident businesses on a unilateral basis, either by offering direct refunds or requiring non-resident businesses to register to make a claim, these measures are often subject to restrictions that undermine their effectiveness. A more effective way to address jurisdictional overlaps in this area is to resort to international cooperation.

Furthermore, the indirect nature of VAT and the requirements of the destination principle are an uneasy fit in the absence of physical borders in international trade. While the formal liability to pay VAT is placed on the supplier, the challenge, in the case of cross-border supplies of services, is how to effectively collect the tax from foreign suppliers who are out of the jurisdictional reach of the importing country. A common response to this challenge with respect to cross-border B2B supplies of services is to use a reverse charge mechanism that shifts the liability to pay VAT from the foreign supplier to the domestic importer.

In contrast, in the context of cross-border B2B sales of goods, the liability to pay VAT is generally placed on domestic importers and, with effective border controls, the VAT is collected at the point of importation without particular difficulty. Nevertheless, this approach imposes a cash flow burden on importers of goods, as the VAT must be paid upfront upon importation and recovered later as input tax through the normal VAT return. Some countries, such as the UK and Australia, introduced a deferred payment option for eligible importers in order to remove the cash flow burden for these businesses. The deferred payment for goods mirrors the reverse charge mechanism for services in its operation. While these mechanisms are designed to ensure the effective application of VAT on a destination basis in cross-border circumstances, they effectively suspend tax collection on B2B supplies and, in doing so, make the VAT functionally resemble an RST in relation to those supplies. Therefore, the deferred payment for goods and reverse charge for services both deviate from the invoice-credit mechanism of VAT.

In response to the dramatic increase in the volume of cross-border B2C sales of low-value goods and digital services driven by the growth of the digital economy, many countries have adopted the vendor/intermediary collection model, which requires foreign vendors and intermediaries, particularly online marketplaces, to register for and pay VAT in the importing country. As is the case with the deemed supplier rules in the context of the sharing economy mentioned above, the requirement for online marketplaces to account for VAT relies on deeming provisions that legally recharacterise the nature of the transactions. Specifically, online marketplaces are deemed to be the suppliers of the underlying supplies they facilitate for VAT purposes. The deemed supplier model, which shifts the liability to pay VAT from the actual supplier to a third party, can also be considered a deviation from the traditional invoice-credit VAT that ordinarily places the tax liability on the actual supplier.

The difficulty of applying the destination principle in the absence of physical borders also arises within economic unions, federations and large countries with multiple tiers of government. A few countries, notably China and Ethiopia, avoided this difficulty by adopting an origin basis system for inter-jurisdictional transactions. While an origin basis system undoubtedly offers the greatest simplicity in terms of administration and compliance, it has been shown to cause significant economic distortion in the context of a single large country or economic union. The application of the origin basis system constitutes a direct break with the core tenets of the destination principle.

In contrast, the EU, where fiscal borders have been eliminated, has made notable progress in transitioning towards a destination-based system for intra-Community transactions over the past few decades. The deferred payment for goods and the reverse charge mechanism for services discussed in the international context are employed within the EU for intra-Community supplies between businesses. However, both these regimes have proven susceptible to cross-border missing trader fraud, in which the importer exploits the opportunity to receive goods or services VAT-free, resell them with the VAT charged, and then disappear without remitting the tax collected to the tax authorities. This type of fraud is particularly pervasive within the EU, where the high degree of economic interdependence among the Member States creates fertile ground for such schemes. Paradoxically, the solution adopted within the EU is precisely the reverse charge mechanism, which partly contributed to the problem in the first place. Specifically, the reverse charge mechanism has been applied more systematically, albeit under strict conditions, to domestic B2B transactions in the sectors that are most vulnerable to fraud. Regardless of the rationale behind its use, the reverse charge mechanism represents a deviation from the standard invoice-credit VAT system.

While the reverse charge mechanism can only be applied to B2B supplies, the EU taxes intra-Community B2C supplies through the One Stop Shop (OSS) schemes. These schemes operate under an origin-based approach to VAT collection, with a clearing house facilitating the redistribution of revenue to the destination countries. Origin-based collection offers the advantage of significantly reducing administrative and compliance costs by eliminating the need for suppliers to comply with VAT rules in multiple jurisdictions and by reducing the total number of registrants in importing countries. Transfers of revenue collected on cross-border B2C sales from the exporting country to the importing country ensure that the allocation outcomes are consistent with the requirements of the destination principle.

The use of the OSS, which combines origin-based collection and destination-based allocation, is worthy of consideration for broader application at the international level to cross-border B2C supplies, potentially through a treaty. While this approach offers a practical means of implementing the destination principle, a key challenge lies in whether countries are willing to rely on other countries to collect a portion of their revenue on their behalf. Nonetheless, globalisation and increasing economic interdependence are likely to make greater international coordination in VAT administration both indispensable and inevitable, a development once considered unnecessary. Despite the practical challenges associated with its implementation, the destination principle remains a theoretically robust and normatively desirable foundation for an ideal VAT system, both in international trade and within federations or economic unions.

Table 8.1 below summarises the deviations from the standard design norms discussed in this book, along with the reasons for these deviations.

**Table 8.1** Deviations from the Design Norms of a Model VAT and Reasons for Deviations

| VAT Features | Deviations from Design Norms | Reasons for Deviations |
|---|---|---|
| **reduced rates and zero-rate (chapter two)** | single rate | social and political objectives |
| **exemptions adopted as subsidies (chapter two)** | broad base and invoice-credit mechanism | social and political objectives |
| **exemptions in the financial and insurance sectors (chapter four)** | broad base and invoice-credit mechanism | technical difficulties |
| **New Zealand's zero-rating of B2B financial services (chapter four)** | invoice-credit mechanism | technical difficulties |
| **registration threshold (chapter three)** | broad base and invoice-credit mechanism | administrative and compliance costs |
| **presumptive input tax entitlement regime (chapters three and seven)** | invoice-credit mechanism | administrative and compliance costs |
| **absence of foreign tax recovery (chapter five)** | invoice-credit mechanism and the destination principle | administrative and compliance costs |
| **reverse charge mechanism and deferred payment (chapters five and six)** | invoice-credit mechanism | administrative and compliance costs |
| **deemed supplier model (chapters five and seven)** | invoice-credit mechanism | administrative and compliance costs |
| **origin principle for inter-jurisdictional transactions (chapter six)** | the destination principle | administrative and compliance costs |

Two key observations emerge from the review of these deviations and the reasons behind them. First, VAT policy in the real world is inevitably shaped by the unique social, political and economic contexts in which it is designed and implemented, and further constrained by the administrative and compliance capacities of each particular jurisdiction. The standard norms of an ideal VAT, which were formulated largely on the basis of economic principles, offer limited practical guidance for real-world VAT design. Second, the standard norms that were developed long before the digital age do not adequately address the new challenges posed by the digital economy in relation to, inter alia, the sharing economy and cross-border trade.

Therefore, a new benchmark that addresses the inadequacies of the standard design norms is needed. Drawing on international experience with VAT, this book examines in detail six important aspects of VAT design and, in doing so, develops a revised benchmark that is more suitable for an increasingly digitalised economy in the twenty-first century. The key elements of this revised benchmark are summarised in Table 8.2 below.

The fact that VAT policy is moulded to a large extent by local social, political and economic conditions helps to explain why there is no one-size-fits-all solution to any of the issues discussed in the book. Key policy considerations, practical constraints and trade-offs between different tax design objectives inevitably vary from country to country. For example, while simplicity quite often stands in tension with other objectives of tax design, such as fairness or neutrality,[5] countries' responses to certain design issues reflect different emphases on these competing objectives. This can be seen, among others, in the design of presumptive input tax entitlement schemes in the UK and Canada;[6] the application of VAT to financial intermediary services in Singapore, Australia, and New Zealand;[7] and the approaches to input tax entitlements for underlying suppliers in the sharing economy under the deemed supplier model in the EU, Canada, and New Zealand.[8] In addition, considerations of simplicity in terms of administration and compliance are likely to carry greater weight in developing countries than in developed countries. Accordingly, although the revised benchmark has been developed with thoughtful consideration of the challenges and constraints commonly faced by VAT jurisdictions, the recommendations in the book must still be tailored to the specific circumstances of individual countries. Even so, the revised benchmark offers a valuable reference point for policymakers as they begin evaluating their existing VAT systems and exploring potential reform options to improve their VAT systems. In a vast majority of countries, there remains significant scope to improve at least some aspects of VAT design.

[5] J Whitting, 'Foreword – Tax Simplification in the United Kingdom: Some Personal Reflections' in C Evans, R Franzsen and E Stack (eds), *Tax Simplification: An African Perspective* (South Africa, Pretoria University Law Press, 2019) xx.

[6] See section V.C in chapter three.

[7] See section II.A.iii.b and c and section II.A.iv in chapter four.

[8] See section IV.C.ii in chapter seven.

**Table 8.2** A Revised Benchmark VAT

| Standard norms | Exceptions |
|---|---|
| **single rate and broad base** | • introduction of a separate rate for loans<br>• exemption for life insurance |
| **registration threshold** | • threshold applies at the platform level where platforms are deemed to be suppliers (for example, in the sharing economy and cross-border B2C sales of low-value goods and digital services) |
| **invoice-credit mechanism** | • deemed supplier rules (as for registration threshold exception)<br>• limited use of the reverse charge mechanism in domestic transactions<br>• limited use of presumptive regimes (for example, in the sharing economy and financial sector) |
| **destination principle** | • no explicit exceptions observed, but more effective implementation of the principle may rely on enhanced international cooperation |

# II. What Does the Future Hold for the VAT?

The economy in which VAT operates today is markedly different from the one that existed when the two most influential treatises on VAT design and implementation were published at the beginning of the twenty-first century.[9] The transformation of the economy means the issues that are pertinent today are not the same as those of 20 years ago, and the solutions to the old problems that made great sense then may no longer hold the same relevance. This shift also explains why the focus of this book differs somewhat from that of earlier works on the subject. Over the past two decades, several important trends have emerged, particularly in policy innovation in the developed world. These developments may offer valuable insights into what the future of the VAT could look like.

## A. The Use of Deeming Rules and Presumptive Schemes

Although the economic objective of VAT is to tax final consumption, the legal approach does not aim to tax the actual consumption. Instead, VAT is imposed on transaction expenditures, which serve as a reasonable proxy for the actual consumption. However, the application of the invoice-credit mechanism becomes challenging

[9] L Ebrill and others, *The Modern VAT* (Washington, DC, International Monetary Fund, 2001); and RM Bird and P-P Gendron, *The VAT in Developing and Transitional Countries* (Cambridge, Cambridge University Press, 2007).

in sectors such as financial services and insurance, where the explicit prices charged cannot be identified on a transaction-by-transaction basis. Special measures are often necessary to bring supplies in these sectors into the scope of taxation. These special regimes must be carefully designed to ensure coherence with the broader invoice-credit system of VAT. Deeming rules could play a useful role in facilitating the integration of such schemes into the standard VAT system. For example, as discussed in chapter four,[10] in the case of general insurance, New Zealand and Australia treat indemnity payment received by an insured person (only unregistered insured in the case of Australia) as deemed consideration for a taxable supply made by the insured person. By treating payouts as deemed consideration for a taxable supply while concurrently taxing insurance premiums, both jurisdictions achieve the correct policy outcome that the Goods and Services Tax (GST) is effectively applied only to the insurer's value added on a pooled basis. It remains to be seen whether this approach will gain broader international acceptance.

More recently, policy innovations in developed countries have increasingly focused on addressing the challenges posed by the rise of the digital economy. VAT was adopted long before the arrival of e-commerce and the digital economy. Since then, the scope of VAT has been expanded to cover circumstances not originally envisaged when the VAT was adopted. The digital economy presents peculiar problems for the design and administration of VAT, particularly in relation to the sharing economy and cross-border B2C transactions. However, the same digital technologies that complicate tax design and administration may also offer solutions. The reliance by sharing economy suppliers and foreign suppliers on digital platforms to reach customers enables comprehensive withholding regimes by treating the platform operators as deemed suppliers for VAT purposes. The deeming rules are, therefore, used to shift the liability from the actual suppliers to a third party (the platform). As platforms become more involved in VAT collection, tax authorities are increasingly able to capture revenue from unregistered businesses more effectively, thereby facilitating base broadening in the long run. Moreover, the deeming rules effectively reduce the threshold to zero for the underlying suppliers, which in turn helps to mitigate undesirable business responses aimed at avoiding crossing the registration threshold, in relation to both cross-border and domestic sales. The successful experience with reliance on platforms in VAT collection may encourage broader adoption of this model across more countries and its extension to other challenging areas in the future.

In addition to deeming rules, presumptive schemes may offer a solution in some of the difficult areas. For example, the separate rate approach proposed for taxing financial intermediary services in chapter four is essentially a presumptive scheme. The tax amount calculated by applying a lower rate to gross loan interest is regarded as an acceptable proxy for the tax that would be collected by applying the standard rate to the actual value of the intermediary services. Another example is New Zealand's approach to taxing sharing economy activities, using a presumptive

[10] See section III.A of chapter four.

regime (the flat rate credit) alongside deeming rules.[11] The flat rate credit acts as the proxy for the input tax credits that unregistered suppliers would have been entitled to if they were fully within the GST system.

The increasing reliance on deeming rules and presumptive regimes in VAT systems suggests that taxing consumption is no longer as straightforward as it was when the VAT was first introduced. Deeming rules construct notional transactions for VAT purposes in situations where it is impractical to apply the VAT directly to the underlying supplies. Likewise, presumptive schemes can be particularly useful where the accurate calculation of VAT liability proves challenging. As economic activities continue to diversify and evolve, countries may increasingly turn to these special measures. Admittedly, any special measure inevitably adds additional complexity to the VAT system. However, both policymakers and businesses may have to accept that the accurate taxation of consumption in a twenty-first century economy is becoming an ever more challenging – and in some cases, a near impossible – task. While the use of deeming rules and presumptive regimes offers opportunities to enhance VAT collection in difficult areas, the key challenge for policymakers is to design these schemes in a way that strikes an optimal balance among often competing tax objectives, most notably, simplicity, neutrality and fairness.

## B. RST-Type Features in Modern VAT Design

Another trend that deserves attention is the increasing incorporation of RST-type features into VAT systems. The RST-like logic is typically reflected in a shift away from full taxation under the standard invoice-credit method towards the suspension of tax between registered businesses, most commonly through zero-rating or the reverse charge mechanism. These features are generally adopted either to simplify the tax collection or to address fraud risks in sectors that are particularly vulnerable.

Table 8.3 below summarises some key RST-type features in VAT systems, along with the rationales for their adoption.

**Table 8.3** Key RST-Type Features in VAT Systems and Their Rationales

| Supplies | Mechanisms | Rationale |
|---|---|---|
| **financial supplies in New Zealand** | zero-rating | simplification |
| **cross-border B2B supplies (both international and within federations or economic unions)** | reverse charge mechanism (for services)<br>deferred payment (for goods) | simplification |

*(continued)*

[11] See section III.C of chapter seven.

**Table 8.3** ***(Continued)***

| Supplies | Mechanisms | Rationale |
|---|---|---|
| **cross-border B2B supplies and domestic supplies that are susceptible to fraud (such as gold and construction services)** | reverse charge mechanism | anti-fraud |
| **intra-group sales; transfer of a business as a going concern** | out-of-scope/zero-rating | simplification |

Unsurprisingly, the rationales for adopting the RST-type features reflect areas in which the RST is perceived to outperform the VAT. The most notable advantage of RST is operation simplicity, as it avoids the churning effect of collecting and refunding the tax on B2B transactions under the VAT. For example, in the case of financial services, subjecting B2B services to either full taxation or zero-rating would produce the same economic outcome for financial service providers and leave the government in an equivalent revenue position. However, zero-rating is likely to reduce compliance costs for financial service providers compared to full taxation, especially when most of their upstream and downstream transactions along the supply chain are zero-rated. The administrative and compliance cost savings are even more pronounced in the case of cross-border B2B services. Without the reverse charge mechanism, foreign suppliers would otherwise be required to register for and remit VAT in the jurisdictions of their business customers.

The operating mechanisms also have different cash flow implications for businesses. On the whole, the VAT is considered no more burdensome on cash flow than the RST.[12] However, in certain circumstances, the imposition of VAT may require more working capital, with input VAT paid before input tax credits or refunds can be claimed. The initial cash outflow for input VAT can be substantial in the case of cross-border B2B imports and the purchase of large assets, such as in the transfer of a business as a going concern (discussed in chapter two).[13] The suspension of tax helps reduce the immediate cash flow burden of paying VAT upfront on these supplies.

The principal advantage of a VAT over an RST, as noted in chapter one,[14] is claimed to be its lower vulnerability to evasion. However, decades of experience with VAT have shown that it is not as resistant to evasion as often believed. The structure of VAT gives rise to distinct incentives and opportunities for evasion, especially through the exploitation of the credit and refund mechanisms, such as fraudulent refund claims.[15]

[12] S Cnossen, 'VAT and RST: A Comparison' (1987) 35 *Canadian Tax Journal* 559, 580; AA Tait, 'VAT Policy Issues: Structure, Regressivity, Inflation, and Exports' in AA Tait (ed), *Value-Added Tax: Administrative and Policy Issues* (Washington DC, International Monetary Fund, 1991) 4.

[13] See the text at nn 7–8 in chapter two.

[14] See the text at nn 20–25 in chapter one.

[15] S Smith, 'VAT Fraud and Evasion' in R Chote and others (eds), *The IFS Green Budget: January 2007* (London, The Institute for Fiscal Studies, 2007) 168.

In addition, the popular belief that the revenue losses are less significant under the VAT in fraud schemes involving a missing trader has also proven illusory.[16] The belief is based on the assumption that tax authorities have already collected the tax on prior stages of the supply chain up to the point where a trader goes missing with the tax collected on their sale, so that the revenue loss is confined to the value added at that stage. In reality, however, fraud schemes are often deliberately structured to maximise revenue losses for the government. Missing trader frauds are typically perpetrated by traders who have acquired zero-rated goods or services, or who provide services with no or very low inputs. As a result, contrary to expectations, the government may not have effectively collected any tax on the transactions involved in the fraudulent schemes. This is particularly evident in international cross-border transactions, where supplies are zero-rated in the exporting country and the importer subsequently disappears with the VAT charged on domestic resales. In such cases, the revenue loss can equal the full amount of VAT due on the supplies.

Ironically, the anti-fraud strategy some countries have adopted is to apply the operating mechanism of an RST by suspending tax on B2B transactions, thereby eliminating the opportunity for a trader to disappear with the tax collected on sales. However, it is crucial to note that the RST is also vulnerable to fraud. The key difference between the two types of taxes lies in the point of vulnerability to fraud within the supply chain. Under the VAT, missing trader fraud tends to occur at intermediary stages of the supply chain, although it may also arise at the final retail stage. By contrast, under the RST, the risk of missing trader fraud is concentrated at the final retail stage, where the tax is legally imposed and collected. Therefore, converting a VAT into an RST may not be the best solution for addressing missing trader fraud, as it may simply shift the risk to a different point in the supply chain. It is worth recalling that the heightened fraud risk at the retail stage under an RST is in fact a prime reason that led many to believe the VAT is a superior form of consumption tax.

The use of RST-like features to address challenges under the VAT raises interesting questions: Does this suggest that VAT may no longer hold the clear superiority as a general consumption tax, a view that was often advanced over two decades ago? And is it now time to revisit the longstanding VAT versus RST debate? In considering these questions, it is also important to acknowledge that RST presents its own implementation challenges in practice.[17] Moreover, over 170 countries around the world already have a VAT in place, making any fundamental shift away from it both complex and unlikely. Therefore, the relevant question is

[16] See the text at nn 23–25 in chapter one.

[17] For example, a common criticism of RST is that, in practice, it proved difficult to exempt all B2B sales from taxation. See CE McLure, 'How to Coordinate State and Local Sales Taxes with a Federal Value Added Tax' (2010) *Tax Law Review* 639, 642; and RM Bird, 'Is a State VAT the Answer? What's the Question?' (Fiscal Research Center, Andrew Young School of Policy Studies, Georgia State University, August 2007).

not which of the two taxes is superior. But rather, whether, and if so, how a hybrid VAT and RST system could enhance the performance of VAT by combining the strengths of both taxes? These questions merit further research in the future. In any case, the trend towards incorporating RST-type features into VAT systems is likely to continue, potentially leading to a de facto merger of the two taxes – still labelled as VAT – in the not-too-distant future. This evolution may open up new opportunities for reforming and strengthening existing VAT systems.

## III. Closing Thoughts

As Bird and Gendron astutely noted some 20 years ago, 'Like most human institutions, VAT is neither perfect nor perfectible'.[18] The characteristics of a well-designed VAT system will vary across countries and evolve over time.[19] Therefore, the goal for any country at any particular time is not to design a VAT system that satisfies all theoretical ideals, but rather, drawing on both the theoretical norms and international experience, to develop one that functions effectively for that jurisdiction at that time.

This book begins this process by examining the key challenges commonly faced by VAT jurisdictions. While much of the conventional wisdom remains valid, there are, in some cases, plausible reasons for deviating from the standard prescriptions. The book presents a revised benchmark for countries to assess their VAT systems, along with recommendations that may be adopted and refined to suit specific needs in a given context. Undoubtedly, challenges remain in improving the VAT system in many countries, and always will. Yet, these challenges also present opportunities to adapt and fine-tune VAT design to better meet the evolving demands of twenty-first century economies.

[18] Bird and Gendron (n 9) at 9.
[19] ibid at 4.

# BIBLIOGRAPHY

## UK Government


European Union Committee (House of Lords), '20th Report of Session 2006-07: Stopping the Carousel: Missing Trader Fraud in the EU' (2006-07, HL 101)

Explanatory Memorandum to the Value Added Tax (Amendment) Regulations 2017

HC Deb 22 May 2012, vol 545, cols 1098-1104

HM Customs and Excise, 'Easing the Impact of VAT: Consultation on a Flat Rate Scheme for Small Firms: HM Customs and Excise Summary of the Responses to the Consultation Document Issued in June 2001' (Parliament Deposited Paper Dep 02/956, 2002)

HM Revenue & Customs, 'Value Added Tax (VAT) annual statistics 2023 to 2024' (6 November 2024)

HM Revenue & Customs, 'VAT: Addressing Borderline Anomalies' (Consultation document, 21 March 2012)

HM Revenue & Customs, 'VAT and Value Shifting: Consultation' (5 January 2021)

HM Revenue & Customs, 'VAT Flat Rate Scheme (FRS): Impact Assessment of Changes to the Flat Rate Percentages in January 2010' (7 December 2009)

HM Revenue & Customs, 'VFOOD6200 – Excepted items: Confectionery: The bounds of confectionery, sweets, chocolates, chocolate biscuits, cakes and biscuits: The borderline between confectionery and cakes' (HMRC internal manual: VAT Food, Updated 24 July 2024)

HM Revenue & Customs, 'VFOOD7590 – Excepted items: beverages: Item 4A: sports drinks' (HMRC internal manual: VAT Food, Updated 24 July 2024)

HM Revenue & Customs, 'VTAXPER36000 – Issues to consider: agency and disbursements: revenue risks associated with agency' (HMRC internal manual: VAT Taxable Person Manual, Updated 13 October 2022)

HM Revenue & Customs, 'VTAXPER68600 – Particular trades: Hairdressing: Who is making the supply? – the three possibilities' (HMRC internal manual: VAT Taxable Person Manual, Updated 13 October 2022)

HM Treasury, 'Budget 2012' (HC 1853, March 2012)

HM Treasury, 'VAT and the Sharing Economy: Call for Evidence' (December 2020)

HM Treasury, 'VAT and the Sharing Economy: Summary of Responses to the Call for Evidence' (July 2021)

HM Treasury, 'VAT Registration Threshold: Call for Evidence' (March 2018)

HM Treasury, HM Revenue & Customs and Department for Transport, 'VAT Treatment of Private Hire Vehicles: Consultation' (April 2024)

The Office of Tax Simplification, 'Review of Value Added Tax: Progress Report and Call for Evidence' (2017)

Office of Tax Simplification, 'Value Added Tax: Routes to Simplification' (2017)


## International Organisations


OECD, *Addressing the Tax Challenges of the Digital Economy, OECD/G20 Base Erosion and Profit Shifting Project Action 1 – 2015 Final Report* (Paris, OECD Publishing, 2015)

OECD, *Consumption Tax Trends 2024: VAT/GST and Excise, Core Design Features and Trends* (Paris, OECD Publishing, 2024)
OECD, *International VAT/GST Guidelines* (Paris, OECD Publishing, 2017)
OECD, *Mechanisms for the Effective Collection of VAT/GST: Where the Supplier is Not Located in the Jurisdiction of Taxation* (Paris, OECD Publishing, 2017)
OECD, *Model Tax Convention on Income and on Capital* (Paris, OECD Publishing, 2017)
OECD, *OECD Economic Survey: Mexico 2007* (Paris, OECD Publishing, 2007)
OECD, *Policy Note on the Introduction of VAT Compensation for Vulnerable Households in Colombia* (Paris, OECD Publishing, 2020)
OECD, *Tax Administration 3.0 and Electronic Invoicing: Initial Findings* (OECD Forum on Tax Administration, Paris, OECD Publishing, 2022)
OECD, *Taxation of SMEs: Key Issues and Policy Considerations* (Paris, OECD Publishing, 2009)
OECD, *Taxation of SMEs in OECD and G20 Countries* (Paris, OECD Publishing, 2015)
OECD, *The Impact of the Growth of the Sharing and Gig Economy on VAT/GST Policy and Administration* (Paris, OECD Publishing, 2021)
OECD, *The Role of Digital Platforms in the Collection of VAT/GST on Online Sales* (Paris, OECD Publishing, 2019)
OECD and Council of Europe, *The Multilateral Convention on Mutual Administrative Assistance in Tax Matters: Amended by the 2010 Protocol* (Paris, OECD Publishing, 2011)

## Foreign Governments

'Collection Models for GST on Low Value Imported Goods: Productivity Commission Inquiry Report' ((Australia) Productivity Commission, 31 October 2017)
'Collection Models for GST on Low Value Imported Goods: Submissions' ((Australia) Productivity Commission)
'Goods and services tax/harmonised sales tax (GST/HST) credit: payments chart effective July 2025–June 2026 (2024 base year)' (Government of Canada)
'GST: Guide for The Banking Industry' 6th edn, (Inland Revenue Authority of Singapore, 7 March 2024)
'GST and general insurance' (The Treasury, Australian Government)
'GST on accommodation and transportation services supplied through online marketplaces' (New Zealand Inland Revenue, Updated 1 April 2025)
'GST on cross-border supplies of remote services' (Policy and Strategy, New Zealand Inland Revenue, May 2016)
'Horizontal Fiscal Equalisation: Productivity Commission Inquiry Report' ((Australia) Productivity Commission, 15 May 2018)
'Options for Strengthening GST Neutrality in Business-to-Business Transactions' (The New Zealand Inland Revenue and the New Zealand Treasury, June 2008)
'Regulatory Impact Statement: Taxation of the Gig and Sharing Economy: GST: Coversheet' (New Zealand Inland Revenue, 25 May 2022)
'Report of the Select Committee on the Goods and Services Tax Bill' [Bill No. 14/93] (Eighth Parliament of Singapore)
'Review of GST on Low Value Imported Goods' ((Australia) The Board of Taxation, December 2021)
'Some International Themes in Fiscal Equalisation: An Australian Perspective' (Australian Government Commonwealth Grants Commission, April 2022)
'Supporting Canadians and Fighting Covid-19: Fall Economic Statement 2020' (Government of Canada, 2020)
'Tax Benchmarks and Variations Statement 2019' (The Treasury, Australian Government, January 2020)
'The Distribution of Major Tax Expenditures in 2019' (The United States Congressional Budget Office, October 2021)

'The Role of Digital Platforms in the Taxation of the Gig and Sharing Economy: A Government Discussion Document' (New Zealand Government, March 2022)

''Value-Added Tax: Administrative Costs Vary with Complexity and Number of Businesses' (United States General Accounting Office, May 1993)

## Books

Adam, S and others, *Tax by Design: The Mirrlees Review* (Oxford, Oxford University Press, 2011)

Arnold, BJ, *International Tax Primer*, 5th edn (The Netherlands, Kluwer Law International, 2023)

Bakker, C and Chronican, P, *Financial Services and the GST – A Discussion Paper* (Wellington, Victoria University Press for the Institute of Policy Studies, 1985)

Bird, RM and Gendron P-P, *The VAT in Developing and Transitional Countries* (Cambridge, Cambridge University Press, 2007)

Cnossen, S, *Modernizing VATs in Africa* (Oxford, Oxford University Press, 2019)

Ebrill, L and others, *The Modern VAT* (Washington, DC, International Monetary Fund, 2001)

Ecker, T, *A VAT/GST Model Convention* (The Netherlands, International Bureau of Fiscal Documentation, 2013)

Ishi, H, *The Japanese Tax System*, 3rd edn (Oxford, Oxford University Press, 2001)

James, K, *The Rise of the Value-Added Tax* (New York, Cambridge University Press, 2015)

Lauré, M, *La Taxe sur la valeur ajoutée* (Paris, Librairie du Recueil Sirey, 1953)

Smith, A, *The Wealth of Nations* (London, W Strahan and T Cadell, 1776)

Sullivan, CK, *Tax on Value Added* (New York, Columbia University Press, 1965)

Tait, AA, *Value Added Tax* (McGraw-Hill Book Company, 1972)

Tait, AA, *Value Added Tax: International Practice and Problems* (Washington, International Monetary Fund, 1988)

von Siemens, W, *Veredelte Umsatzsteuer* (Berlin, Siemensstadt, 1919)

von Siemens, CF, *Veredelte Umsatzsteuer*, 2nd edn (Berlin, Siemensstadt, 1921)

## Chapters in Edited Volumes

Brooks, N, 'The Under-Appreciated Implications of the Tax Expenditure Concept' in C Evans and R Krever (eds), *Australian Business Tax Reform in Retrospect and Prospect* (Sydney, Thomson Reuters, 2009)

Cnossen, S, 'The Technical Superiority of VAT over RST' in JG Head (ed), *Australian Tax Reform in Retrospect and Prospect* (Sydney, Australian Tax Research Foundation, 1989)

Crawford, I, Keen, M and Smith, S, 'Value Added Tax and Excises' in S Adam and others, *Dimensions of Tax Design: The Mirrlees Review* (New York, Oxford University Press, 2010)

Crossley, TF, Phillips, D and Wakefield, M, 'Value Added Tax' in R Chote and others (ed), *The IFS Green Budget: January 2009* (London, The Institute for Fiscal Studies, 2009)

de la Feria, R and Krever, R, 'Ending VAT Exemptions: Towards a Post-Modern VAT' in R de la Feria (ed), *VAT Exemptions: Consequences and Design Alternatives* (The Netherlands, Wolters Kluwer, 2013)

Due, JF, 'The Implications for Australia of the Experience in the United States, Canada and Other Countries with Retail Sales Tax' in JG Head (ed), *Changing the Tax Mix* (Sydney, Australian Tax Research Foundation, 1986)

Edgar, T, 'The Search for Alternatives to the Exempt Treatment of Financial Services under a Value Added Tax' in R Krever and D White (eds), *GST in Retrospect and Prospect* (Wellington, Brookers Ltd, 2007)

Evans, C and Krever, R, 'Counting the Costs of VAT Compliance' in RF van Brederode (ed), *Virtues and Fallacies of VAT: An Evaluation after 50 Years* (The Netherlands, Kluwer Law International, 2021)
Heady, C, 'Tax Expenditures: Definitional and Policy Issues' in L Philipps, N Brooks and J Li (eds), *Tax Expenditures: State of the Art* (Toronto, Canadian Tax Foundation, 2011)
Krever, R, 'Designing and Drafting VAT Laws for Africa' in R Krever (ed), *VAT in Africa* (South Africa, Pretoria University Law Press, 2008)
——, 'VAT and Financial Investments' in RF van Brederode and R Krever (eds), *VAT and Financial Services: Comparative Law and Economic Perspectives* (Singapore, Springer, 2017)
R Krever, and Teoh, J, 'Financial Loan Intermediary Services: Australia' in RF van Brederode and R Krever (eds), *VAT and Financial Services: Comparative Law and Economic Perspectives* (Singapore, Springer, 2017)
Krever, R and White, D, 'Preface' in R Krever and D White (eds), *GST in Retrospect and Prospect* (Wellington, Brookers Ltd, 2007)
——, 'GST and Insurance: Australia' in RF van Brederode and R Krever (eds), *VAT and Financial Services: Comparative Law and Economic Perspectives* (Singapore, Springer, 2017)
Millar, R, 'Echoes of Source and Residence in VAT Jurisdictional Rules' in M Lang, P Melz and E Kristoffersson (eds), *Value Added Tax and Direct Taxation: Similarities and Differences* (The Netherlands, IBFD, 2009)
——, 'Jurisdictional Reach of VAT' in R Krever (ed), *VAT in Africa* (South Africa, Pretoria University Law Press, 2008)
Morse, G, 'The Origins, Development and Future of Zero-Rating in the UK' in G Loutzenhiser and R de la Feria (eds), *The Dynamics of Taxation: Essays in Honour of Judith Freedman* (Oxford, Hart Publishing, 2020)
Mukherjee, S, 'India: The Challenges of Implementing VAT in a Federal State' in RF van Brederode (ed), *Virtues and Fallacies of VAT: An Evaluation after 50 Years* (The Netherlands, Kluwer Law International, 2021)
Poddar, S, 'Consumption Taxes: The Role of the Value-Added Tax' in P Honohan (ed), *Taxation of Financial Intermediation* (Washington and New York, The World Bank and Oxford University Press, 2003) 352
——, 'VAT on Financial Services – Searching for a Workable Compromise' in R Krever and D White (eds), *GST in Retrospect and Prospect* (Wellington, Brookers Ltd, 2007)
Smith, S, 'VAT Fraud and Evasion' in R Chote and others (eds), *The IFS Green Budget: January 2007* (London, The Institute for Fiscal Studies, 2007)
Swift, ZL, Brixi, HP, and Valenduc, CMA, 'Tax Expenditures: General Concept, Measurement, and Overview of Country Practices' in HP Brixi, CMA Valenduc and ZL Swift (eds), *Tax Expenditures – Shedding Light on Government Spending through the Tax System: Lessons from Developed and Transition Economies* (Washington, The World Bank, 2004)
Tait, AA, 'VAT Policy Issues: Structure, Regressivity, Inflation, and Exports' in AA Tait, (ed), *Value-Added Tax: Administrative and Policy Issues* (Washington DC, International Monetary Fund, 1991)
van Brederode, RF and Krever, R, 'Taxing Load Intermediary Services: Theory and Design Considerations' in RF van Brederode and R Krever (eds), *VAT and Financial Services: Comparative Law and Economic Perspectives* (Singapore, Springer, 2017)
Whitting, J, 'Foreword – Tax Simplification in the United Kingdom: Some Personal Reflections' in C Evans, R Franzsen and E Stack (eds), *Tax Simplification: An African Perspective* (South Africa, Pretoria University Law Press, 2019)
Zee, HH, 'Inter-jurisdictional Sharing of the VAT' in R Krever (ed), *VAT in Africa* (South Africa, Pretoria University Law Press, 2008)
Zu, Y, 'China's VAT in the Digitalized Economy' in Y Xu (ed), *VAT in the Digital Era: Unilateral and Multilateral Options for Reform* (Oxford, Oxford University Press, 2023)

## Articles


Adams, TS, 'Fundamental Problems of Federal Income Taxation' (1921) 35 *The Quarterly Journal of Economics* 527

Alley, C, Bentley, D and James, S, 'Politics and Tax Reform: A Comparative Analysis of the Implementation of a Broad-Based Consumption Tax in New Zealand, Australia and the United Kingdom' (2014) 24 *Revenue Law Journal*

Arnold, BJ, Sasseville, J and Zolt, E, 'Summary of the Proceedings of an Invitational Seminar on Tax Treaties in the 21st Century' (2002) 50 *Canadian Tax Journal* 65

Auerbach, A and Gordon, R, 'Taxation of Financial Services Under a VAT' (2002) 92 *The American Economic Review* 411

Barham, V, Poddar, S. N. and Whalley, J, 'The Tax Treatment of Insurance Under a Consumption Type, Destination Basis VAT' (1987) 40 *National Tax Journal* 171

Bird, RM and Gendron P-P, 'Sales Taxes in Canada: The GST-HST-QST-RST "System"' (2010) 63 *Tax Law Review* 517

——, 'CVAT, VIVAT, and Dual VAT: Vertical "Sharing" and Interstate Trade' (2000) 7 *International Tax and Public Finance* 753

——, 'Dual VATs and Cross-Border Trade: Two Problems, One Solution?' (1998) 5 *International Tax and Public Finance* 429

Brashares, E and others, 'Calculating the Optimal Small Business Exemption Threshold for a U.S. VAT' (2014) 67 *National Tax Journal* 283

Buettner, T and Erbe, K, 'Revenue and Welfare Effects of Financial Sector VAT Exemption' (2014) 21 *International Tax and Public Finance* 1028

Bury, Y, Feld LP and Burret HT, 'Skimming the Achieved? Quantifying the Fiscal Incentives of the German Fiscal Equalization Scheme and Its Reforms since 1970' (2024) 25 *Economics of Governance* 291

Carroll, R and Viard, A, 'Value Added Tax: Basic Concepts and Unresolved Issues' (2000) 126 *Tax Notes* 1117

Caspersen, E and Metcalf, G, 'Is a Value Added Tax Regressive? Annual Versus Lifetime Incidence Measures' (1994) 47 *National Tax Journal* 731

Chia, NC and Whalley, J, 'The Tax Treatment of Financial Intermediation' (1999) 31 *Journal of Money, Credit and Banking* 704

Cnossen, S, 'VAT, RST, or a Reverse Charge Mechanism: Which is Best?' (2017) *Tax Notes International* 453

——, 'A Proposal to Apply the Kiwi-VAT to Insurance Services in the European Union' (2013) 20 *International Tax and Public Finance* 867

——, 'The Technical Superiority of VAT over RST' (1987) 4 *Australian Tax Forum* 419

——, 'VAT and RST: A Comparison' (1987) 35 *Canadian Tax Journal* 559

D'Ascenzo, M, 'Making the Value Added Tax Happen' (2020) 18 *eJournal of Tax Research* 2

Davidson, P, 'Tax Reform: A Retrospective' (2000) 23 *UNSW Law Journal* 264

de la Feria, R, 'Editorial: The New VAT General Reverse-Charge Mechanism' (2019) 28 *EC Tax Review* 172

de la Feria, R and Walpole, M, 'Options for Taxing Financial Supplies in Value Added Tax: EU VAT and Australian GST Models Compared' (2009) 58 *International & Comparative Law Quarterly* 897

——, 'The Impact of Public Perceptions on General Consumption Taxes' [2020] *British Tax Review* 637

de Mello, L, 'The Brazilian "Tax War": The Case of Value-Added Tax Competition among the States' (2008) 36 *Public Finance Review* 169

Editors, 'Deferred GST Scheme for Importers' (2000) 3 *Manifest: Journal of the Australian Customs Service* 17

Eriksen, NP, 'Should Tax Treaties Play a Role for Consumption Taxes?' (2005) 33 *Intertax* 166

Gendron, P-P, 'Policy Forum: Canada's GST and Financial Services – Where Are We Now and Where Could We Be?' (2016) 64 *Canadian Tax Journal* 401

Grubert, H and Krever, R, 'VAT and Financial Services: Competing Perspectives on What Should be Taxed' (2012) 65 *Tax Law Review* 199
Grubert, H and Machie, J, 'Must Financial Services be Taxed Under a Consumption Tax?' (2000) 53 *National Tax Journal* 23
Heinemann, M, and Stiller, W, 'Digitalization and Cross-Border Tax Fraud: Evidence from E-Invoicing in Italy' (2025) 32 *International Tax and Public Finance* 195
Hill, R and Rushton, M, 'Harmonizing Provincial Sales Taxes with the GST: The Problem of Interprovincial Trade' (1993) 41 *Canadian Tax Journal* 101
Hoffman, LA, Poddar, SN and Whalley, J, 'Taxation of Banking Services Under a Consumption Type, Destination Basis VAT' (1987) 40 *National Tax Journal* 547
Huizinga, H, 'A European VAT on Financial Services?' (2022) 17 *Economic Policy* 497
Ilzetzki, E, 'Tax Reform and the Political Economy of the Tax Base' (2018) 164 *Journal of Public Economics* 197
Jack, W, 'The Treatment of Financial Services Under a Broad-Based Consumption Tax' (2000) 53 *National Tax Journal* 841
Jenkins, G and Khadka, R, 'Value Added Tax Policy and Implementation in Singapore' (1998) 9 *VAT Monitor* 35
Jenkins, P, 'VAT Treatment of Financial Services' (2006) 866 *Tax Journal* 15
Kanbur, R and Keen M, 'Thresholds, Informality and Partitions of Compliance' (2014) 21 *International Tax and Public Finance* 536
Kassim, L and Mansour, M, 'Tax Expenditure Reporting in Developing Countries: An Evaluation' (2018) 26 *Revue d'économie du développement* 103
Keen, M, 'The Anatomy of the VAT' (2013) 66 *National Tax Journal* 424
Keen, M and Hellerstein, W, 'Interjurisdictional Issues in the Design of a VAT' (2010) 63 *Tax Law Review* 359
Keen, M and Lahiri, S, 'The Comparison between Destination and Origin Principles under Imperfect Competition' (1998) 45 *Journal of International Economics* 323
Keen, M and Mintz, J, 'The Optimal Threshold for a Value-Added Tax' (2004) 88 *Journal of Public Economics* 559
Keen, M and Smith, S, 'The Future of Value Added Tax in the European Union' (1996) 11 *Economic Policy* 373
Kualizadeh-Shirazi, J and Shah, A, 'Tax Reform in Developing Countries: What Constitutes Successful Tax Reform? A Review of Developing Country Experience' (1991) *Finance & Development* 44
Lamensch, MCS, 'Is There Any Future for the Vendor Collection Model in the 21st Century Economy?' (2016) 27 *International VAT Monitor* 182
Li, N, Teoh, J and Krever, R, 'VAT Reform in China Reaches a Critical Turning Point' (2016) 82 *Tax Notes International* 387
Liu, L and others, 'VAT Notches, Voluntary Registration, and Bunching: Theory and U.K. Evidence' (2021) 103 *The Review of Economics and Statistics* 151
McLure, CE, 'How to Coordinate State and Local Sales Taxes with a Federal Value Added Tax' (2010) 63 *Tax Law Review* 639
——, 'Implementing Subnational Value Added Taxes on Internal Trade: The Compensating VAT (CVAT)' (2000) 7 *International Tax and Public Finance* 723
Okunogbe, O and Santoro, F, 'The Promise and Limitations of Information Technology for Tax Mobilization' (2023) 38 *The World Bank Research Observer* 295
Onji, K, 'The Response of Firms to Eligibility Thresholds: Evidence from the Japanese Value-Added Tax' (2009) 93 *Journal of Public Economics* 766
Perry, VJ, 'International Experience in Implementing VATs in Federal Jurisdictions: A Summary' (2010) 63 *Tax Law Review* 623
Poddar, S and English, M, 'Taxation of Financial Services Under a Value-Added Tax: Applying the Cash-Flow Approach' (1997) 50 *National Tax Journal* 89
Pomeranz, D, 'No Taxation without Information: Deterrence and Self-Enforcement in the Value Added Tax' (2015) 105 *American Economic Review* 2539

Salo, M, 'The Ideas of Maurice Lauré on VAT in the 1950s' (2014) 3 *World Journal of VAT/GST Law* 130
Sandford, C, 'The Administrative and Compliance Costs of the United Kingdom's Value Added Tax' (1990) 38 *Canadian Tax Journal* 1
——, 'The Administrative and Compliance Costs of Taxation: Lessons from the United Kingdom' (1985) 15 *Victoria University of Wellington Law Review* 199
Satterthwaite, EA, 'Electing into a Value-Added Tax: Evidence from Ontario Microentrepreneurs' (2018) 66 *Canadian Tax Journal* 761
Schenk, A, 'Taxation of Financial Services Under a Value Added Tax: A Critique of the Treatment Abroad and the Proposals in the United States' (1994) 9 *Tax Notes International* 823
Teoh, J and Krever, R, 'Court Favors Broad Application of Antiavoidance Rule in GST Case' (2013) 70 *Tax Notes International* 737
Turnier, WJ, 'Accommodating to the Small Business Problem under a VAT' (1994) 47 *Tax Lawyer* 963
van Brederobe, RF and Pfeiffer, S, 'Combating Carousel Fraud: The General Reverse Charge VAT' (2015) 26 *International VAT Monitor* 146
Xu, Y, 'A Multilateral Option for VAT in International Trade?' (2022) 71 *International and Comparative Law Quarterly* 857
Xu, Y and Krever, R, 'Applying VAT to Financial Services in China: Opportunities for China and Lessons for the World?' (2016) 45 *Australian Tax Review* 38
Yesegat, WA and Krever, R, 'Value Added Tax and Fiscal Federalism in Ethiopia' (2020) 28 *African Journal of International and Comparative Law* 147
Zee, HH, 'A New Approach to Taxing Financial Intermediation Services Under a Value-Added Tax' (2005) 58 *National Tax Journal* 77
——, 'VAT Treatment of Financial Services: A Primer on Conceptual Issues and Country Practices' (2006) 34 *Intertax* 458
Zodrow, GR, 'The Sales Tax, the VAT, and Taxes in Between – or, Is the Only Good NRST a "VAT in Drag"?' (1999) 52 *National Tax Journal* 429
Zu, Y, 'Developing VAT Treaties: International Tax Cooperation in Times of Global Recovery' (2022) 42 *Legal Studies* 159
——, 'VAT/GST Thresholds and Small Businesses: Where to Draw the Line?' (2018) 66 *Canadian Tax Journal* 309
Zu, Y and Krever, R, 'GST Cash and Accrual Mismatches: Avoiding the Avoidance' (2017) 46 *Australian Tax Review* 271

## Miscellaneous

Abramovsky, L, Philips, D and Warwick, R, 'Redistribution, Efficiency and the Design of VAT: A Review of the Theory and Literature' (London, The Institute of Fiscal Studies, 2017)
Andrew, C and Baer, K, 'How to Combat Value-Added Tax Refund Fraud' IMF How to Notes 23/01, August 2023)
Baert, P, 'Filling the Gap: The EU's Fight against VAT Fraud' (European Parliament Briefing, 29 January 2025)
Bird, RM, 'Is a State VAT the Answer? What's the Question?' (Fiscal Research Center, Andrew Young School of Policy Studies, Georgia State University, August 2007)
Brondolo, J and Konza, M, 'Administering the Value-Added Tax on Imported Digital Services and Low-Value Imported Goods' (International Monetary Fund Technical Notes and Manuals, March 2021)
Caragher, J, 'How Many Countries have VAT or GST? 175' (*VATCalc*, August 2024)
Carter, A (ed), 'International Tax Dialogue: Key Issues and Debates in VAT, SME Taxation and the Tax Treatment of the Financial Sector' (Paris, International Tax Dialogue, 2013)
Clougherty, T and others, 'A Framework for the Future: Reforming the UK Tax System' (Centre for Policy Studies & Tax Foundation, 2020)

Commission of the European Communities, 'A Common System of VAT: A Program for the Single Market' COM (1996) 328 final
Commission of the European Communities, 'Commission Staff Working Paper on Measures to Change the VAT System to Fight Fraud' COM (2008) 109 final
Commission of the European Communities, 'Completing the Internal Market' COM (85) 310 final
Conlon, M QC, 'Apportionment of Consideration for Supplies in UK Value Added Tax' (Australian Bar Association Conference Paper, June 2017)
Council of the European Union, 'VAT in the Digital Age Package: = Statements' (30 October 2024)
Daley, J and Wood, D, 'A GST Reform Package' (Grattan Institute, 2015)
The Davis Tax Committee, 'Final Report on Value-Added Tax for the Minister of Finance' (March 2018)
de la Feria, R and Swistak, A, 'Designing a Progressive VAT' (IMF Working Paper WP/24/78, April 2024)
Deloitte, 'Special Scheme for Small Enterprises under the VAT Directive 2006/112/EC – Options for Review: Final Report Volume I' (European Commission, May 2017)
Directorate-General for Taxation and Customs Union, European Commission, 'EU VAT Rules for E-commerce Two Years On: Updated Revenue Figures Point Again to a Successful Implementation' (*News*, 30 June 2023)
Due, JF, 'The Choice Between A Value Added Tax and A Retail Sales Tax' (Faculty Working Paper No. 1205, College of Commerce and Business Administration, University of Illinois at Urbana-Campaign, November 1985)
Dunne P, 'GST: Business-to-Business Neutrality across Borders – A Government Discussion Document about GST on Cross-Border Supplies between Businesses' (New Zealand Policy Advice Division of Inland Revenue, August 2011)
Eloi, JO, 'A Global VAT One Stop Shop: Boosting Development' (*Tax Adviser Magazine*, 21 August 2024)
European Commission, 'Commission Staff Working Document Impact Assessment: Generalised reverse charge mechanism – Accompanying the document Proposal for a Council Directive amending Directive 2006/112/EC on the common system of value added tax as regards the temporary application of the generalised reverse charge mechanism in relation to supplies of goods and services above a certain threshold' (21 December 2016) SWD (2016) 457 final
European Commission, 'Commission Proposes New Tax Rules to Support E-commerce and Online Businesses in the EU' (Press release, 1 December 2016)
European Commission, 'Modernising VAT for E-Commerce: Question and Answer' (5 December 2017) MEMO/16/3746
European Commission, 'Proposal for a Council Directive amending Directive 2006/112/EC as regards VAT rules for the digital age' COM/2022/701 final
European Commission, 'Proposal for a sixth Council Directive on the harmonization of Member States concerning turnover taxes – Common system of value added tax: Uniform basis of assessment' COM (73) 950
European Commission, 'Questions and Answers: VAT Gap 2022 Report' (8 December 2022) QANDA/22/7519
European Commission, 'Questions and Answers: VAT in the Digital Age' (8 December 2022) QANDA/22/7518
European Commission, 'Reduced rates of VAT: frequently asked questions' (2003) MEMO/03/149
European Commission, 'Report from the Commission to the Council and the European Parliament on the effects of Articles 199a and 199b of Council Directive 2006/112/EC on combatting fraud' (8 March 2018) COM (2018) 118 final
European Commission, 'Report from the Commission to the Council and the European Parliament, Experimental application of reduced rate of VAT to certain labour-intensive services' COM (2003) 309 final
European Commission, 'VAT Compliance Gap due to Missing Trader Intracommunity (MTIC) Fraud – Final Report. Phase II' (2024)
EY, 'Assessment of the Application and Impact of the VAT Exemption for Importation of Small Consignments' (European Commission, May 2015)

EY, 'European Commission – Assessment of the Application and Impact of the Optional 'Reverse Charge Mechanism' within the EU VAT System' (Final Report, November 2014)

Gadenne, L, Nandi, TK and Rathelot, R, 'Taxation and Supplier Networks: Evidence from India' (IFS Working Paper W19/21, August 2019)

Gerard, F and Naritomi, J, 'Value Added Tax in Developing Countries: Lessons from Recent Research' (International Growth Centre Growth Brief Series 015, May 2018)

Harju, J, Matikka, T and Rauhanen, T, 'The Effects of Size-Based Regulation on Small Firms: Evidence from VAT Threshold' (CESifo Working Paper No. 6115, 2016)

Heady, C and Mansour, M, 'Tax Expenditure Reporting and Its Use in Fiscal Management: A Guide for Developing Economies' (IMF How to Notes 19/01, March 2019)

Huber, N, 'Bakers Protest Vote on Pasty Tax' (*AccountingWEB*, April 2012)

Independent Panel of Experts for the Review of Zero Rating in South Africa, 'Recommendations on Zero Ratings in the Value-Added Tax System' (Recommendations to the Minister of Finance, 6 August 2018)

Institute for Fiscal Studies and others, 'A Retrospective Evaluation of Elements of the EU VAT System' (December 2011)

Keen, M, 'VIVAT, CVAT and All That: New Forms of Value-Added Tax for Federal Systems' (IMF Working Paper WP/00/83, April 2000)

——, 'Targeting, Cascading, and Indirect Tax Design' (IMF Working Paper WP/13/57, February 2013)

Keen, M and Smith, S, 'VAT Fraud and Evasion: What Do We Know, and What Can be Done?' (IMF Working Paper WP/07/31, February 2007)

Klahr, R and others, 'Behaviours and Experiences in Relation to VAT Registration: Final Report' (HM Revenue and Customs Research Report Number: 446, November 2017)

Lee, HC, 'Can Electronic Tax Invoicing Improve Tax Compliance? A Case Study of the Republic of Korea's Electronic Tax Invoicing for Value-Added Tax' (World Bank Group Policy Research Working Paper 7592, March 2016)

Liu, L, Lockwood, B and Tam, EHF, 'Small Firm Growth and the VAT Threshold: Evidence for the UK' (IMF Working Paper WP/24/33, February 2024)

Luchetta, G and others, 'VAT in the Digital Age: Final Report. Volume 1, Digital Reporting Requirements' (European Commission, March 2022)

——, 'VAT in the Digital Age: Final Report. Volume 2, The VAT Treatment of the Platform Economy' (European Commission, March 2022)

Lukic, MR, 'Tax Reform in Brazil and the Unique Federal Arrangement to Implement Its Dual-VAT' (*Kluwer International Tax Blog*, 26 February 2024)

Malan, J and Bosch Chen, I, 'Possible Solutions for Missing Trader Intra-Community Fraud' (Committee on Budgetary Control, European Parliament, 2022)

Mattauschová, B, 'Implementation of the Reverse Charge Regime' in 'Closing VAT GAP through Reverse Charge Mechanism: Collection of the tax conference of the Ministry of Finance with the support of International Fiscal Association, CR' (December 2015, Prague)

Mehta, D and Mukherjee, S, 'Emerging Issues in GST Law and Procedures: An Assessment' (NIPFP Working Paper Series No. 347, 24 August 2021)

OECD, 'Global Revenue Statistics Database' (2024)

Office for Budget Responsibility, 'Economic and Fiscal Outlook' (March 2023)

PwC, 'How the EU Exemptions Impact the Banking Sector: Study to Assess whether Banks Enjoy a Tax Advantage as a Result of EU VAT Exemption System' (18 October 2011)

PwC, 'Sharing or Pairing? Growth of the Sharing Economy' (2015)

Rahim, N and others, 'Research on the Sharing Economy' (HMRC report 453, 05 May 2017)

Redonda, A and Neubig, T, 'Assessing Tax Expenditure Reporting in G20 and OECD Economies' (CEP Discussion Note 2018/3, November 2018)

*Report of the Committee on Turnover Taxation* (Cmnd 2300)

Sinhal, A, 'The Atrocity of Section 49(5), Clause (e) & (f): When GST Credit Utilization Becomes a Trap' (Tax Management India, 9 May 2025)

Tax Expert Commission, 'Tax Expenditures Report: Colombia 2021' (OECD, DIAN and Ministry of Finance)

'Tax Harmonization in the European Community' (Community Topics 29, July 1968)

Thomas, A, 'VAT Rate Structures in Theory and Practice' (World Bank Policy Research Working Paper 10677, January 2024)

Tyson, J, 'Reforming Tax Expenditures in Italy: What, Why, and How?' (IMF Working Paper WP/14/7, January 2014)

Vale, R and others, 'Distributional Impacts of Brazil's Tax Reform: Scenarios regarding *Cesta Básica* Exemption' (World Bank Group Poverty and Equity Notes, October 2023)

Villela, L, Lemgruber, A and Jorratt, M, 'Tax Expenditure Budgets: Concepts and Challenges for Implementation' (Inter-American Development Bank Working Paper Series No. IDB-WP-131, April 2010)

Werner, J, 'Fiscal Equalisation among the States in Germany' (Institute of Local Public Finance Working Paper 02-2008, January 2008)

# INDEX

www.ingramcontent.com/pod-product-compliance
Ingram Content Group UK Ltd.
Pitfield, Milton Keynes, MK11 3LW, UK
UKHW020817290926
15470UKWH00003B/1203

9 781509 969579